P9-EMD-932

DISCARDED

Building An Effective Middle School

• • • • • • • • • • • • • • • • • • • •

DISCARDED

Building An Effective Middle School

• • • • • • • • • • • • • • • • •

Louis G. Romano
Michigan State University

Nicholas P. Georgiady
Miami University

WCB Brown & Benchmark
PUBLISHERS

Madison, Wisconsin • Dubuque, Iowa

Book Team

Editor   *Sue Pulvermacher-Alt*
Production Editor   *Jayne Klein*
Visuals/Design Developmental Consultant   *Marilyn A. Phelps*
Visuals/Design Freelance Specialist   *Mary L. Christianson*
Publishing Services Specialist   *Sherry Padden*
Marketing Manager   *Steven Yetter*
Advertising Manager   *Brett Apold*

WCB Brown & Benchmark

A Division of Wm. C. Brown Communications, Inc.

Executive Vice President/General Manager   *Thomas E. Doran*
Vice President/Editor in Chief   *Edgar J. Laube*
Vice President/Sales and Marketing   *Eric Ziegler*
Director of Production   *Vickie Putman Caughron*
Director of Custom and Electronic Publishing   *Chris Rogers*

Wm. C. Brown Communications, Inc.

President and Chief Executive Officer   *G. Franklin Lewis*
Corporate Senior Vice President and Chief Financial Officer   *Robert Chesterman*
Corporate Senior Vice President and President of Manufacturing   *Roger Meyer*

Cover design by Fulton Design

Cover image by James L. Shaffer

Copyedited by Rebecca Christian

Copyright © 1994 by Wm. C. Brown Communications, Inc. All rights reserved

A Times Mirror Company

Library of Congress Catalog Card Number: 93–70650

ISBN 0–697–15179–4

No part of this publication may be reproduced, stored in a retrieval
system, or transmitted, in any form or by any means, electronic,
mechanical, photocopying, recording, or otherwise, without the
prior written permission of the publisher.

Printed in the United States of America by Wm. C. Brown Communications, Inc.,
2460 Kerper Boulevard, Dubuque, IA 52001

10 9 8 7 6 5 4 3 2

This book is dedicated to our parents. As immigrants, they brought with them to America a great respect for education, which they always shared with us. This has inspired us throughout our careers.

CONTENTS

PART II CURRICULAR EXPERIENCES FOR THE TRANSESCENT

---

8   Evaluating Student Progress in the Middle School   139

9   Physical Activities and Intramurals   169

PART IV   GUIDANCE FOR A TROUBLED AGE

---

13   Guidance for the Middle School   235

14   Social Development of Transescents   257

PREFACE

This book is designed to provide important information for use by middle school teachers and administrators in a variety of ways. Its material is based on the results of ongoing field research conducted over the past twenty-five years, analyzing middle school organization, curriculum, staffing, and other important aspects of middle school education. This long-range study has centered on several important sources of information. First, the basic theoretical principles of effective middle school education, along with the evolving nature of middle school age students, have been examined and reexamined over this time. Leading educators in middle school education have been consulted with regard to the bases of middle school education as well as the desirable long-range goals for the middle school. Second, middle schools identified by educators as being exemplary and noteworthy for particular aspects of their programs have been studied and these observations have been used in forming specific conclusions regarding key aspects of desirable middle school education. Third, the professional literature including books, articles, research reports, and conference proceedings have been systematically studied to further define what is desirable and what has been successful in middle school education. Next, and certainly not the least important, is the consideration of the nature, the characteristics of the youth to be served, and the kind of society in which they live. As in any worthwhile educational program, this is a most important consideration.

All of these data have been compiled and analyzed with the goal of formulating a list of the most important characteristics of an effective middle school program. Each item in the refined final list of fourteen characteristics so identified has been used as the focus for one chapter in the book. In addition to discussing the general nature of each characteristic, ideas are set forth on procedures for developing that particular aspect of middle school education as well as ways of dealing with some problems that might arise in the development process. An important further provision is that numerous examples from successful middle schools using each idea are provided for the reader along with sources for further reading and information on the subject of that chapter.

At all times in the preparation of this book, stress has been placed on making it as practical and usable as possible for middle school administrators and teachers who seek to either improve an existing middle school program or embark on the initial planning for one. In addition, the ideas and materials in this book should be well suited for use in preservice education of prospective middle school teachers as well as for in-service education of practicing teachers in need of professional improvement and refinement.

Each of the chapters in the book has been carefully prepared by a selected writer who is recognized for particular expertise in the practices described in the chapter. A number of these writers are actively practicing middle school educators in the field. The others are university educators widely recognized for their middle school knowledge and for their ongoing involvement with middle schools in the United States and abroad. The ideas and materials suggested by the writers have been tested and retested in actual programs in numerous schools.

This acknowledges the writers and the chapters which they prepared.

Chapter 1
What Is a True Middle School?
Dr. Nicholas P. Georgiady
Miami University
Oxford, Ohio

Chapter 2
Growing Up in Difficult Times: The Transescent Today
Dr. Marie Smith
Grand Rapids Public Schools
Grand Rapids, Michigan

Chapter 3
Changing from a Traditional Junior High School to a True Middle School
Dr. Louis G. Romano
Michigan State University
East Lansing, Michigan

Chapter 4
Basic Skill Repair and Extension
Dr. Charles A. Sloan
Northern Illinois University
DeKalb, Illinois

Chapter 5
Multimedia Materials Approach
Dr. Louis G. Romano
Michigan State University
East Lansing, Michigan

Chapter 6
Creative Exploratory and Enrichment Activities
Dr. Nicholas P. Georgiady
Miami University
Oxford, Ohio

Chapter 7
Independent Study
Dr. John Swaim
University of Northern
Colorado
Greeley, Colorado

Chapter 8
Evaluating Student Progress
in the Middle School
Dr. Nicholas P. Georgiady
Miami University
Oxford, Ohio

Chapter 9
Physical Activities and
Intramurals
Dr. Glen Gerard
Educational Consultant
Grand Rapids, Michigan

Chapter 10
Middle School Organizational
Patterns
Dr. Karen Dornbos
Traverse City Schools
Traverse City, Michigan

Dr. Lorraine Kaminski
Central Michigan University
Mt. Pleasant, Michigan

Chapter 11
Flexible Scheduling
Dr. Michael Samulski
Assistant Superintendent
Chippewa Valley Schools
Clinton Township, Michigan

Chapter 12
Continuous Progress
Dr. David Killian
Miami University
Oxford, Ohio

Chapter 13
Guidance for the Middle
School
Leon Klein
Larson Middle School
Troy, Michigan

Chapter 14
Social Development of
Transescents
Dr. Corey Lock
University of North Carolina
at Charlotte
Charlotte, North Carolina

Chapter 15
Auxiliary Staffing
Dr. G. Wayne Swezig
Eastern Kentucky University
Richmond, Kentucky

Chapter 16
Student Services
Dr. Cynthia Mee
University of
Wisconsin–Platteville
Platteville, Wisconsin

Chapter 17
Community Relations
Dr. Samuel A. Moore
Michigan State University
East Lansing, Michigan

The authors wish to express their gratitude to their wives, Shirley Romano and Bee Georgiady, for their understanding and patience throughout the trials and tribulations of the development of this book. Thanks goes to Jan Clegg, Lorraine Hull, and Linda Baker for their invaluable work in typing and preparing the manuscript while it was in progress.

For their help in reviewing our book, we are indebted to:

Charles E. Jaquith
    Central Michigan University
    Mt. Pleasant, Michigan

Richard Negangard
    Marshall University
    Huntington, West Virginia

James E. Heald
    University of Florida
    Gainesville, Florida

Michelle Maksimowicz
    Central Michigan University
    Mt. Pleasant, Michigan

George P. White
    Lehigh University
    Bethlehem, Pennsylvania

It is important to recognize that there is no single model for an ideal middle school. In a nation of so many varied communities and settings, what has been designed for one community, and functions well there, may not work well in a different setting. Therefore, we expect the ideas and materials set forth in this book to be carefully reviewed and, where appropriate, revised and adopted for a specific situation. The wide range of suggestions offered by the authors makes it reasonable to expect that educators in any middle school setting will find a great deal of material in this book to consider in their planning. It is hoped that it will provide a valuable stimulus for their ongoing professional discussions and evaluations.

The book is organized into five parts:

Part I—The Middle School and Its Boys and Girls

Part II—Curricular Experiences for the Transescent

Part III—Class Organization for Instruction

Part IV—Guidance for a Troubled Age

Part V—Student Services and the Community

The Middle School and Its Boys and Girls

PART I

Chapter One begins with a brief review of the origins and history of the middle school as it evolved from the earlier junior high school. The major elements of a model middle school are identified and discussed.

Chapter Two identifies the developmental characteristics of middle school age youth today. It stresses the critical importance of using these as the sound basis for planning middle school programs which are current to the times of youth and relevant to their needs.

Chapter Three follows with a detailed explanation of the best procedures for changing from a traditional junior high school to a true middle school, giving attention to factors such as planning the whole process and each step in it, and timing the actions and personnel involved at various points in the process.

What Is a True Middle School?

WHY DID THE MIDDLE SCHOOL EMERGE?

For much of the existence of this nation, a two-tiered educational system prevailed, consisting of an elementary school of eight years and a secondary or high school of four years. Generally, only the elementary years were compulsory. Early in the twentieth century, there was a growing realization that the changing nature of life made it necessary to reconsider the scope of the educational ladder. The result was the move from an 8–4 pattern to a 6–3–3 pattern, with six years devoted to elementary education and six years for secondary education. The secondary phase was divided into three years for the upper or senior high school and three years for the lower or junior portion of the secondary school program. Thus the term ''junior'' high school was born.

As originally conceived, the junior high school was intended to provide for the educational needs of 12- to 15-year-old students in grades 7, 8, and 9 or the first three years of the secondary school. These early junior high schools were generally student-centered and flexible in scheduling with a strong emphasis on guidance as an important staff function.

However, as time passed—most particularly following the end of World War II—a rapid increase in the numbers of students in our schools was accompanied by gradual abandonment of the original goals and characteristics of the junior high school. Junior high schools adopted many characteristics of the senior high school that were not appropriate for the early adolescents. Dissatisfaction with these conditions increased and the early 1960s saw the emergence of a new educational program for the early adolescent, namely, the middle school.

As conceived by the leaders in this educational movement, the middle school was designed to be just what its name suggested—a school in the middle. This was not an elementary school, for while the elementary school fit the needs of young children, it was not appropriate for older students who were preadolescent or early adolescent. Neither did the senior high school organization and program fit these pre- or early adolescent needs. The term "transescence" was originated by Donald Eichhorn to emphasize the unique characteristics of this age group. No longer children, but not yet fully adolescent, they were in *trans*ition from childhood to adol*escence,* hence, *transescence* which Eichhorn[1] describes as

> the stage of development which begins prior to the onset of puberty and extends through the early stages of adolescence. Since puberty does not occur for all precisely at the same chronological age in human development, the transescent designation is based on the many physical, social, emotional and intellectual changes in body chemistry that appear prior to the puberty cycle to the time in which the body gains a practical degree of stabilization over these complex pubescent changes.

The middle school became not only a school in the middle of the educational ladder, but it also served an important bridging function. It took the students who were no longer children—but not yet fully adolescent—and provided them with a school organized and programmed to lead them successfully through the troubled years leading to full adolescence.

In the three decades since its inception, there has been a strong and rapid movement toward adoption of the middle school in many communities across the nation. The early years of the 1960s saw the first middle schools begin to appear, numbering in the low hundreds. A 1968 national study by Alexander[2] reported 1,101 schools identifying themselves as middle schools. This was remarkable progress in a period of less than ten years since the first middle schools were established. Even more rapid growth took place in the next decade, as Brooks[3] reported, with 4,060 middle schools reported in a national survey. More recently, various estimates regarding the continued rapid growth of middle schools have placed the total numbers of such schools at around 12,000.

SOME REASONS FOR CHANGING TO A MIDDLE SCHOOL

Several factors motivate the movement toward middle schools:

1. *Problems of declining enrollments.*
   Many school districts in the country have empty or underused classrooms. Consolidation of the fewer students becomes necessary with older, less efficient buildings sometimes being closed,

sold, demolished or converted to other community uses. In the process, the rearrangement of student population makes it feasible to consider establishment of a middle school.

2. *Problems of crowding in existing buildings.*

    School districts that are experiencing rapid growth in population sometimes turn to the middle school concept to provide relief in terms of needed classroom space. Rather than adding to existing school buildings, needed classrooms can take the form of a new middle school.

3. *Problems of desegregating schools now racially segregated.*

    Where school attendance lines coincide with racially segregated living patterns, some districts turn to the middle school as a means of providing more mixed racial populations in schools. In this way, a new middle school district can be superimposed on existing elementary school attendance areas that may be racially homogeneous.

4. *Problems of hand-me-down, obsolete high school buildings no longer needed for secondary education.*

    The completion of a new high school facility frequently presents a community with the problem of what to do with an obsolete building that is no longer needed, but for a variety of sentimental reasons, cannot be demolished. A common practice is to convert such a facility to a middle school.

5. *The "bandwagon effect" or "faddism."*

    We have popular styles in education just as we do in clothing and cars. At present, middle schools are considered a sign of being in the forefront of educational change. Some communities simply change the name of an existing junior high school to "middle school" as a quick but superficial way of gaining public recognition for being "innovative." Such innovation is cosmetic at best.

6. *Problems of better meeting the needs of preadolescent or early adolescent youth.*

    A change to a middle school provides a means for developing a program that better meets the needs of a unique group of students who are no longer children and not yet true adolescents. It also makes better use of teacher talents and community resources in a well-coordinated, soundly based educational program.

In examining the above, it becomes readily apparent that there may be a number of factors in a community that prompt it to move toward a middle school program. These frequently may be of a purely political or economic nature. Serious questions can be raised as to the appropriateness of such reasoning. The only valid reason for the adoption of the middle school concept is that it provides the best approach to meeting the unique needs of the youth who constitute the population of such a school. It should be designed to recognize the true nature of the present society in which these youth must live.

A further point requiring attention is the matter of terminology. The term ''middle school'' is not intended as an exclusive term but rather as a generic term. The term ''middle school'' is not intended to replace completely the established ''junior high school'' since many junior high schools continue to carry on effective programs for the education of the ''between-ager'' or transescent student. The term ''middle school'' is used throughout this book for the reason that it is not encumbered with stereotypes of traditional education that so often prove inadequate. We hope that in time the term ''middle school'' will become as firmly established as the terms ''elementary school'' and ''secondary school.'' Meanwhile, consider the ideas set forth in this book equally applicable to junior high and middle school programs.

THE TRUE MIDDLE SCHOOL CONCEPT

Quite logically, the middle school concept draws its major strengths from the very nature of the transescent individual and his interaction with society. Three elements become apparent as we study the transescent and his society in an effort to find the bases for a truly relevant educational program.

1. As we observe and analyze the ways in which the child grows and develops, we conclude that the physical maturation of children, particularly in the years from 11 to 14, has been considerably accelerated. Improved diet and upgraded health care have seen to this. As a result, children today are larger, stronger and in many ways more mature physically than children of the same ages in previous generations. These observations are further substantiated by reports of anthropologists based on statistical evidence they have gathered.

2. Along with these physical changes, we also note sociopsychological differences between transescent children of today and those of previous generations. Increased family travel, not only travel within this country but abroad as well, contributes to this. More numerous cultural and informational resources provided by more extensive mass media are also a factor. Books are available today in quantities never present before. The paperback revolution is apparent everywhere. Reading material and the information, ideas, and stimulation that these provide contribute significantly to the

more rapid social development of children. The almost universal availability of television is also a factor in the environment of the transescent. The many hours spent in viewing television often exceed those spent in actual classrooms.

3. Educating larger and larger numbers of students has become necessary as our population has grown. Unfortunately, there has been a growing impersonalization of education as well. The individual has lost his identity in many schools. This lies at the heart of much of the present dissatisfaction with schools and is nowhere more true than in the middle grades. There is growing recognition for the basic principle of education which stresses the importance of providing differentiated treatment of young people of varied maturity levels. Educators have begun to consider the differences between transescents and younger and older children. An examination of the kinds of educational programs called for by such identified developmental characteristics naturally follows.

Regrettably, the rapid growth of the middle school movement has in far too many instances meant a mere change of the name of the school to ''middle school'' without significant changes in program organization or staffing. The pattern of regression to the highly departmentalized, subject-centered, rigid schedules of the secondary school is occurring in the middle school today, just as it occurred for the junior high school earlier in this century.

A MAJOR TASK FORCE REPORT

While much has been written in this regard no viewpoint has been more strong and eloquent than that expressed in *Turning Points,*[4] the report of the Carnegie Council Task Force on Education of Young Adolescents.

> Middle grade schools—junior high, intermediate, and middle schools— are potentially society's most powerful force to recapture millions of youth adrift, and help every young person thrive during early adolescence. Yet all too often these schools exacerbate the problems of young adolescents.
>
> A volatile mismatch exists between the organization and curriculum of middle grade schools and the intellectual and emotional needs of young adolescents. Caught in a vortex of changing demands, the engagement of many youth in learning diminishes, and their rates of alienation, substance abuse, absenteeism, and dropping out of school begin to rise.

As the number of youth left behind grows, and opportunities in the economy for poorly educated workers diminish, we face the specter of a divided society: one affluent and well-educated, the other poorer and ill-educated. We face an America at odds with itself.

The recommendations contained in this report will vastly improve the educational experiences of all middle grade students, but will most benefit those at risk of being left behind. The Task Force calls for middle grade schools that:

- *Create Small Communities for Learning* where stable, close, mutually respectful relationships with adults and peers are considered fundamental for intellectual development and personal growth. The key elements of these communities are schools-within-schools or houses, students, and teachers grouped together as teams, and small group advisories that ensure that every student is known well by at least one adult.

- *Teach a Core Academic Program* that results in students who are literate, including in the sciences, and who know how to think critically, lead a healthy life, behave ethically, and assume the responsibilities of citizenship in a pluralistic society. Youth service to promote values for citizenship is an essential part of the core academic program.

- *Ensure Success for All Students* through elimination of tracking by achievement level and promotion of cooperative learning, flexibility in arranging instructional time, and adequate resources (time, space, equipment, and materials) for teachers.

- *Empower Teachers and Administrators to Make Decisions about the Experiences of Middle Grade Students* through creative control by teachers over the instructional program linked to greater responsibilities for students' performance, governance committees that assist the principal in designing and coordinating schoolwide programs, and autonomy and leadership within sub-schools or houses to create environments tailored to enhance the intellectual and emotional development of all youth.

- *Staff Middle Grade Schools with Teachers Who Are Expert at Teaching Young Adolescents* and who have been specially prepared for assignment to the middle grades.

- *Improve Academic Performance through Fostering the Health and Fitness of Young Adolescents* by providing a health coordinator in every middle grade school, access to health care and counseling services, and a health-promoting school environment.

- *Reengage Families in the Education of Young Adolescents* by giving families meaningful roles in school governance, communicating with families about the school program and student's progress, and offering families opportunities to support the learning process at home and at the school.
- *Connect Schools with Communities,* which together share responsibility for each middle grade student's success, through identifying service opportunities in the community, establishing partnerships and collaborations to ensure students' access to health and social services, and using community resources to enrich the instructional program and opportunities for constructive after-school activities.

A MIDDLE SCHOOL VERSUS A TRADITIONAL JUNIOR HIGH

We can vividly illustrate the contrast between a true middle school and a traditional, secondary oriented junior high school by comparing the two on a number of important educational characteristics.

A middle school is an educational unit with a philosophy, structure and program that will realistically and appropriately deal with 11 to 14 year olds as they indeed are and behave. Its commitment is primarily to the youth it seeks to serve. A traditional junior high school is patterned after the senior high school and utilizes an approach and organization best suited for students older and more mature than the 11 to 14 year olds found in the middle grade years.

A True Middle School Includes	A Traditional Junior High School Includes
1. Continuous progress.	1. Graded structure.
2. Multimaterial approaches with students learning at different rates.	2. Single text approach with all students on same page at the same time.
3. Flexible schedules.	3. Rigid block schedules.
4. Team teaching—teachers plan together.	4. Departmentalization—teachers plan individually.
5. Appropriate social experiences—fitting 11–14 year olds.	5. Social experiences emulating high school.
6. Intramural activity for all.	6. Interscholastic sports mainly for more athletically skilled boys.

A True Middle School Includes	A Traditional Junior High School Includes
7. Physical education activity based on needs of students in this age group.	7. Physical education activity that emulates the high school program.
8. Planned gradualism in the transition from childhood to adult independence.	8. A preplanned adult environment.
9. Exploratory and enrichment experiences meeting individual interests of students.	9. Minimal opportunities for exploratory and enrichment experiences—emphasis on ''covering the material.''
10. Individualized and group guidance services led by teacher-advisors.	10. Guidance services limited to academic performance.
11. Independent study opportunities for all students.	11. Independent study usually limited to the bright students.
12. Student-centered, student-directed, and student-developed creative activities.	12. Teacher-centered, teacher-directed, and teacher-developed ''creative'' activities.
13. A security group and a teacher who knows students well.	13. A homeroom setting for administrative purposes.
14. Evaluation of student achievement that is personal, positive in nature, and strictly individualized.	14. Student evaluations based on a letter grade in comparison to others.
15. A varied program of community involvement to develop awareness and understanding of school goals.	15. Parent involvement limited to sports, music, and open house activities.
16. Greater use of specialized student services (county, state, and local).	16. Limited use of specialized student services.

A True Middle School Includes	Traditional Junior High School Includes
17. Use of volunteers (parents/students) and aides to facilitate and augment the teaching staff.	17. Limited use of diversified services.
18. Teacher/student planning of lessons.	18. Teacher planning of lessons.[5]

Guidelines for a Middle School

The findings of several studies have led to the identification of varying numbers of characteristics of the middle school. For the purposes of this book, we identified fourteen characteristics as being most viable and as representing the scope of a desirable set of guidelines. Use them for planning new or revised programs as well as for evaluating existing middle school or junior high school programs.

FOURTEEN CRITERIA FOR EVALUATING THE MIDDLE SCHOOL

1. *Provide for Continuous Progress*
   Regardless of chronological age, students should be allowed to progress at their own individual rates. This transescent state of growth is one where individual differences are most pronounced. Forcing students into a rigid chronological grouping pattern ignores this important developmental characteristic and defeats the effectiveness of educational plans. Instead, the curriculum must be built on continuous progress, permitting each student to move through sequential learning activities at his own rate.

2. *Flexible Class Schedules*
   In the traditional school, rigid time schedules often interfere with learning rather than serving it. Logically, the schedule should be based on instructional needs for various activities. To do this, the schedule should be varied and flexible, with changes made in class periods where necessary to fit the kinds of study activities going on.

3. *Use of Team Teaching*

   Every teacher possesses certain teaching strengths as well as weaknesses. In addition, transescent students benefit from a carefully planned schedule that puts them in contact with more than one teacher. However, they are not yet ready for the highly departmentalized approach of the high school. Therefore, a team teaching approach which utilizes teacher strengths in working with students individually and in groups is the logical way to meet the transescent's needs.

4. *Use of Multimedia Materials Approach*

   While the basal text approach to teaching is the dominant approach today, it has disadvantages which give cause for serious concern. One of the major disadvantages is its inflexibility. It assumes that all students respond to the same approach equally and progress through the text at the same rate. More consistent with the nature of the transescent is the use of a wide range of easily accessible instructional materials and a variety of activities to appeal to the varied abilities and interests of students. The multimaterial approach is consistent with the wide intellectual and physiological range of middle school age students, who may compare with seven to nineteen year olds.

5. *Provide for Basic Skill Repair and Extension*

   Because of individual rates of growth, some youngsters have not entirely mastered the basic skills. These students require an extension of the program of basic skills development begun in the elementary school. There should be many opportunities to practice reading, listening, map and arithmetic skills, questioning, debate, etc. In some instances, the special services of remedial teachers may be necessary.

6. *Provide for Creative Exploratory and Enrichment Studies*

   Transescents have a strong interest in and curiosity about the world in which they live. To provide for this, the middle school should offer a wide range of educational opportunities for the student. Electives should be part of the program of every student so that unique needs can be met. Time should be spent in enriching the students' concept of themselves and the world around them rather than confining them to learning only required subject matter in traditional form. The creative talents of transescents require opportunities for expression. Students should be free to explore interests in many areas and to do so without pressures. Student newspapers, dramatic activities, art, musical programs, and others should be carried on in such a way that they encourage students to select, conceive, plan, and carry out activities in these areas.

7. *Provision for Independent Study*
Strong individual interests and curiosity characterize the transescent. This serves as a highly effective motivational force when there is adequate provision for independent study by the student, with the teacher available for assistance in planning and as a resource person. The value that this has in fostering self-direction by students makes it an important provision of the middle school.

8. *Full Provision for Evaluation of Pupil Growth*
The middle school program should provide a system of evaluation that is personal and positive in nature. If an individualized program is to be carried on, then the evaluation should be individualized. Students should be encouraged to assess their own progress and plan for future progress as well. The present common grading system using letters provides little information useful in understanding progress and areas of needed improvement. As part of an effective evaluation system, student–teacher conferences on a regularly scheduled basis should be available. Additional conferences including parents can aid in reporting progress. The whole atmosphere in conducting evaluation should be constructive and positive rather than critical and punitive.

9. *Guidance for a Program of Planned Gradualism*
Another characteristic of the transescent is eagerness to make more decisions concerning behavior, social life, choice of friends, and learning activities. While students are ready for some decision making at this stage, they are not quite ready for assuming the full burden of such planning as the high school student must do. The transescent still requires some security and continues to depend heavily upon adult guidance. Therefore, the program of experiences in the middle school should satisfy the transescent's needs for more independence while it also continues to offer the assurance of sound adult guidance.

    The transescent has many problems troubling him. Often these stem from the rapid physical changes. These problems require careful counseling from teachers and from trained guidance counselors. Group and individual counseling services are an important part of a successful middle school program.

10. *An Appropriate Program of Physical Experiences and Intramural Activities*
Highly competitive athletic programs are not appropriate for transescents who are generally unprepared for the serious pressures these activities generate. Instead, physical education classes should center on helping students to understand and use their bodies. A strong intramural program which encourages widespread

participation is greatly preferred to a competitive, selective program of athletics which benefits only a few in a "star" system. The stress should be on the development of body management skills.

11. *Appropriate Social Experiences*

Some middle school age students are still children, immature and not yet ready for more sophisticated social activities. Others are already adolescents with strong interests in social contacts with members of the other sex. Many are in transition between these two stages. Therefore, a program of social activities based on a high school model is inappropriate. Instead, there should be a program which provides, for the unique needs of the transescent. These include wholesome social contact with members of the other sex through interaction in small groups, large group activities in common areas of the school, club activities, dancing of the "mixer" type such as square dancing, and others. Serious dating and pairing off of couples is more appropriate at later ages.

12. *Auxiliary Staffing*

Every community has many human resources that can be useful to a school program. The middle school recognizes this and seeks to utilize people from the community in many ways. Volunteer parents, teacher aides, clerical aides, student volunteers, and others can do a great deal to facilitate the operation of the middle school program.

13. *Student Services*

Providing adequately for the many needs of middle school students calls for a broad spectrum of specialized services. These should include health services, counseling services, testing services, and opportunities of both a curricular and a cocurricular nature. The important point is that the major needs of every student should be met by the school through services available to schools.

14. *Emphasize Community Relations*

The truly effective middle school is community-minded. It seeks to develop and maintain a varied program of community relations. Programs to inform, to entertain, to educate, and to understand the community are part of the basic operation of the school.

Many communities today are considering the development of middle school programs. Other communities have begun programs which they feel are middle school programs. Unfortunately, the pressures of time and an inadequate understanding of the true nature of a sound middle school program may result in a disappointing or inappropriate program in some of these communities.

In the chapters which follow, one of the fourteen criteria outlined above has been used in each as the focal point for discussion. Each chapter gives recommendations to guide educators in planning and evaluating the programs it discusses. A general discussion of the criterion is developed so as to establish it in a context of the all-school setting. Then specific recommendations are made for consideration in specific planning for educators. Where appropriate, sample materials from middle schools recognized as successful, quality institutions are also included. By no means are the possibilities for planners limited to those set forth in this book. There are no limitations to the creative planning which is possible for a group of dedicated, imaginative, and informed planners.

SUMMARY

The junior high school's original purpose has undergone gradual change in the fifty years since its founding. Dissatisfaction with these changes has led to a rapid movement toward a redefined school for the middle years of the educational ladder for students who are 11 to 14 years of age.

While some middle schools have rapidly been established for varied reasons, some of which may be questioned, the only valid reason for a middle school is the better education of this important age group.

Studies of effective middle schools have resulted in the identification of fourteen characteristics of schools that can be useful in evaluating existing middle school programs or in establishing such programs.

ENDNOTES

1. Eichhorn, Donald H. *The Middle School.* New York: The Center for Applied Research in Education, Inc., 1966; Special Printing by the National Association of Secondary School Principals and the National Middle School Association, 1987, 3.

2. Alexander, William M. *A Survey of Organizational Patterns of Reorganized Middle Schools.* Final Report, USOE Project 7-D-026, Gainesville, Fla.: University of Florida, July, 1968.

3. Brooks, Kenneth, and Francine Edwards. *The Middle School in Transition: A Research Report on the Middle School Movement.* Lexington: College of Education, University of Kentucky, 1978.

4. Carnegie Council on Adolescent Development. *Turning Points: Preparing American Youth for the 21st Century.* The Report of the Task Force on Education of Young Adolescents, Carnegie Corporation of New York, 1989.

5. Romano, Louis G., Nicholas P. Georgiady, and James E. Heald. *The Middle School: Selected Readings on an Emerging School Program.* Chicago: Nelson-Hall Co., 1973.

Growing Up in Difficult Times
The Transescent Today

THE TRANSESCENT CHILD

Description of the Transescent

Middle schools have developed in response to the growing realization that during and just before adolescence, children have unique needs that an appropriate program must meet. Examining these developmental changes and their implications for education is a necessary and valuable first step in studying the middle school.

The characteristics and needs of young children until the age of about eleven seem to be adequately provided for within the elementary school as it presently functions. However, it is in the years that follow the elementary grades that we find great cause for concern. The result is the challenge to seek more appropriate education. These are the years when our children experience the greatest and the most rapid body changes of their entire life. The continuing development of a positive self-concept is extremely critical during these years. Our youth should feel capable, responsible, and appreciated by the time they become full adolescents.

This section will consider the nature of the transescent in terms of physical, intellectual, emotional, and social development. Following a discussion of these areas is a chart depicting physical, intellectual, emotional, and social characteristics, and their implications for middle school curriculum and organization.

Physical Development

The rather steady physical growth of the elementary school years is radically altered by a new pattern which begins to emerge in the developing early adolescent or transescent. For one, boys generally show a spurt in height between the ages of twelve and thirteen. At the same time, they find themselves behind girls of the same ages who have experienced this rapid increase in height one or two years earlier. The average gain in height of young adolescents is from two to four inches per year; the average weight gain per year is eight to ten pounds. Adjustment to this rapid and somewhat disproportionate change in body structure presents many problems for individuals experiencing it. Suddenly they have longer legs and arms, with larger hands and feet. They need to accept this changed physical appearance and to adjust to manipulation of these enlarged extremities. As a result, awkwardness and self-consciousness are characteristic of the growing individual. The bones in the young person's body often grow more rapidly than the muscles attached to them. In such instances, it is not uncommon for the individual to suffer frequent muscle cramps because of the disparity. Parents and teachers are painfully conscious of these changes as they observe youngsters who stumble over their own feet and have difficulty in carrying on ordinary activities in the classroom and in the home. Disturbed coordination is common in the rapidly growing individual.

Studies in the rate of maturation of children in the middle years show that the onset of puberty occurs earlier in today's youth than in previous generations. Fifty percent of all girls will have begun breast development at age 11 years, 3 months; will have pubic hair at age 11 years, 6 months; and will have begun to menstruate by age 12 years, 8 months. The average age in boys for the beginning of the enlargement of the testes is 12 years; for the growth of the penis, 12 years, 3 months; and for the appearance of pubic hair, 12 years, 6 months. There is tremendous variation as to when sexual changes begin to occur and how rapidly they take place.[1] To prevent the unhealthy effects of feeling ''different,'' we should let transescents know that a broad range in the rate of sexual development is normal.

Health and body management become of increasing concern to the transescent. Sweat glands in the body become highly active, often resulting in unpleasant body odors when bathing habits are not adjusted accordingly. This is also the age when that scourge of youth, acne, makes its unwelcome appearance. The changed chemical composition of the body and the increased activity of sweat and other glands result in eruptions in the facial skin which cause great distress for many. The disproportionate growth of the jaw, ears, and nose cause a great deal of concern and anxiety for the transescent. The subject of one's facial appearance becomes a matter of deep concern and is accompanied by many hours of detailed study before a mirror.

The rapid physical growth takes its toll in terms of stamina. The child becomes tired more easily and requires frequent periods of rest. To fuel the growing body, children eat more. Not only is the quantity of food which is consumed increased, but the nature of the diet becomes altered and often erratic. Overloading the digestive system with large quantities of poorly selected foods is typical of this age.

This is also the age at which rapid body changes create apprehension. Worry about changes in appearance and the general body chemistry tend to make transescents highly susceptible to fad medicines as well as diets. Peer group opinions and cures are more readily accepted than advice from close adult sources. Prescriptions in magazines which prey upon these fears and anxieties are unfortunately often used. The need for constructive health information found in reliable sources is urgent in these years.

Intellectual Development

There are a number of notable characteristics associated with the intellectual development of transescents. The development stages suggested by Piaget and the subsequent findings of Epstein and Toepfer hold major implications for the middle school.

Piaget theorized that logical reasoning is composed of stages: Sensorimotor (birth to two years of age); preoperational (two to seven years of age); concrete operational (seven to eleven years of age); and formal operational (eleven years of age and above). Fundamental differences in reasoning exist at each of these levels. Lower levels of reasoning must develop prior to the development of higher levels of reasoning.[2] Bondi and Tocco point out that practically all youngsters in the ten to fourteen age group make progress, but the gap between the good student and the poor student continually widens.[3] Thus, it is at this period in their development that chronological age should be of the least importance. Each individual should be allowed to travel toward their goal at their own rate of educational growth. Wavering concluded that ''a very small number of middle school students are beginning to develop formal operational structures and even these rely mainly on concrete operational reasoning, especially under stress.''[4]

Toepfer reported that the empirical research conducted by Epstein has borne out that brain growth is consistent with increase in body size. A set of five periods of growth occur in the age intervals three to ten months, two to four years, six to eight years, ten to twelve years, and fourteen to sixteen years.[5] Toepfer goes on to report that during each of the age ten to twelve and fourteen to sixteen periods of great brain growth, youngsters experience an average growth of thirty-eight months in mental age. However, during the intervening age of twelve to fourteen years, a plateau period in brain growth, youngsters experience an average growth of only seven months in mental age.[6] Certainly this alone provides strong reason to reconsider expectations for learning between the ages of twelve and fourteen years and to develop a curriculum consistent with this reality.

A major preoccupation of transescents is the drive to utilize their growing maturity in shaping a life more independent of adult direction. There is a transition from childhood with its well-ordered, organized, systematic and largely directed life shaped by adults. The drive for independence makes youth want to shape decisions formerly made by adults. Transescents tend to view adults somewhat differently than does the child. They seek more frequently to engage in adult activities and conversations as an exercise of their developing intellectual maturation and interests. The early adolescent period is a time of transition from the "concrete operations" stage to the "formal operations" stage. The young person begins to think about thinking.

Transescents also show growth in the ability to reason and generalize from observing and analyzing data. Pure data do not satisfy them as they did in childhood. They seek to find relationships beyond the facts. Along with this, there is a stronger tendency to arrive at decisions based on conscious or unconscious criteria.

Adults working with transescents are frequently impressed with the amazing intellectual curiosity of young persons and their ability to function creatively and effectively when educational challenges appeal to them. They display a growing insight into themselves and eagerly assume a greater responsibility for self-direction.

A strong tendency also develops for planning one's own life. Part of this is the growing preoccupation for earning money and being able to spend it on items deemed important by the individual and the peer group. As a further outgrowth of this increasing responsibility for self-direction, transescents seek a greater freedom to make decisions about clothes, grooming, leisure time activities, friends, and others. The justification for these choices becomes very clear to them, largely on the basis of what the peer group dictates. The choices are often perplexing if not aggravating to parents.

Attention spans tend to grow at this age, another aspect of intellectual development. This is by no means constant or consistent—other aspects of development can and do affect it. For one, the rapid physical growth and the accompanying need to exercise the growing body more frequently makes it difficult to remain sitting for long periods of time. Classes where some movement is permitted are far more likely to be free of conflict between students and teacher. Students concentrate better when they aren't worried about changing appearances and other personal problems.

Emotional and Social Development

The approach and onset of puberty signals a rapid move away from parental influence and toward greater independence. Sometimes transescents reject and defy adult authority. They criticize opinions, suggestions, and actions of adults. The questions of what young transescents should wear, say, and do are often considered beyond the scope of adult authority.

However, this rapid movement away from adult authority and towards greater independence is not accomplished smoothly. It is often accompanied by problems which develop because of the lack of judgment needed to handle their new roles of independence. These young people still have a strong need for a home base to which they can return for comfort in times of stress. Their lack of readiness for severing home ties completely makes it imperative that they have the security of the family and home or other adult role models to turn to, even as they struggle to develop their new independence. The situation is basically one of transition and change, and there is frequent evidence of the need for the security of childhood to balance out the emerging young adolescent role.

The importance of parents and school staff who understand this changing role cannot be overstated. Young transescents require freedom. Yet they must be assured of a secure base to turn to when the need to do so becomes urgent. Our changing society and the increasing number of disrupted homes further mandates the need for security in our young people. A quality guidance program in the middle school is one means of dealing with the transescent's efforts to exercise more independence in decision-making.

Transescents frequently fluctuate between emotional peaks of exuberance and depths of moodiness. Joy or happiness can give way to quiet and silence. The transescents seek greater privacy in this period. A place to store one's clothes, correspondence, and other possessions becomes important. Open sharing of these items becomes less frequent. The use of the telephone, television, and stereo becomes a matter of possession, often to the annoyance and inconvenience of other members of the family.

Discussion of the day's events at school or play is less readily volunteered as the transescent pursues privacy. Conversation is less spontaneous with members of the family. Periods of reticence are often followed by other periods of near monopoly of family discussions. Close questioning by adults will often be resented and followed by silence or a negative response. Transescents prefer to talk when they feel like it.

The peers with whom transescents spend time are now gradually taking the place of family and home. More and more, the concern of the growing young individual is with what his age group—not his family—thinks, does, and says. During these years, the young transescent often develops a close friendship with a peer of the same sex. According to Brendt's survey of the research on the features and effects of friendship in early adolescence, there is a striking increase in intimate communication and cooperation from what is found in middle childhood. Girls have more intimate and exclusive friendships than boys. Friendships tend to be relatively stable, at least over several months.[7]

Peer groups greatly influence clothes, hair, and grooming styles in this period. While clothing was only incidentally regarded in childhood, now it becomes a crucial matter that one wears what the others wear and that one's hairstyle and general appearance conform with the modes of the day for the age group. This strengthens the feeling of belonging to the group, of being "one of them," and equally of being less dependent upon adult direction. Crockett, Losoff, and Petersen found the clique, or friendship group, to be an important feature of the peer group. The importance attributed to cliques and positive attitudes towards cliques increases over time. Boys and girls considered the same qualities to be important for success in the peer group.[8]

Boys and girls alike seek out places where they can congregate with their interest mates. If such facilities are not provided by the school or another recognized community agency, transescents will meet at drive-in restaurants, parking lots, shopping malls, or other convenient locations. The more fortunate youngsters will find opportunities to gather together in homes where this is encouraged or tolerated. Here, they can talk, listen to popular music, play games, and enjoy themselves. The unmistakable point here is that the urge to meet with peers is a strong one, which will be satisfied by congregating in less wholesome places if these are the only ones available.

On a somewhat negative yet normal note, middle level students may be cruel to others, deliberately make fun of those who are different from them, or may hassle teachers to gain peer acceptance. In the extreme, they may be willing to commit acts of violence, take drugs, become sexually precocious, or become dependent on alcohol to be accepted by peers.[9] The need for social acceptance by peers dominates the transescent's behavior. Perhaps for no age group other than the emerging adolescent is there greater concern for peer acceptance.[10]

At this time an individual learns to feel, think, and act according to congruent sex roles.[11] There is little evidence to suggest that hormones directly influence gender roles and gender role identity. These constructs are embedded in sociocultural norms and expectations, which have a strong impact on hormonal influences.[12]

While the members of the opposite sex are regarded with growing interest and curiosity, the distance between them for the present remains considerable. It will be narrowed in following years. Transescents tend to make exaggerated responses to anything with sexual implications. However, at this age, since girls are often a year or more physically mature than boys, they experience a peculiar problem. Their interests in the opposite sex find more response from older boys. As a result, it is not uncommon for girls to associate with senior high school boys, who are more nearly their peers in terms of physical and emotional maturity. This has considerable implication for social events conducted both on and off the school property, and for the potential sexual dangers of younger girls associating with older boys.

One of the fascinating developments of this age group is a growing interest in ethics and morality. While childhood was characterized by an acceptance of adult-formulated standards or values, transescents begin to deviate from this pattern. They develop their own views on these matters that may be in conflict with previously held standards.

As individuals grow through the transescent years, increased dependence upon their own judgment and less dependence on that of their parents creates some uncertainties and anxieties. Are the transescents and their peers right, or are the parents? Dual standards are not acceptable to them. Standards which respond to reason and logic are acceptable. More than in any other way, the generation gap becomes vividly evident in this respect as transescents develop their own ideals and standards of behavior. As Havighurst suggests, the most significant lessons of transescence are emotional and social, not academic.[13]

THE TRANSESCENT AND OUR SOCIETY

The school is society's major institution for transmitting our cultural heritage and preparing our youth for participation in society. The general objectives of the school reflect our understanding and beliefs concerning the individual and society. The school reflects new insights and understandings that grow out of experience, observations, and research.

The previous section of this chapter described physical, intellectual, social, and emotional changes experienced by the middle school age student. It is also important to note the fact the vast changes transescents undergo take place in the unsettled environment of a troubled society. Recent reports present alarming statistics. The problems of school failure, substance abuse, violence, early sexual activity and resultant pregnancies and sexually transmitted diseases, and of single-parent families, pose a significant, immediate challenge for those designing middle schools. Statistics from the *Encyclopedia of Adolescents,* the Census Bureau, and the Child Defense Fund show that half of the 28 million Americans between 10 to 17 engage in two or more categories of risk behavior, ranging from unsafe sex to drug abuse to crime. According to Marion Wright Edelman, Children's Defense Fund president, some examples of the daily fate of neglected and deprived American children are:

> Every 8 seconds of a school day, a child drops out.
>
> Every 26 seconds a child runs away from home.
>
> Every 47 seconds, a child is abused or neglected.
>
> Every 67 seconds, a teenager has a baby.
>
> Every 8 minutes, a child is arrested for a drug offense.
>
> Every 30 minutes a child is arrested for drunken driving.
>
> Every 36 minutes a child is killed or injured by guns.
>
> Every day, 135,000 children bring guns to school.[14]

Joy Dryfoos sums up the problem poignantly:

> It appears that school failure begins to occur at very early ages, and that once failure occurs, other events begin to take place. . . . Doing poorly in school and minor delinquent offenses seem to fit together, and as these high-risk children grow older, substance abuse and sexual activity enter the picture, and the major negative consequences—early childbearing, heavy substance abuse, serious delinquency, school dropout—ensue. Obviously patterns differ dramatically. But what emerges is at least one central stream of high-risk children who are at particularly high risk of at least several of these difficulties.[15]

The transescent student is the most vulnerable to the above scenario. The physical and sexual self has matured at a rate exceeding the responsible social and emotional self. The educational institution becomes the primary hope for successfully addressing the unique needs of transescents. No longer can our society afford to sit back and assume that these needs will be met through the family or church.

Even though the school is in the best position to make the necessary difference with our students in this critical stage of transescence, the school cannot do it alone. As the report issued by the Carnegie Council on Adolescent Development (1989) states:

> All sectors of the society must be mobilized to build a national consensus to make transformation of middle grade schools a reality. . . . Through their efforts a community of learning can be created that engages those young adolescents for whom life already holds high promise, and welcomes into the mainstream of society those who might otherwise be left behind.[16]

A wide variety of social service agencies already exists for the purpose of serving children and youth at risk. However, services are often narrow in focus, cumbersome to access, and minimally effective. At a time when resources are decreasing as needs are increasing, it is incumbent on schools and community agencies to join together in a collaborative effort to address the complex needs of today's students.[17] Self-preserving separate bureaucracies no longer have a place in the human services field.

THE ROLE OF THE MIDDLE SCHOOL

The basic ways in which the middle school achieves its objectives are, of necessity, cast in terms of the task to be done, the individual students to be served. In dealing with 11 to 14 year olds, the middle school, the place to begin is with what has been observed and learned about them. Utilizing this knowledge, a general statement of objectives as follows may be developed.

1. Students should learn what they need to know to live present and future lives that are happy and useful to themselves and to their various communities—local, state, national, and world. Schools should facilitate the development of experiences, understandings, attitudes, and skills necessary to meet students' personal and social needs. Knowledge of our social and cultural heritage and of the skills of democratic decision making will help them function as democratic citizens.
2. Students need to acquire the basic tools of learning. These include subject matter and other skills which permit them to think rationally, clearly express thoughts, solve problems, and observe understandingly.
3. Schools can assist the growing transescent in moving from childhood dependence to adolescence and later to adult independence by providing opportunities for continued development of skills, attitudes, and understandings which were begun in the elementary school. They also need to provide opportunities for students to assume greater responsibility for themselves appropriate to their maturity.
4. Schools must provide students with the opportunity to explore interests through educational experiences, vocational choices, and social and recreational interests.
5. Counseling and positive experiences permit the growing young individual to develop the wholesome social competencies needed to enter young manhood or womanhood. Assistance is needed here, too, in accommodating the rapid physical changes so characteristic of imminent adolescence.

6. Also important are experiences which will assist changing and questioning young people as they seek to develop value systems acceptable both to themselves and to society, and to find their own unique philosophy for living.
7. At all times, schools must allow for individual differences. Flexible grouping, specially designed courses and materials, and increased use of electives all contribute to the accomplishment of this goal.

The most immediate data and information concerning the middle schooler derive from their visibly rapid physical maturation, cognitive development stages (Piaget), and brain growth periodization (Epstein). These physiological and intellectual changes are by no means uniform among different individuals. Neither do they occur with a consistent and constant pattern in any given individual. However, through observations of large numbers of transescents, it is possible to identify characteristics which are typical of the age group. Using these, then, schools can develop middle school programs intended to accommodate such changes. Following are listed a number of developmental characteristics of 11 to 14 year olds which educators need to consider. These are organized into the groups discussed in the previous pages, namely physical development, intellectual development, and social and emotional development. The aspects of growth in each of the three categories are briefly cited in Table 2.1. Then, following each cited characteristic, the implications that it bears for the transescents themselves and for the middle school's educational program are explored. Suggestions are given for consideration in planning the middle school program.[18]

TABLE 2.1 Relating the Curriculum to the Transescent

I. Physical Growth Characteristics	Implication for the Transescent (11–14 Years)	Curriculum Implications for the School
A. Body Growth		
The average gain in height of young adolescents is from 2 to 4 inches per year; the average weight gain per year is 8 to 10 pounds.	Develop an awareness that individuals grow at varying rates of speed and begin this rapid growth at different ages.	Emphasize self-understanding throughout the curriculum. This can be done by:
The growth pattern usually is the same for all boys and girls, but there are wide variations in the timing and degree of changes. The sequential order in which they occur stimulates overall growth of bones and tissue.	Learn to accept one's own body; realize, too, that classmates may develop differently; each individual is unique.	a. Providing health and science experiences that will develop an understanding of growth such as: (1) weighing and measuring at regular intervals and charting gains or losses; (2) observing growth of plants and animals; (3) learning about individual differences in growth.
The growth stimulating hormone of the pituitary gland is largely responsible for the growth rate.		b. Providing guidance at the classroom level and utilizing school counselor as a resource person.
		c. During physical education classes, providing for individual differences by having several groups of differing abilities.
Certain parts of the body, most notably, the extremities, develop earlier and more rapidly. This obviously affects movement.	Understand that others will be changing as well as oneself and that all preadolescents have similar difficulties in coping with these changes.	Provide opportunities for interaction among students of multiages.
Bones grow fast, muscles slower; the skeletal structure is extending more rapidly than the muscular structure.		Because of the vulnerability to bone fractures or breaks, young adolescents should not be pushed to their "limits."
The skeletal structure also begins to harden. The tail bone takes on its final form.		Transescents should not be expected to sit still for long periods of time. Classroom activities should be varied and provide for movement.

TABLE 2.1—*Continued*

I. Physical Growth Characteristics	Implication for the Transescent (11–14 Years)	Curriculum Implications for the School
B. Sexual Development—Puberty		
The onset of puberty is occurring earlier in today's youth than in past generations.		
Fifty percent of all girls will have begun breast development at age 11 years, 3 months; will have pubic hair at age 11 years, 6 months; and will have begun to menstruate at age 12 years, 8 months.	Understand that reproductive organs are developing. Girls should know that menstruation will soon occur and should know how to deal with it.	Provide instruction related to growth of the body so that one can better understand changes in him/herself and in others and be prepared for future changes and problems.
The average age in boys for the beginning of the enlargement of the testes is 12 years; the growth of the penis is 12 years, 3 months; and the appearance of pubic hair is 12 years, 6 months.	Boys should know that they may have nocturnal emissions.	
There is tremendous variation as to when sexual changes begin to occur and how rapidly they take place.	Understand that a wide range exists.	Provide instruction in the wide range of events to reduce any anxiety of not being normal.
Girls are usually taller and proportionately heavier than boys. Boys are growing broad-shouldered, deep chested and heavier with a more noticeable voice change than in girls. Most rapid growth has occurred by 13 1/2–14 and most have experienced ejaculation.	Develop the habit of periodic visits to the doctor and dentist.	
C. Health and Body Management		
The typical middle school student craves food; this tendency is reinforced by the draining off of nutrients into the rapid growth of body organs. Overtaxing the digestive system with large quantities of poorly selected foods is a normal experimental activity at this age.	Understand that stomach does become longer and increased in capacity. Select food carefully.	Provide instruction in proper nutrition. Provide nutritious, well-balanced selection of food in school cafeteria.

TABLE 2.1—*Continued*

I. Physical Growth Characteristics	Implication for the Transescent (11–14 Years)	Curriculum Implications for the School
Excessive perspiration becomes a problem as sweat glands become active and emit offensive odor.	Learn good health habits such as bathing regularly and using deodorant.	
The appearance of acne may cause students to feel extremely sensitive.	Be aware of sales propaganda for beauty aids which may be harmful or ineffective.	
Endurance is usually not high, perhaps because of the rapid growth spurt. Pre-adolescents can overtire themselves in exciting competition. Heart and circulatory system develop more slowly than bones and muscles, so symptoms of fatigue may be displayed.	Develop good habits for diet, exercise and rest. Nine hours of sleep is usually needed.	Formulate school policy regarding homework assignments to ensure adequate play and rest time.
Extreme restlessness and alternating periods of almost hyperactivity and fatigue reflect variations in basal metabolic rates.	Develop a balance between mental and physical activities.	Provide instruction in the wide range of events to reduce any anxiety of not being normal.

II. Intellectual Growth Characteristics	Implication for the Transescent (11–14 Years)	Curriculum Implications for the School
A. Intellectual Development		
The early stages of transescence (ages 10–12 years) are usually characterized by success in initiating new and higher level cognitive processes because of the brain growth spurt experienced by about 85% of youngsters during this time.		Provide learning experiences for transescents at their own intellectual levels, relating to immediate rather than remote academic goals.
About 85% of 12–14-year-olds experience a plateau in brain growth.	Be aware of this characteristic and do not become discouraged when some learning tasks are difficult.	Concentrate upon reinforcement of existing cognitive skills and reinforcement of psychomotor, affective, and self-concept development.

TABLE 2.1—*Continued*

II. Intellectual Growth Characteristics	Implication for the Transescent (11–14 Years)	Curriculum Implications for the School
The transescent is gradually moving from the period of concrete operations to formal operations, still relying heavily on concrete operational reasoning.	Engage in activities which enable one to grow in the ability to carry out concrete operations. Grow in the ability to solve problems.	Learning objectives should be sequenced to allow for transition from concrete to formal operations. Instruction should rely heavily on hands-on activities that require the student to reason about interrelationships that are present or are being created.
		Provide activities in both the formal and informal situations to improve the student's reasoning powers.
Transescents display wide ranges of skills, interests, and abilities. Slow-rate and fast-rate learners both continue to grow toward mental maturity at their own rates.	Understand that others will differ in intellectual interest and abilities. Learn to be tolerant of these differences. Continue to expand interest by selecting books which challenge.	Individualized instruction should be provided so that the student can proceed successfully at his or her own pace and level of ability without undue competitive pressures.
		Provide experiences to challenge each youngster's thinking abilities in the instructional program. Keep an adequate number of books at all levels of reading ability.
Transescents are curious and enjoy both intellectual and manipulative activities appropriate to their stage of development. They prefer active involvement in learning rather than passive recipiency.		Provide a diversified curriculum of exploratory and fundamental activities resulting in daily successful experiences that will stimulate and nurture intellectual development. Encourage personal curiosity, with one learning experience inspiring subsequent activities.
Transescents enjoy discussing experiences with adults. They are able to evaluate issues critically, though not always objectively.	Realize that one's experience is limited, and that others who have more experience may have something to offer.	Adults who covertly role-model their own emergence through sharing perspectives, information, and points-of-view rather than directing without involvement are vital for the growth and development of middle school youth. Provide positive feedback to individuals about learning activities that will help build a sense of self-worth for the individual, of the process, and of the product.

TABLE 2.1—*Continued*

II. Intellectual Growth Characteristics	Implication for the Transescent (11–14 Years)	Curriculum Implications for the School
Transescents display a heightened egocentrism which is often balanced through peer interaction. They argue to clarify personal thinking as much as to convince others.		Provide a balanced program of exploratory experiences and other activities and services for personal development, and provide appropriate attention to the development of values.
Interests, attention span, and concentration alter during transescence, generally assuming shorter rather than longer periods of focus.	Participate in many activities so that attention span will increase in those activities most enjoyed.	Recognize that students have varying attention spans and make provisions for this variation in the instructional program, homework, etc. Teach students how to study.
		Combine previously departmentalized areas of the curriculum and teach around integrative themes, topics, and experiences.
Learners are concerned with intellectual, philosophical, biological, sociological, moral and ethical issues. They have an increased ability to see through situations and seek to find causal and correlative relationships.		Show consideration for who the student is and who he or she becomes, his or her self-concept, self-responsibility, and attitudes toward school and personal happiness; and for how much and what he or she knows.

B. Interests, Creative Ability, Appreciations

Interests are related to accelerating physical growth, increasingly strong emotional reactions, and the awareness of new roles awaiting them in society.		Provide reading materials which contain examples of emotional problem solving, various occupations, and problems of human relations.
There is a wide variety of interests and individual differences become greater.	Recognize that everyone does not have the same interests.	Provide reading instruction which is individualized. This is more effective than level grouping.
Reading and collecting equal or exceed the high rates of later childhood.	Recognize that reading can be an avenue to open up many new experiences.	Provide opportunities for reading individually and in organizing clubs in various interest areas.
This is the period of excessive daydreaming.	Excessive day dreaming can be avoided through involvement in many activities.	Provide a program of learning which is exciting and meaningful.

TABLE 2.1—*Continued*

II. Intellectual Growth Characteristics	Implication for the Transescent (11–14 Years)	Curriculum Implications for the School
Transescents become more preoccupied with themselves and their appearance.		Provide experiences in clothing and textiles, food and nutrition.
Individual differences in creative ability are pronounced. Exceptional talent, if given opportunity and training, develops rapidly. Some students are self-conscious and highly critical of themselves.	Do the best you can when expressing yourself. Recognize that mistakes will happen. Be tolerant of the mistakes of others.	Provide experiences for individuals to express themselves by writing and participating in dramatic productions.
Writing, dramatizing, and painting are particularly appealing for self-expression and creative expression.		Aesthetic components of the curriculum, such as art and music, should be considered basic ingredients of the middle school program and not treated as "frills."
Diaries, poetry, and letters are used for expressing thoughts.	Recognize that these forms of expression are useful in organizing thoughts.	Encourage journal and diary as part of the curriculum.

III. Emotional and Social Characteristics	Implication for the Transescent (11–14 Years)	Curriculum Implication for the School
A. Emotional Status		
Transescents experience an extreme variance in moods. They frequently appear unable to control their emotions and lose themselves in anger, fear, love, joy, sadness, etc. Often no relationship exists between the importance of the situation and violence of reaction.	Understand that one is in a period of extreme violent moods with emphasis on exerting some control. Understand that peer friends who "blow up" are not necessarily bad. They are only doing what is natural to all peers.	Discuss values, morality, and what's important. Get children's feelings on these. If consideration emerges, stress this for children to remember in relationships. Surprise students often with different activities; make creative use of the strangeness of the age. Help children find activities at which they excel. Provide for ample variety of outlets to emotions and for educational learning.

TABLE 2.1—Continued

III. Emotional and Social Characteristics	Implication for the Transescent (11–14 Years)	Curriculum Implication for the School
Uncertainty may begin along with strict self-criticism and strict criticism of others. Criticisms from adult sources are not easily tolerated, even when they concern things the transescent is prone to criticize.	Learn to judge self and others with less criticism.	When criticism is necessary, it should be delivered privately and constructively.
		Provide dramatic experiences which allow the child to release tension, to take different roles, and to achieve satisfaction in the eyes of peers.
Frustrations grow out of conflicts with parents or peers, an awareness of lack of social skills, or in failure to mature as rapidly as others.	Realize the turmoil of the period they are in, the gap that exists between older and younger, and that younger sibling has feelings, too.	
Anger is common and may grow out of feelings of inadequacy, fatigue, rejections, or uncertainty.		
The transescent desires attention, at times without regard to how it is secured.		Provide a wide range of awards and recognition activities. Give praise publicly. Find reason for positive reinforcement daily.
Fears are more in form of worries, primarily over non-acceptance. The transescent also worries because of increasing demands of self as well as of school and home.	Realize that there are scientific causes for the things that are happening. Understand that everyone worries and that fear is natural. Learn to discover those sources where one can seek personal assistance such as counselor, teacher, parent. See how worry tends to beget worry and that emotional outlet in some form is necessary for everyone—physical activity, involvement with others, reading, other.	Discuss worries and fears in class. Encourage freedom of expression of feelings and in communicating problems. Show examples of people who have had problems and have learned to overcome them. Explain that many adults strive to help this group. Attempt to build faith in home, school and agencies, with emphasis on parents, teachers and counselors. Tell students who to consult when necessary.

TABLE 2.1—*Continued*

III. Emotional and Social Characteristics	Implication for the Transescent (11–14 Years)	Curriculum Implication for the School
B. Independence		
The transescent begins to cut loose from parents. Adult standards and conventions may be ignored, ridiculed and at times, defied.	Give opportunity for each child to be independent at times and yet attempt to help each develop security within the group.	Understand that it is normal at this age to want to be independent. Provide learning activities which include independent study.
Transescents vacillate between their desire for regulation and direction, and their demand for independence.		In successful schools, limits are clear but unobtrusive and the school day is structured but not regimented. Consequences for undesirable behavior should be predictable. Positive reinforcement should be given for desirable behavior. Advisor-advisee programs provide needed security in the struggle for independence.
Home hostilities are expanded but if channeled by giving choice, transescents are more apt to select an activity to do. They generally hate to work early in period, especially at home.	Show youngster the need for responsibility in group situations and in own. Let child know that their feelings in situations may be another's feelings in another situation.	Provide opportunities to discuss feelings displayed at home and how to cope with them. Try to get students to empathize and to be fair and considerate.
They begin to accept views of others and to live in harmony with those with whom they disagree.	Learn how to live with others in many different life situations.	Provide many situations where they grow in their ability to work with the group or other individuals.
The acceptance of work becomes natural.	Acceptance of work responsibility is part of growing up.	Provide activities which help student to work well, complete jobs, and to be increasingly responsible.
The transescent wishes to preserve a self-identity; often wishes to be alone; spends time in reflective thinking toward end of the transescent period of development.	Understand that at times they want to be alone rather than with the group.	Provide a quiet corner for independent study both in the classroom and in the Instructional Materials Center.

TABLE 2.1—*Continued*

III. Emotional and Social Characteristics	Implication for the Transescent (11–14 Years)	Curriculum Implication for the School
Self-concept is affected by personal appearance, attitude expressed toward family and other adults, and acceptance by peers and adults.		Provide advisor-advisee program which uses discussions to provide a chance to hear how others think and feel without taking excessive risks. In successful advisory programs, students learn as much about themselves as they do about each other.
Conscience becomes more apparent at this stage. The transescent exhibits strong feelings about fairness, honesty and values in adults but "relaxes" their own. Example: Cheating in school, shoplifting. This dichotomy may grow out of greater need for wide variety of articles, greater chance of success in not getting caught, pressure of gang, general emotional stability of age.	Realize that nearly everything is not absolutely right or wrong, black and white, but that there are many gray areas. Learn that there are two sides to every situation.	Let the students help develop a method for establishment of some classroom rules. Show the need for rules in a simple society and for a complex society.
The transescent's sense of simple justice is strong—wants fair teachers and is quick to challenge anyone unfair.	Develop a respect for self, for self-inspection, and plans for improvement.	Develop sense of responsibility, that each of us is responsible to someone or something every minute of our lives.
		Teaching-learning situations (consistent with basic democratic principles) will provide the surroundings conducive to positive individual personality development.

C. Peer Acceptance

Family allegiances diminish and peer allegiances become stronger.	Help transescent learn polite meaningful ways of persuasion, to talk and express self to parents, peers, and others with a minimum of antagonistic characteristics.	Provide role playing activities to understand personal and family problems.

TABLE 2.1—*Continued*

III. Emotional and Social Characteristics	Implication for the Transescent (11–14 Years)	Curriculum Implication for the School
Much behavior is role-playing and cannot be taken at face value. The transescent must respond as the group would expect. They may say "the rest of the kids are doing it." They could show lack of concern for family but look out if one is in bad health or needs help. Much concern is displayed.		Gain the support of student leaders. Set up student advisory committees and initiate special projects.
The desire for social acceptance leads to attempts to become effectively gregarious. Efforts are made to gain acceptance by sub-groups with whose standards they wish to conform. Individuality is surrendered in a desire to be accepted.		Provide for positive social interaction (i.e., a "friendly, not-so-quiet" lunchroom). Never embarrass or humiliate students. Provide opportunities for them to be many different people in a non-threatening environment.
The group is all important. Transescent group loyalty carries out group will with indifference and sometimes cruelty to outsiders. Conformity to the groups in terms of mannerisms, dress, speech and behavior often runs counter to social expectations of adults.	Learn that group behavior means giving as well as taking, that there are "rules" in any society. Recognize those conformists who are tied to the group, help them realize this is natural, help each to become confident within themselves somewhat as well.	Analyze the behavior of the group and attempt to sort out desirable and undesirable characteristics.
Transescents are willing to work hard and sacrifice, especially if social rewards are involved. Altruism and high ideals in the search for beauty and truth are directed toward institutions such as school, community, church, and government.		
In play, the competitive spirit and the will to excel are primary at early stages.	Encourage all to participate in some game.	Provide opportunities for a variety of activities, especially lifetime activities, so that a student may excel in one.

TABLE 2.1—*Continued*

III. Emotional and Social Characteristics	Implication for the Transescent (11–14 Years)	Curriculum Implication for the School
	Encourage all to be considerate of each other in the game with understanding that some are naturally better at game than others.	Provide opportunity for all girl, all boy games; for mixed activity; and for activity where each can succeed to the best of one's ability.
Team play is understood and practiced. Transescents can work reasonably well together but ground rules should have first been established and a supervisor should be in charge.	Attempt to provide at least one group activity in which each person can excel and one where each will experience some sense of inferiority.	Provide activity for increasingly difficult coordination in both boys' and girls' interests.
	Learn that on a team, all must contribute.	
	Learn that criticizing each other on a team can cause internal decay. Building each member is a way to win.	
Near end of period, group play is still appreciated, but not for winning. Participants are more concerned about how well each did. Rules are not needed as much; the group is more able to make up rules as needed.	Learn to develop leadership qualities and also follower qualities. Participate in vigorous exercise but also in the quiet and spectator games.	Provide active and quiet team activities in curricular and noncurricular learnings.

D. Friendship and Sex Role Identification

Transescents begin to develop intimate friendships (caring and cooperation) with members of their own sex. Girls have more intimate and exclusive friendships than boys. Friendships do appear to be relatively stable, at least over several months.

TABLE 2.1—Continued

III. Emotional and Social Characteristics	Implication for the Transescent (11–14 Years)	Curriculum Implication for the School
As emerging adolescents formulate a self-concept, they also encounter what it means to be a male or female. At this time an individual learns to feel, think, and act in a role congruent with his or her sex. Although sex roles are changing, certain types of behavior are still associated with a particular sex.	Understand that sex roles are changing and are embedded in socio-cultural norms and expectations.	Provide exposure to non-traditional careers for men and women. Invite resource persons to interact with students, e.g. female fire fighter, male secretary.
The period begins by boys loathing girls but girls liking boys. Much teasing occurs between sexes, e.g. "stealing" loose articles of clothing.	Learn how one functions with the opposite sex.	Develop an understanding of the opposite sex through readings, discussions, role playing, etc.
Transescents tend to make exaggerated responses to anything with sexual implications.		
Interests in the other sex increase with time. By end of period, both prefer mixed parties.		Activities should be carefully planned to promote the acquisition of social skills and to minimize elitism.

SUMMARY

The school years that follow the elementary grades and precede high school are a cause for concern on the part of parents and teachers. Rapid changes, not only physical but emotional, social, and intellectual as well require understanding of the nature of such changes and the means for dealing with them. With this understanding, transescents can adjust to these changes and accept them in a wholesome way.

The drive for independence, the continual search for peer acceptance, the adjustment to the onset of puberty and a growing awareness of the other sex all occupy a major portion of the attention of the transescent. All are a source of anxiety and concern for the individual. Provision for these rapid changes and emerging drives should be reflected in the curriculum, class schedules and other organizational and operational arrangements of the middle school.

ENDNOTES

1. Van Hoose, John, and David Strahan. *Young Adolescent Development and School Practices: Promoting Harmony.* Columbus, Ohio: National Middle School Association, 1988.

2. Wavering, Michael J. "Research and Logical Reasoning of Middle School Students," in Deborah A. Butler (Ed.), *In the Middle: Perspectives on Transescence and Middle School Education.* ERIC Document #250 078 (June 1984).

3. Bondi, Joseph C., and Thomas S. Tocco. "The Nature of the Transescent as it Affects Middle School Program Evaluation." ERIC Document #3 094 462 (1974).

4. See note 3.

5. Toepfer, Conrad. "A Realistic Expectation for Cognitive Growth During Transescence." ERIC Document #141 316 (March 1977).

6. Toepfer, Conrad. "Brain Growth Periodization—A New Dogma for Education." *Middle School Journal,* 10:3 (August, 1979).

7. Brendt, Thomas J. "The Features and Effects of Friendship in Early Adolescence." *Child Development* 77 (1982): 1447–1460.

8. Crockett, Lisa, Mike Losoff, and Anne C. Petersen. "Perceptions of the Peer Group and Friendship in Early Adolescence." *Journal of Early Adolescence* 4:2 (1985): 155–181.

9. See note 2.

10. Gatewood, Thomas E., and Charles A. Dilg. "The Middle School We Need." A Report from the A.S.C.D. Working Group on the Emerging Adolescent. ERIC Document #113 821. (1975).

11. See note 10.

12. McNeill, Suzanne, and Anne C. Petersen. "Gender Role and Identity in Early Adolescence: Reconsideration of Theory." *Academic Psychology Bulletin* (Winter, 1985): 7.

13. Havighurst, R. J. *Developmental Tasks and Education,* 3rd Edition. New York: David McKay Co., 1979.

14. Machacek, John. "Advocate says U.S. needs to be more aware of kids' needs." *Lansing State Journal* (Monday, November 19, 1990): 3A.

15. Dryfoos, Joy. "Making the Middle Grades Work." An Adolescent Pregnancy Prevention Clearinghouse Report. Washington D.C., 1988.

16. Carnegie Council on Adolescent Development. "Turning Points: Preparing American Youth for the 21st Century." New York: Carnegie Corporation of New York. June, 1989.

17. Guthrie, Grace Pung, and Larry F. Guthrie. "Streamlining Interagency Collaboration for Youth at Risk," *Educational Leadership,* 49:1 (September, 1991): 17–22.

18. The following sources were used in the development of Table 2.1.

Physical Development

Bondi, J., and T. Tocco. (1974). *The Nature of the Transescent as It Affects Middle School Program Evaluation.* ERIC Document #ED 094 462.

Gatewood, T., and C. Dilg. (1975). *The Middle School We Need.* A report from the A.S.C.D. Working Group on the Emerging Adolescent. ERIC Document #ED 113 821.

NMSA (1982). *This We Believe.* Columbus, Ohio: National Middle School Association.

Romano, L., J. Hedberg, and M. Lulich. (1973). "Developmental Characteristics of Pre-Adolescents and Their Implications," in L. Romano, N. Georgiady, and J. Heald, Eds. *The Middle School.* Chicago, Illinois: Nelson-Hall Co., Publishers.

VanHoose, J., and D. Strahan. (1988). *Young Adolescent Development and School Practices: Promoting Harmony.* Columbus, Ohio: National Middle School Association.

Intellectual Development

Gatewood and Dilg. (1975)

NMSA. (1982)

Romano. (1973)

Toepfer, C. (1979). "Brain Growth Periodization—A New Dogma for Education." *Middle School Journal.* Volume 10, No. 3.

Educational and Social Development

Brendt, T. (1982). "The Features and Effects of Friendship in Early Adolescence." *Child Development.* Volume 53, pages 1447–1460.

Gatewood and Dilg. (1975)

Romano. (1973)

REFERENCES

Bondi, Joseph C., and Thomas S. Tocco. "The Nature of the Transescent as It Affects Middle School Program Evaluation." ERIC Document #094 462 (1974).

Brendt, Thomas J. "The Features and Effects of Friendship in Early Adolescence." *Child Development,* 53 (1982): 1447–1460.

Carnegie Council on Adolescent Development. *Turning Points: Preparing American Youth for the 21st Century.* New York: Carnegie Corporation, June, 1989.

Crockett, Lisa, Mike Losoff, and Anne C. Petersen. "Perceptions of the Peer Group and Friendship in Early Adolescence." *Journal of Early Adolescence* 4:2 (1985): 155–181.

Dryfoos, Joy in "Making the Middle Grades Work." An Adolescent Pregnancy Prevention Clearinghouse report by the Children's Defense Fund. Washington, D.C., 1988.

Edelman, Marion Wright in John Machacek, "Advocate says U.S. needs to be more aware of kids' needs." *Lansing State Journal* (Monday, November 19, 1990): 3A.

Eichorn, Donald. *The Middle School.* New York: The Center for Applied Research in Education, Inc., 1969.

Eichorn, Donald in John H. Lounsbury, (Ed.), *Perspectives: Middle School Education.* Columbus, Ohio: National Middle School Association, 1984.

Epstein, Herman in John H. Lounsbury, (Ed.), *Perspectives: Middle School Education.* Columbus, Ohio: National Middle School Association, 1984.

Gatewood, Thomas E., and Charles A. Dilg. "The Middle School We Need." A Report from the A.S.C.D. Working Group on The Emerging Adolescent. ERIC Document #113 821. (1975).

Guthrie, Grace Pung, and Larry F. Guthrie. "Streamlining Interagency Collaboration for Youth at Risk." *Educational Leadership,* 49:1 (September, 1991): 17–22.

Havighurst, R. J. *Developmental Tasks and Education,* 3rd Edition. New York: David McKay Co., 1979.

Lerner, Richard in Darci McConnell, "Director of MSU institute pushes for youth programs." *Lansing State Journal.* (October 2, 1991).

McNeill, Suzanne, and Anne C. Petersen. "Gender Role and Identity in Early Adolescence: Reconsideration of Theory." *Academic Psychology Bulletin* 7 (Winter, 1985).

Piaget, Jean. *Science of Education and the Psychology of the Child.* New York: Orion Press, 1970.

Romano, Louis G., James D. Hedberg, and Mark Lulich. "Developmental Characteristics of Pre-adolescents and Their Implications." In L. Romano, N. Georgiady, and J. Heald, (Eds.), *The Middle School.* Chicago, Illinois: Nelson-Hall Co., 1973.

Toepfer, Conrad. "A Realistic Expectation for Cognitive Growth During Transescence." ERIC Document #141 316 (March, 1977).

Toepfer, Conrad. "Brain Growth Periodization—A New Dogma for Education." *Middle School Journal,* 10:3 (August, 1979).

Van Hoose, John, and David Strahan. *Young Adolescent Development and School Practices: Promoting Harmony.* Columbus, Ohio: National Middle School Association, 1988.

Wavering, Michael J. "Research and Logical Reasoning of Middle School Students," in Deborah A. Butler, (Ed.), "In the Middle: Perspectives on Transescence and Middle School Education." ERIC Document #250 078 (June, 1984).

3

Changing from a Traditional Junior High School to a True Middle School

PREPARING FOR THE CHANGE TO A MIDDLE SCHOOL

The best reason for the development of a middle school is that it provides for an educational organization and program consistent with the needs of youngsters between 11 and 14 years of age.

Unfortunately, not all middle schools have been planned with this important goal in mind. As pointed out in Chapter 1, middle schools have been established for reasons not related to the nature and needs of students in this critical age group. In addition, some communities may presently be considering a move to a middle school organization.

This chapter is intended to assist in both kinds of situations. It provides important criteria for (1) the reexamination of the organization and function of an existing middle school and (2) for the systematic transition from a traditional junior high school to a true middle school, with each important step in the process identified and clearly explained. To make the process more pragmatic and to assist educators and lay citizens in following the steps, we will use a hypothetical program in ''Middle Town,'' a small city, with two traditional junior high schools. We will show how the change-over to middle schools was planned and carried out there.

First and foremost, the new program should be one that meets the needs of these unique students. It is critical, therefore, that from the start, attention should focus on what the nature and needs of the students in this age group are. Throughout the process, any question about an organizational, curricular, or instructional concern should be decided by how well it fits with these characteristics of this age group.

MAKING THE DECISION TO CHANGE

This planning process in Middle Town begins with a decision by the Board of Education to move to a middle school organization. The decision becomes a charge to the Superintendent or a designee, with the first step being the appointment of personnel who will make up the Middle School Planning Council (MSPC). This will include administrators, teachers and interested members of the community. The purpose of the Middle School Planning Council is to organize and coordinate the activities of the various working subcommittees that will be appointed.

APPOINTING THE MIDDLE SCHOOL PLANNING COUNCIL

In this hypothetical case of Middle Town, the Superintendent of Schools appoints the Director of Instruction to chair the MSPC. She or he is chosen because of the following qualifications:

1. A concern about the total educational program from kindergarten through grade twelve.
2. A strong interest in the orderly, sequential development of learning, including those of the middle school level.
3. The leadership skills needed to bring together a diverse group of people and enable them to work effectively.

It is agreed that the Middle School Planning Council should be limited to 8 to 13 people so that it can be representative district-wide, but not so large as to be cumbersome and unworkable. Using 12 as an example, there would be four lay people, six teachers representing grades 6, 7, and 8, and the two junior high principals, providing a good balance in membership. The principals ask for volunteers from the teaching staff. Those not chosen for the Council could later be included on the study committees for more specific planning tasks.

At the first planning session of the MSPC, the Superintendent of Schools or the Chairperson of the MSPC outlines the charge to the council. It is emphasized that the council is responsible to the Superintendent of Schools, serving as an *advisory group* on the implementation of middle schools. Once the tasks are completed, the council, which is an ad hoc or temporary body, will be dissolved. (See Figure 3.1.)

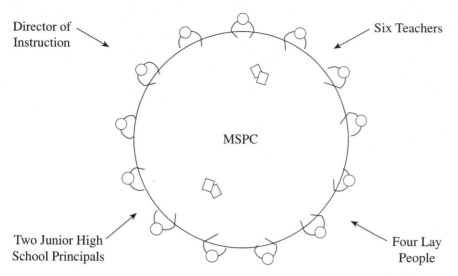

Director of
Instruction

Six Teachers

MSPC

Two Junior High
School Principals

Four Lay
People

FIGURE 3.1
Middle School Planning
Council.

C. William Brubaker, Perkins
and Wills Architects,
Chicago, IL.

Furthermore, the resources and constraints of the MSPC will be spelled
out. These include funds for resource materials, such as books and audiovisual materials, costs involved in visitations to other middle schools and
attendance at middle school conferences. Also included are funds to secure
the services of a competent consultant or consultants as well as secretarial
assistance when needed. (See Figure 3.2.)

The Chairperson of the MSPC suggests to the group that it would be
advisable to have one or two knowledgeable persons come in and meet with
them to insure arriving at a common understanding of what a middle school
is. Furthermore, it is suggested that a number of resource materials be sent
to each member of the Council so they can do some advance reading. The
council agrees.

GATHERING INFORMATION

A well-known university professor or a successful middle school principal or
teacher who has an in-depth understanding of a middle school is asked to
speak with the MSPC. Prior to this visit, a list of questions concerning a
middle school is collected from council members. Answers to the questions

FIGURE 3.2
Resources Needed by
the MSPC.
C. William Brubaker,
Perkins and Wills
Architects, Chicago, IL.

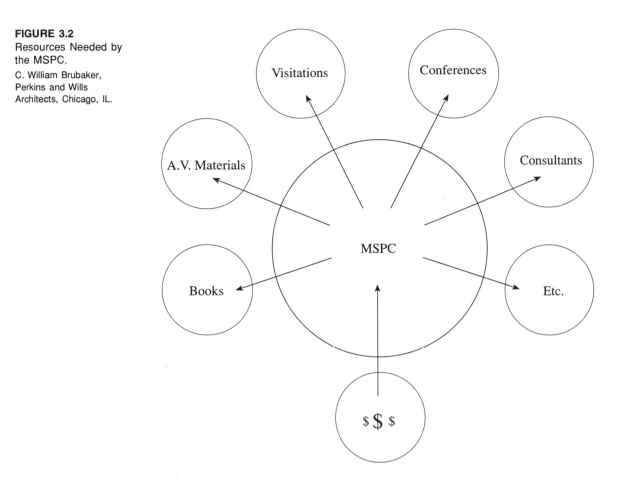

are incorporated into the speaker's presentation. Following the presentation and discussion, the chairperson asks the council and the speaker how they might proceed with their responsibility.

A member of the council recommends that a presentation be made to the present junior high parents and the incoming sixth grade parents. This presentation will center on (a) Why a middle school? (b) What makes these pre-adolescents so unique? and (c) What instructional strategies best meet the needs of these youngsters? The council agrees, but also adds that at least two more sessions should be planned with parents. These will give them an overview of the progress of the various committees toward building a middle school program.

FORMING WORKING COMMITTEES

At another meeting, the MSPC agrees to have the following committees formed:

> Philosophy of a Middle School
> Language Arts, including Reading
> Social Studies
> Mathematics
> Science
> Unified Arts
> Physical Education and Intramural
> Music
> Scheduling
> Instructional Media Center
> Guidance
> Enrichment Activities
> Social Activities
> Reporting Pupil Progress
> Instructional Strategies

Philosophy Committee

One of the most important committees would be the Middle School Philosophy Committee. The philosophy statement is a position paper on what a middle school is. It should serve as an important guideline for the efforts of all of the other study committees. The membership of this committee might typically include one Board of Education member, one central office administrator, two teachers from each grade 6, 7, and 8, both junior high school principals, one elementary principal, one senior high principal, and two parents. (See Figure 3.3.)

The Philosophy Committee should begin its work immediately and complete its report as quickly as possible. The committee should report on the nature of the pre-adolescent student today and tell how a middle school can provide for the unmet needs of this individual. It should include a discussion of the teaching-learning strategies which promote greater learning for these youngsters and give some important elements of the curriculum of the middle school.

Periodic reports should be shared with the teachers for constructive suggestions and reactions.

FIGURE 3.3
Philosophy Committee.
C. William Brubaker, Perkins
and Wills Architects,
Chicago, IL.

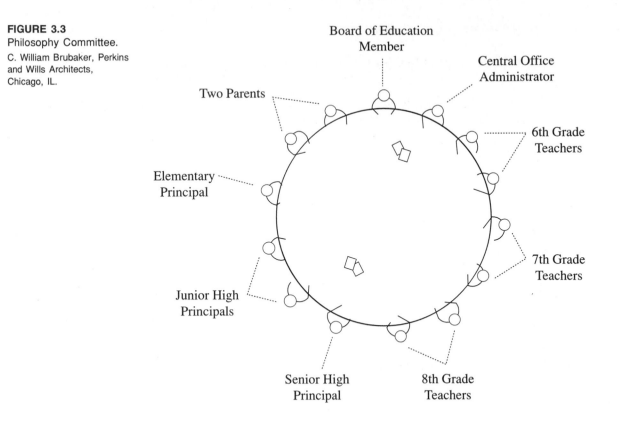

Planning for Math

The council decides that each study committee should be given a list of carefully prepared questions designed to assist them. For example, the math committee may be asked;

"What math skills should be developed in grades six to eight?"

"Are these skills part of the sequential development of math skills grades 1 through 12?"

"What teacher aids should be developed to be used in math teaching?"

These questions are suggested. The math committee may want to revise or elaborate further.

The committee membership should be made up of two teachers from grades 6, 7, and 8, one administrator and two parents. Some school districts may want to include an elementary teacher and a high school teacher to insure full continuity in the teaching of math skills.

Planning for Language Arts

The Language Arts Committee is asked ''What are the skills to be developed in reading, writing, speaking, and listening from the 6th grade to the 8th grade?'' ''What units of study should be included in English and Spelling?'' Because of the extensive work needed here, the study committee is often made up of four teachers from each grade 6, 7, and 8, one administrator, one reading consultant, and four parents.

Planning for Social Studies

The Social Studies Committee is asked to define the units of study to be covered in grades 6, 7, and 8 and to keep in mind what is being taught in the elementary grades and the high school. Once the units are defined, the committee is asked how to use the following format for the units. Each unit should include the behavioral objectives to be taught, at least five activities for achieving the particular objective, and the materials of instruction needed for each activity. Each unit will include a pretest so as to regroup students into cooperative learning groups. A posttest would also need to be included to determine if the students met the objectives of the unit.

The membership of the Social Studies Committee would include two teachers from each grade 6, 7, and 8, one administrator, and two parents. The size of the membership and the general tasks would be the same for the Science Study Committee.

Planning for Unified Arts

The Unified Arts Committee would determine what units of study need to be included in industrial arts, home economics, and art. Furthermore, this committee should study the possibility of an integration of these instructional areas into a Unified Arts block. This committee would be made up of two industrial arts teachers, two art teachers, two home economics teachers, two regular teachers, and two parents. The regular classroom teachers can assist in determining interrelated activities.

Planning for Music

The Music Committee should be concerned with the development of units of study in music for grades 6, 7, and 8. They will also be concerned with how music can be integrated with other instructional areas such as social studies, science, and language arts, along with integration with the elementary and high school programs. The committee membership will include the two junior high music teachers, one elementary traveling music teacher, one high school music teacher, two parents, and two regular classroom teachers.

Planning for Physical Education

The Physical Education Committee will be concerned with the definition of physical education skills to be developed in grades 6, 7, and 8. This committee should also define what health concepts can best be taught in the physical education classes. Another important concern of this group is the development of a strong intramural program for both boys and girls. The membership will include one physical education teacher from each grade 6, 7, and 8, one elementary physical education teacher, one high school physical education teacher, two regular junior high classroom teachers, and three parents.

Planning for Instructional Strategies

The Instructional Strategies Committee will be concerned with how the middle school staff should be organized to teach the students. Some of the problems they must deal with include:

What is team teaching?
What forms of teaming are presently in operation?
Should interage grouping be employed?
How do we meet individual differences?
What is interdisciplinary teaching?
If we team teach, how do we provide time for planning as a team?

The membership of this committee includes two teachers from each grade 6, 7, and 8, one junior high administrator, and two parents.

Planning for Scheduling

The Scheduling Committee will be concerned with these problems as well as others:

How should the various instructional areas be scheduled?
How are large blocks of time included to facilitate team teaching?
How can the schedule be opened for enrichment activities?

The members of the committee will include one teacher from each grade 6, 7, and 8, one junior high administrator, and two parents. We recommend that

	1	2	3	4	5	6	7
M	Team Subjects				Lunch	SAS	SAS
T	Team Subjects				Lunch	SAS	SAS
W	Team Subjects			Lunch	SAS	SAS	SAS
T	Team Subjects				Lunch	Special	
F	Team Subjects			Lunch	SAS	Area Subjects	

FIGURE 3.4
Team Teaching Schedule.
C. William Brubaker, Perkins and Wills Architects, Chicago, IL.

this committee and the Instructional Strategies Committee should meet together occasionally because of the related nature of the problems to be studied.

In Figure 3.4 the team subjects (math, science, social studies, and language arts) are taught in large blocks enabling team members to work with the same students for longer periods of time. The students complete their studies in other specialized subject areas such as music, art, physical education, computer instruction, industrial arts, and home economics.

Planning for Enrichment Activities

The Enrichment Activities Committee will explore the type of enrichment activities from which to choose other than those included in the regular instructional program. They will also survey staff members to determine what skills or knowledge they possess that would be available for this program. One teacher from each grade 6, 7, and 8 plus two parents will be the membership of this committee.

Instructional Media Center

In the Middle School, the Instructional Media Center (IMC) plays a significantly different role from that of the traditional school library. Therefore, the Instructional Media Center Committee will study the following problems:

What is the role of the Instructional Media Center in a middle school?

What software and hardware are essential to meet the varying interests of these students?

What services should be offered to students? To teachers?

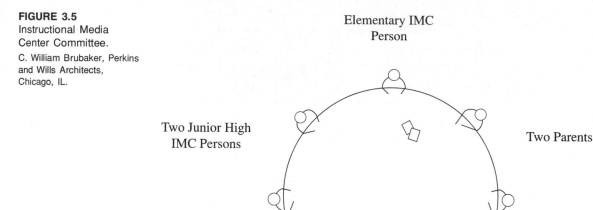

FIGURE 3.5
Instructional Media
Center Committee.

C. William Brubaker, Perkins
and Wills Architects,
Chicago, IL.

How do the IMC personnel function to facilitate teaching and learning done in the regular classroom situation?

What inventories and other information are needed to assist teachers in finding learning materials and other resources?

What procedures are needed to facilitate the acquisition of materials of instruction by teachers and students?

How can centers for various instructional areas be used effectively in the IMC?

The membership of this committee will include the two IMC personnel from the junior highs, one IMC person from the elementary school, two parents, and three classroom teachers. (See Figure 3.5.)

Other MSPC Actions

The same process is used for the remaining committees. Other study and action procedures recommended by the MSPC are as follows:

> All curriculum committees will be concerned with career education. Within each unit of study an instructional objective which is career oriented will be defined. For example, in the science unit "Astronomy," the objectives would be: "The student will be able to discuss the various job opportunities in the field of astronomy. Such jobs as: astro-chemist, astrophysicist, astrophotographer, etc. will be discussed.

Principals for the planned middle schools will each be asked to serve on more than one committee, while central office staff members will serve as consultants to committees that need their input.

As soon as committees have defined scope and sequence, other staff members will be asked to volunteer to write or modify existing specific units of study. These committees will need writers in the subjects of science, social studies, math, language arts, and physical education. Consistency of writing style and format will receive attention.

It is imperative for the MSPC to remind each committee of the following:

1. The tasks outlined for each committee are suggestions. Any major changes in task must be submitted to the Council for study and approval.
2. All reports represent recommendations to be approved by the MSPC.
3. Final approval of recommendations rests with the Board of Education.

One of the important issues which needs to be resolved is the time provided for these committees to meet. It is recommended in Middle Town that sufficient funds be provided for teachers to have at least eight half-days of released time. It is hoped that the teachers will match the released time with their own time for meetings after school hours at their convenience. The MSPC will coordinate these dates so that not all committees are released from school on a particular day, but rather that released time is distributed throughout the year.

SETTING A TIME TABLE AND BEGINNING WORK

As further illustration of the process, here is a timetable and summary of the jobs to be done. Phase one includes the task of approving the in-service plan developed by the MSPC and the consultant. The proposal must be approved by September 1.

The second phase should include a presentation by the general consultant on ''What is a Middle School?'' not only to the MSPC but also junior high staff members and the sixth-grade teachers who will become part of the middle school. Another presentation will be made to junior high parents and elementary grade parents of incoming students. A position paper on what a middle school is will be distributed widely prior to every presentation.

The third phase will include membership selection for the various committees. These committees will include parents, teachers, and administrators.

The fourth phase should include the planning of the committee work, beginning with the selection of a chairperson and secretary. It should also include accepting or revising the tasks as recommended by the MSPC.

The fifth phase has to do with evaluation and revision. As progress reports are made to the MSPC, both groups are to consider ''Where are we?'' ''Where should we go?'' and ''What do we do to get there?'' They should keep in mind what plans need to be made for summer work by certain committees.

In the sixth phase, much of the work should be completed, except for the teams of teachers who will work during the summer months to write units of study or to develop other teacher help materials. The committees will present verbal and written recommendations to the MSPC.

COMMITTEES REPORT PROGRESS TO MSPC AND BOARD OF EDUCATION

In the seventh phase, each chairperson will have turned in a report to the MSPC. Because the MSPC was functioning so closely with the committees, each chairperson was also asked to give an oral report to the Board of Education on June 15.

In phase eight, after presenting the reports to the Board of Education, it will be necessary for the Superintendent of Schools and Board Members to determine if all of the recommendations can be implemented. In the case of Middle Town, not all of the recommendations could be implemented in one year because of financial problems. Therefore, using the priority lists provided by each committee, the Superintendent, with the assistance of the Director of Instruction, recommended to the Board of Education which changes could be implemented at a later date.

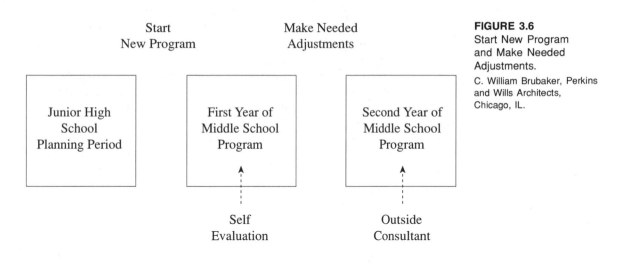

FIGURE 3.6
Start New Program
and Make Needed
Adjustments.
C. William Brubaker, Perkins
and Wills Architects,
Chicago, IL.

THE SUMMER WEEKS ARE USED TO MAKE THE CHANGE FOR THE FALL SEMESTER

In phase nine, two weeks prior to the opening of school, there is an in-service program for all middle school staff members. They review the concept of what a middle school is. Then they meet in smaller groups to discuss various changes in units of study, to study improvements in scheduling, to discuss in detail how a team functions, and to examine any other details related to the middle school program.

The First Year Actions

On September 8, the middle schools open officially, with, it is hoped, the young people ready to attend a more inviting environment for them. Although the eighth-graders have been together previously, they now have a new group of sixth and seventh-graders who were previously fifth and sixth-graders. Now we may wonder, although we have a new population in our school, do we necessarily have a middle school? The careful planning by the staff and community should insure that the change will be real and substantive.

Periodically, it is essential that the staff addresses itself to this important question. During the first year, a more thorough self-evaluation of the middle school should be completed by April 15 so that any adjustments can be planned for introduction in the beginning of September. Sometimes during the second year, it might be advisable to have an outside consultant come in to determine if the Middle Town School District truly has middle schools.

The timing and schedule contained in the outline of procedures in Figure 3.6 is only suggested. Local circumstances and other factors may very well make it necessary to modify this.

All of the efforts of the Middle School Planning Council and the various study committees should result in a school program designed to meet the specific needs of boys and girls in the middle school. These efforts should result in a school designed to help children not only discover themselves as people, but also to develop positive attitudes toward learning. In this environment, children should reach a developmental stage where they are able to make the kind of choices necessary to achieve fulfillment, not only as unique individuals but also as members of the society in which they live.

SUMMARY

In the development of a Middle School, it is imperative that all persons who will be affected by the change will be involved through staff representatives on various committees. The committees must have financial and other resources available in order to reach their goals.

As various committees develop a first draft of their materials, time should be provided to share the progress of the committee with all middle school staff. This procedure will insure the development of programs consistent with the needs of the transescent or preadolescent.

The cooperative efforts of teachers, administrators, and parents can spell success in moving from a junior high to a middle school.

PART

II

Curricular Experiences for the Transescent

4

Basic Skill Repair and Extension

5

Multimedia Materials Approach

6

Creative Exploratory and Enrichment Activities

7

Independent Study

8

Evaluating Student Progress in the Middle School

9

Physical Activities and Intramurals

PART II

Chapter Four begins with a discussion of the importance of continued development and repair of basic skills in the middle school curriculum. Many students are still in the process of mastering these skills. They continue to require the assistance of teachers and tutors in doing so. Ideas to strengthen skills development programs are offered, along with examples for illustrative purposes.

Chapter Five points out that planned use of a variety of materials and media in instruction can increase learning. Suggestions are also offered for effectively incorporating such materials in programs at the middle school level.

Chapter Six discusses the critical importance of providing learning experiences of a creative, exploratory, and enrichment nature for this age group. This is particularly important, since recent research indicates relatively slow brain growth at this age level, with diminished capacity for higher level thinking tasks. It becomes logical to provide for the expanding interests and curiosity these students exhibit. Suggestions of activities and examples are provided.

Chapter Seven is concerned with the transescent's growing need for and interest in independent study. This in part reflects a striving for recognition and status as an individual, as well as in part the drive for independence occurring at this time. Suggestions are offered for the planning of this in the classroom, using a variety of techniques.

Chapter Eight deals with the problems of evaluating middle school students and their work. The importance of an evaluation system which is consistent with the pupil-centered middle school philosophy is discussed, along with suggestions for planning and developing an appropriate evaluation system. The problem of parental understanding and acceptance of a system, as well as teacher acceptance, are also discussed.

Chapter Nine cites the rapid physiological changes in students in the middle school years and stresses the importance of a program of physical activities and intramurals to help students adjust to their changing bodies. The importance of encouraging all students to participate and feel they belong is stressed. Activities are also suggested.

Basic Skill Repair and Extension

PURPOSE AND OBJECTIVES

Some people insist that the middle school is probably the most challenging yet exasperating professional assignment in the teaching field. As pointed out in *An Agenda for Excellence at the Middle Level,*[1] schools which are successful in fully developing students' potential in any subject area should be sensitive to the expressed and unexpressed needs of those students. This makes the job at the middle school a difficult assignment. In an effort to understand effective practices in middle schools, it is necessary to review research on effective curriculum and instruction. Probably the most complete assessment of middle school research was published in June 1989 by the Carnegie Corporation of New York and entitled, *Turning Points: Preparing American Youth for the Twenty-First Century: The Report of the Task Force on Education of Young Adolescents.*[2] Young adolescents face significant turning points. For many youths, early adolescence offers opportunities to choose a path toward a productive and fulfilling life. For many others, it represents their last chance to avoid a diminished future. This added dimension of teaching for the middle school teacher creates challenge after challenge. During this time in a young person's education, there is still time to mold, develop, and stimulate the minds of young people. The very nature of preadolescent children offers a challenge to every person who relates to them. This chapter considers the actions of the teacher, an authority figure who attempts to transmit in a meaningful, understanding manner academic and social-cultural concepts. At the same time, these children represent a wide variety of individuals who are themselves on a roller coaster in their cognitive, affective, and psychomotor development. *An Agenda for Excellence at the Middle Level*[3] points out that as middle schools establish expectations for the behavior and cognitive growth of the transescent, a knowledge of the characteristics and needs of the early adolescent learner is necessary. This knowledge helps develop a responsive school program.

The topics to be discussed here represent the very essence of the middle school years and an outline of the academic opportunities to meet these children at their peaks and valleys. The middle school program should provide opportunities for students to receive the help needed for learning and extending the basic skills. The skills fostered by the elementary school program(s) should be built upon to further both the self-concept and the academic development of each student. Cognitively, the transescent is moving from concrete to formal learning with the emerging capability to deal with greater levels of abstraction. While the 10- to 11-year-old student functions at literal thinking levels, the 14-year-old student may typically be able to see relationships among similar concepts, make inferences, and critically evaluate information.[4] Moreover, because of the vast individual differences among youngsters in basic skill development, a careful program must be undertaken at this level. These students should be provided with organized experiences to improve their basic skills as well as their personal development. The Carnegie Report[5] suggests that the young adolescent is maturing intellectually at a rapid rate. These youths can analyze problems and issues, examine the component parts, and reintegrate them into either a solution or into a new way of stating the problem or issue. In developing thinking skills, these youths will master self-expression and be able to ''hear'' others' expressions through diverse media. Recent studies have further identified ''multiple intelligences'' or personal abilities not only in the traditional academic area, but also in performance or nonlinear cognitive abilities.[6]

The major focus of this chapter is on basic skills assessment and development at the middle school level. Areas of concern reviewed are (1) reading, (2) language arts, (3) study skills and/or thinking skills, and (4) organizing for mastery learning. Each section has components that review the basic objectives for middle school programs. The second component of each area focuses on teaching, diagnostic ideas, and suggestions that aid the teacher(s) in deciding where to start with their students. The chapter concludes with a summary. However, before the specific areas of study are considered, a brief discussion is offered to demonstrate the need for program change and improvement.

NEED FOR CHANGE

Eichhorn[7] suggests that the transitional school has been a dynamic movement in American education. From the beginning it has been in some respects an innovation. Later Eichhorn states that groundwork for the middle school has been laid, but some educators have been unable to place wide-spread realization of these schools in action. Toepfer and Marani[8] suggest that middle schools will continue to suffer if there is continued failure to validate the accomplishments of such schools. Further, Toepfer and Marani suggest a continued quest to meet and use all available means of research. One such suggestion was the documentation of developments in the schools themselves, with some results summarized here.

First, Humm[9] found that junior high schools were organizationally con-fused with middle schools and that only 10 percent of the schools tended to have a structure different from the uniform class period schedule. Fabri and Sloan[10] studied one hundred schools and found much the same a decade later. Ninety-one schools reported regular class periods of 40 to 50 minutes in length. It is also still true that rural and small schools are less likely to report alternate programs. All schools reported a concern about the reduced spending for elementary and middle/junior high school programs in the past ten years.

Sloan and Walker[11] studied middle/junior high schools for develop-mental skills in reading, math, and work study skills. This study was repeated as a part of the Fabri and Sloan[12] study. In 1979, 89 percent of the schools had developmental/remedial programs. The 1988 study found that 94 percent of the schools had some form of extra help. It was found that 65 of 100 schools had remedial help in both reading and math. In addition, 26 schools had remediation programs in reading only and three schools in math only. The remaining six schools reported that reduced funding caused the loss of additional help, but that they were providing ''in class'' assistance to young-sters. Further, there was a wide range of skill levels covered by the various programs. Thirty-eight schools were taking advantage of Chapter I funding and they complied with state and federal guidelines. Twenty-seven schools reported levelized programs, that is, they tended to work only with students who were two or more years below grade level. However, 67 schools reported that they provided individualized assistance for students one year below grade level. The latter finding in 1988 is very comparable to the 1979 study.

The Fabri and Sloan study also sought to determine whether critical thinking skills were taught. The vast majority, over 80 percent, *did not* have such offerings as special courses. However, 60 percent of the schools re-ported some attempt at teaching critical thinking skills in reading and/or the other content areas. About 40 percent of the schools reported that some teachers have attended courses and workshops in order to implement the teaching of critical thinking skills. These teachers tended to be involved in gifted education programs.

The remainder of this chapter seeks to identify ideas and materials to assist the regular classroom teachers in their efforts, because of the wide variety of programs to aid middle school youngsters to improve their performance. The focus has been on reading, math, study skills, and/or critical thinking skills. Moreover, emphasis was given to classroom organization and practical teaching skills and ideas.

READING INSTRUCTION

Back to the Basics! Competency testing! Cooperman,[13] in *The Literacy Hoax,* suggests that American education has seen a nationwide deterioration in the basic skills and that the post-Sputnik gains have quickly disappeared. Critics and criticism pervade society and haunt the educational community. More recently, there is a new call for effective schools research. At any rate, the thrust here was to review objectives and effective practices in middle school reading programs in order to improve instruction.

Duffy[14] states that much progress has been made in defining developmentally appropriate reading instruction for early adolescents. However, in order to avoid past and present criticisms that middle-level practices are inadequate, educators must determine how to enter the twenty-first century with the nation's middle schools implementing appropriate teaching practices. Too many middle schools fall short in practices such as providing abundant time and materials for wide exploratory reading, teaching reading across the curriculum through interdisciplinary teaming, teaching comprehension strategies explicitly, providing enriched opportunities for writing, and eliciting thinking.

In order to grasp the totality of reading instruction at the middle school level, a review of (1) present statements about the nature of reading in middle school reading programs are examined and (2) suggested diagnostic teaching procedures are offered to the reader. As reading has always been the center of attention, the perception of ideal versus real was considered. The goal here was to review concisely the suggested purposes of reading instruction at the middle school level.

Heilman[15] has suggested fifteen specific principles for reading instruction at the middle school level. They are:

1. Individual evaluation should take place to determine the capacity of students and the present level of achievement in all facets of reading including:
   a. sight-word vocabulary
   b. word-attack skills
   c. level of silent reading
   d. meaning of vocabulary and concepts
   e. ability to profit from listening situations, including oral directions
   f. oral reading skills

     g. facility in finding information, use of reference materials

     h. work habits and attitudes

     i. rate at which curricular materials can be read.

2. Following diagnosis, the teacher should devise a flexible reading program to take care of the individual differences and needs the diagnosis revealed.

3. Reading instruction must be deliberate and systematic. Inestimable damage to children can result from the philosophy that "Children learn to read in the primary grades and read to learn at the intermediate level." They must do both at each level.

4. In addition to specific reading instruction per se, instruction must also be incorporated into the teaching of all subject matter. Children must be "taught to read" science, mathematics, health, and social science materials. It is not intended that reading instruction be seen or treated as dichotomous, but rather that items three and four be complementary parts of the whole program.

5. The child should be helped to expand a stock of concepts. This is essential in all content areas.

6. Practice should be provided in various types of functional reading— in newspapers, magazines, and books—to supplement basic texts in subject areas.

7. Guidance should be supplied in reading for recreation, pleasure, and personal growth.

8. The child's reading interest should be widened to build a sound foundation for lifelong personal reading activities.

9. Appreciation should be developed for good literature, poetry, and drama.

10. A wide selection of materials should be made available in all fields—science, literature, biography, current events, social studies, and the like.

11. A program should be devised for guiding the growth of intellectually-gifted children.

12. Children should be helped to increase the rate at which they can comprehend printed word symbols in combination. This skill becomes increasingly important at this instructional level since the curriculum materials in the various content areas make ever-widening demands on readers.

13. Steps should be taken to improve critical reading skills such as:

     a. coping with figurative or picturesque language

     b. drawing inferences

     c. classifying ideas and selecting those that are germane to the reader's purpose

d. evaluating ideas and arriving at the author's purpose or intent

e. detecting bias and differentiating between fact and opinion.

14. The following reading study skills should be developed and extended:

    a. using books effectively—making maximum use of the index, table of contents, and appendix

    b. acquiring facility in the use of a dictionary

    c. using reference books effectively

    d. understanding graphs, maps, charts, and tables

    e. using library resources, card catalogue, and periodical indexes

    f. taking notes and outlining materials for a given purpose

15. Diagnosis should be continuous and ongoing throughout each instructional year. An initial diagnosis serves only for initial procedures.

These fifteen principles were formulated to be representative of a theory and direction for reading instruction in the middle schools. Moreover, the principles of instruction suggested by Heilman seem to be utilized in a number of middle schools today. Middle school teachers become more effective reading instructors when the following are put into practice: the primary objectives of diagnosis of and prescription for instruction; the use of materials at or near the instructional level of the students; the development of skills and abilities as needed; the development of appreciation of literature; interests; recreational reading; and the integration of the reading program into all aspects of the school curriculum.

It appears that a definite reading program needs to be implemented at the middle level. The basics seem to be that:

1. All upper grade students need some help in developing specific reading skills.

2. General reading abilities profit from direct instruction.

3. Only through a broad-based program of diagnosis and sound instruction can reading be improved.

With the foregoing in mind, the section which follows focuses on specific suggestions for middle school teachers.

IMPORTANT SUGGESTIONS FOR READING INSTRUCTION

First, it is very important to place in perspective the teacher's role and the importance of reading. Bond and Tinker[16] clarified these aspects as well as a general guideline for a schoolwide philosophy of reading. These four guidelines are described in the following paragraphs.

Bond and Tinker estimate that 25 percent of the children who become students in remedial reading cases could be helped successfully by the classroom teacher before they reach that stage. The necessary conditions are as follows.

1. All pressure from the teacher for every child to complete the same work in the same amount of time with the same amount of practice must be eliminated.
2. Each child must be accepted as an individual and be permitted to work at his or her instructional level of reading, moving only as fast as the child is able to learn.
3. The teacher's effort should be bent toward providing many learning activities at many levels of difficulty so that each child is challenged at his or her growing edge of learning.
4. The philosophy of the school should be that other personnel are also concerned about each child's learning, so that no teacher need operate alone (p. 245).

Many of these well-known and established teaching ideas are long-standing and are suggested by many specialists and teachers. An effort was made to classify and categorize these. The four major categories selected were: (1) factors affecting general motivation in reading, (2) in-class reading ideas, (3) suggestions for working with poor readers, and (4) reading in the content areas.

1. Factors affecting motivation for reading.[17] Teachers are reminded that the use of the following are important.
   a. Teacher enthusiasm: Setting an example or model is very important. One of the best and easiest ways for a teacher to communicate enthusiasm and appreciation for literature is by being a good model for students. Ask yourself the following questions:
      1) Do I freely choose to spend my spare time reading?
      2) Do I read to my students regularly?
      3) Do I reach for a book when I need information?
      4) Am I knowledgeable enough about children's books to make recommendations based upon students' interests and achievement levels?
      5) Do I discuss my interest in reading with my students?
      6) Do my personal attitudes and my classroom environment demonstrate that I value reading?
      7) Am I enthusiastic and positive in my approach to reading?[18]
   b. Booklists, librarians, and reading specialists for suggestions about books and supplementary materials of various levels and interest.

    c. Motivational devices such as classroom atmosphere. Surround the students with a wide variety of interesting books. Set up a browsing area.

    d. Magazines and newspapers: Provide a variety of topics and current subjects for the classroom.

    e. Uninterrupted, sustained reading periods where students may select their own reading materials for pleasure.

    f. Use of the laboratory approach.[19] It is characterized by:

       1) Wide variety of reading goals.

       2) Self-direction and responsibility where "every pupil may plan an individual program with the teacher" (p. 20).

       3) Used by all of the students, but flexible and appropriate for all individual levels.

    g. Developing and using interests in and related to reading.[20]

       1) Oral reading by the teacher: Expose the students to good literature. Read "selectively and widely . . . from a broad variety of readings . . . and carefully selected experts" (p. 106).

       2) Use tapes, records, filmstrips, and other non-book media: Expose the students to what is available in printed form. Stimulate interest. Give poorer students practice in reading along with tapes, etc.

       3) Oral reading by students to one another, grouped by interests or cross interests, and across grade levels.

       4) Sharing literature through reading, writing, speaking, dramatization, and visual arts.

2. Regular Classroom "In Class" Reading Ideas. The following suggestions are offered for regular classroom teachers. They are:

    a. Out of class special instruction is necessary, but it must be co-ordinated with classroom program.

    b. Realistic, individualized goals must be set.

    c. "Total Programs" have been implemented where the regular classes (social studies, mathematics, science, etc.) also emphasize good reading and study skills.[21]

    d. Content teachers can also help in the classrooms.[22] In setting individualized teaching and learning methods, it is important to "distinguish inability to understand the concepts and inability to read the concepts in the first place" (p. 10).

    e. Better readers may read aloud to others, or poor readers could read silently along with a tape recording. Learning concepts may be presented through some avenue other than reading.

    f. The teacher may emphasize the transfer of information from reading to thought.

g. Reading materials need to be varied, with different levels and interest.

h. Reading assignments need to be adjusted to fit all of the students.[23] The teacher may utilize:

   1) Study guides to help the students focus on particular information.

   2) Structural overviews, which involve using a graphic arrangement of terms that apply to the important concepts in a passage.

     a. Analyze vocabulary and list important words.

     b. Arrange the concepts to be learned.

     c. Add any other vocabulary terms that you believe the students understand.

     d. Evaluate the overview.

     e. Introduce students to the learning task.

     f. As you complete the learning task, relate new information to the overview.[24]

   3) Direct reading approaches, including:

     a. Motivation and building background.

     b. Guided reading of the story (silent and/or oral).

     c. Skill development activities.

     d. Follow-up activities.

The importance of the "teacher ingredient" in the reading process cannot be overestimated. Successful teachers have particular qualities that are the basis for their success: They are enthusiastic, careful planners, and they strive toward continued improvement in their teaching methods. Above all, good teachers meet individual needs and are aware that it is the children they teach who are the "products" of their teaching.[25]

3. Suggestions to Use with Poor Readers.[26]

a. Discover each poor reader's reading strengths and weaknesses. Use a combination of assessment procedures including standardized tests, informal diagnosis from a conference with the reader, basal reader tests, multilevel kits, etc.

b. Give poor readers encouragement and the opportunity to read materials of their own choosing, with no comprehension checks or other penalties to pay after reading.

c. Teach poor readers to rely heavily on context clues to get the meaning of unfamiliar words. Allowing the child to concentrate on contextual clues instead of phonetic analysis and "sounding out" words will give him the success of understanding what he is reading. It will eventually help students to learn to use both contextual clues and phonetic analysis skills.

d. Before poor readers begin reading a selection, alert them to specific linguistic structures likely to cause interpretation difficulties (e.g., figurative language, unusual or long sentence structures, specialized vocabulary, punctuation, etc.). Note: The teacher should read the assigned material in advance to be able to prepare poor readers for potential ''trouble spots'' in the linguistic structure of the material.

e. Provide poor readers with information that relates to the ideational content of their reading material. Poor readers often possess meager experiential backgrounds. Time spent talking about concepts, viewing film, or looking at pictures can provide a cognitive framework into which the ideas in a reading selection can fit.

f. Teach poor readers to pause periodically to reflect on what they have just read and to make some predictions about what they will read next.

g. Do not require poor readers to read orally in front of their classmates. Many students with reading problems are better silent readers than they are oral readers, and an embarrassing display of their greatest weakness is a degrading experience of no instructional value.

h. Give poor readers opportunities to be successful with tasks or projects that do not require reading. This is to preserve the poor reader's self-concept and give him a useful place in the classroom.

i. Assemble a library of audiotapes, filmstrips, phonograph records, and films to help poor readers get the information they need without reading.

j. Poor readers should, whenever possible, be provided with content area related reading materials at easy readability levels instead of the more difficult materials good readers use. Besides giving the poor readers successful reading experiences at their own level, class discussions are often more interesting and meaningful when they bring out the students' different reading experiences relative to a broad common topic.

k. Give poor readers many opportunities to discuss reading experiences with better readers in small groups. This will provide the poorer reader with the model he needs to learn what a good reader does when he reads and what he gets from his reading experience.

l. Refer seriously disabled readers to remedial instruction and coordinate classroom programs with remedial programs.

4. Reading in the Content Areas. It is clear from the literature and recent studies that a need exists for reading instruction at the middle

school level in all subject areas. Teachers in all content areas must be drawn into active reading instruction. If content area teachers accept the responsibility and opportunity to increase reading ability, the independence of the student and the mastery of the subject matter will occur. It is especially necessary to help students develop requisite comprehension skills in the content areas. Bush and Huebener[27] suggest that these student skills are:

a. Setting his own purpose.
b. Acquiring the special or technical vocabulary of the subject matter.
c. Understanding the concepts specific to the content area.
d. Noting main points and supporting details.
e. Noting sequence and interrelationships in the presentation of ideas.
f. Being alert to ways of making new learnings functional in his own life.

In addition to the above basic skills suggestions, teachers in the various content areas need to be mindful of their special content and the special knowledge and reading skills they require.

LANGUAGE ARTS INSTRUCTION

The thesis of this text and chapter hinges on the notion that formal specialized instruction in basic skills is necessary for middle school age students. The language arts are related and an integral aspect of all teaching. Therefore, they deserve attention even though they are taught as a separate subject. It is not the author's intent to review the whole of language arts, but to present basic tenets that all teachers can utilize in their teaching. In addition, a few selected ideas and references are put forward for consideration for the reader's use.

Burns[28] proposes that the following are aspects that are more or less unique to language instruction. Other notes and ideas that supplement these ideas follow.

1. Oral language development is fundamental to other language arts. Children who express themselves effectively in speech tend to succeed in other areas of language arts. However, oral language development depends in a great measure on the various aspects of a student's environment. "It is especially noteworthy for teachers at the middle school level to be cognizant of the 'gang' and other social pressures. . . ."[29] Moreover, Polley suggests that teachers

who recognize the influence of social pressure will avoid an "only-one-way-is-right attitude. . . ." Further, he suggests that the teacher's task is to:

    a. Make the student an observer of the language spoken about him.

    b. Instruct the student in standard usage patterns.

    c. Lead the student to establish goals which are realistic.

2. Pupils should work with content in practical situations before the ideas are analyzed. In this way, pupils are encouraged to see a pattern for themselves and form their own conclusions or generalizations about the accepted use of words.

3. For fuller language development, the child must participate actively in the process of learning. Growth in any curriculum requires action; growth in language skills requires greater action.

4. Because of the creative, intimate nature of the relationship between language and the child, a feeling of abiding regard and respect for the worth of each child must be maintained.

Many language arts teachers subscribe to the diagnostic point of view as a tenet of teaching. Burns[30] relates that the word "diagnostic" is derived from two Greek roots which mean "to know thoroughly." As related earlier, knowing the child thoroughly and their progress is essential to preparation for teaching. Here, too, in the language arts, this concept is essential. For example, Triplett[31] has developed a diagnostic checklist as an aid to regular classroom and language arts teachers. This checklist is offered as a means to assist teachers in evaluating and recording individual student progress. Further, this checklist on oral and written language can serve as a planning guide. (See Box 4.1.)

Finally, Burns' 1974 text, *Diagnostic Teaching of the Language Arts*,[32] is suggested as a practical guide for further assistance in each of the areas in language arts for all teachers. This text has a wealth of excellent teaching ideas.

STUDY AND CRITICAL THINKING SKILLS/CONTENT AREAS

There are many programs available today designed for the teaching of study skills and/or critical thinking skills. Although they are useful and show that educators are aware of fostering these skills, the number of options and varying definitions can be confusing. What has been missing is an organizational framework for the teaching of critical thinking. An appropriate framework would allow practitioners in different subject areas to develop a common knowledge base and a common language for teaching thinking.

BOX 4.1
Diagnostic Checklist

ORAL LANGUAGE

1. Listens for the following purposes:
   a. To follow directions.
   b. To identify main ideas.
   c. To remember sequence.
   d. To remember details.
   e. To distinguish relevant and irrelevant information.
   f. To predict outcomes, make inferences, and draw conclusions.
   g. To sense sounds, rhyme, rhythm, images, moods, and prejudices.
   h. To detect speaker's purpose—information, persuade, and entertain.
   i. To detect fact from opinion.
   j. To judge the validity of information.
2. Uses language creatively:
   a. To express needs, concerns, and thoughts.
   b. To make individual presentation—dictating, recording, reading, and reporting.
   c. To share ideas interactively—dramatic play, discussion, debate, and conversation.
   d. To entertain—puppets, plays, poems, literature, readers' theater, storytelling, choral reading, and singing.

WRITTEN LANGUAGE

1. Writes for the following purposes:
   a. To label: pictures, titles, descriptions, forms, and directions.
   b. To request or inform: letters, notes, telegrams, announcements, and advertisements.
   c. To react: editorials and reviews.
   d. To record: messages, outlines, logs, minutes, diaries, notes, and reports.
   e. To entertain: stories, poetry, music, plays, and essays.
2. Uses writing techniques and devices:
   a. To employ rhyme, rhythm, and alliteration.
   b. To express feelings: humor, nonsense, amusement, pathos, distress, lament, and sadness.
   c. To generate figuration language: idioms, similes, metaphors, imagery, and onomatopoeia.
   d. To influence work choice: pronouns, tense forms, meanings, and usage.
   e. To interpret relationships: cause-effect, general-specific, time-place, and part-whole.

**BOX 4.1
(Continued)**

    f. To differentiate fact and opinion: news stories and advertising.

    g. To employ a literary genre: realism, fantasy, fable, folk tale, and mystery.

    h. To achieve time and tone: flashbacks, foreshadowing, irony, and suspense.

    i. To establish an interpretation: mood, point-of-view, and characterization.

3. Writes words:

    a. To express ideas: accuracy, vividness, specificity, appropriateness, and variety.

    b. To communicate effectively: tense forms, plurals, possessives, and spelling.

4. Writes sentences:

    a. To express intent: declarative, imperative, interrogative, and exclamatory.

    b. To offer variety: simple, compound, and complex.

    c. To lend interest: varied patterns, lengths, and contrasts.

    d. To achieve coherence: meaning, sequence, transition, coordination, and subordination.

5. Writes paragraphs:

    a. To develop unity of thought: introductory, supporting, and concluding sentences.

    b. To express a unifying theme: logical progression, supporting data, consistency of viewpoint, and sense of audience.

    c. To indicate transitions: conversations, change in time, place, setting, or topic.

6. Uses of knowledge of mechanics:

    a. To punctuate: periods, commas, question marks, apostrophes, hyphens, and colons.

    b. To capitalize: I, first word of a sentence, proper nouns, proper adjectives, important words in titles, and words and letters in outline.

    c. To execute form: margins, paragraph indentations, handwriting, spelling, and usage (Triplett 1980).

Accordingly, five dimensions of thinking have been identified by Marzano et al.[33] as follows.

1. *Metacognition:* our awareness and control of own thinking. For example, students' beliefs about themselves and about such things as the value of persistence and the nature of work will heavily influence their motivation, attention, and effort for any given task.
2. *Critical and Creative Thinking:* two different but related ways of characterizing thinking. Regardless of the particular processes or skills involved, an individual's thinking can be described as more or less creative or critical.
3. *Thinking Processes:* Box 4.2, Thinking Processes, is a pictorial view of knowledge acquisition and knowledge production or application.
4. *Core Thinking Skills:* basic cognitive operations used in metacognitive reflection and in the thinking processes. The skills of comparing and classifying, for example, are used frequently in decision making and problem solving. Box 4.3, from Rankin and Hughes,[34] is a categorical system to aid in organizing one's thinking. It is also a means of developing lessons to meet the various levels of operation while teaching.
5. *The Relationship of Content Area Knowledge to Thinking:* The first four dimensions do not exist in isolation. Individuals must think about something. The content of our thinking greatly influences how we think. For example, our ability to classify and order data probably depends more on our knowledge of the topic than on our knowledge of the skills of classifying and ordering. Knowledge is related to the other dimensions in complex and subtle ways.

According to Ennis,[35] critical thinking is logical, reflective thinking that is focused on deciding what to believe or do. Critical thinking so defined involves both dispositions and abilities.

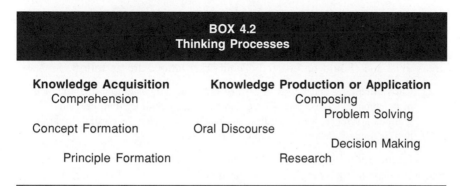

BOX 4.2
Thinking Processes

Knowledge Acquisition	Knowledge Production or Application	
Comprehension		Composing
		Problem Solving
Concept Formation	Oral Discourse	
		Decision Making
Principle Formation		Research

BOX 4.3
Core Thinking Skills as they Frequently Occur in Thinking Processes

---

Focusing Skills

Defining Problems	Setting Goals

Information Gathering Skills

Observing	Formulating Questions

Remembering Skills

Encoding	Recalling

Organizing Skills

Comparing	Classifying	Ordering	Representing

Analyzing Skills

Identifying Attributes and Components	Identifying Relationships and Patterns
Identifying Main Ideas	Identifying Errors

Generating Skills

Inferring	Predicting	Elaborating

Integrating Skills

Summarizing	Restructuring

Evaluating Skills

Establishing Criteria	Verifying

The point of view taken in this section is that all teachers, regardless of academic discipline, can assist middle school age students in their development. Friedman and Rowls[36] suggest that commonalities among content areas exist and should be utilized. Their observations are as follows:

> Current thinking and trends in each of the content areas emphasize a number of common concerns. The curricula in English (including literature and grammar), science, social studies, and mathematics have, according to current thinking, many factors in common.

Recognition of common factors can crystallize how middle school teachers relate to the overall program at their level. In addition, there is always a concern of how study/critical thinking skills relate to the several areas of study. A comprehensive analysis was conducted by Van Dongen.[37] This summary is included to further integrate the use of study/critical thinking skills and the content areas. Van Dongen surveyed several graded series of readers to find out which study skills are commonly taught. From this research, he synthesized the following outline.

I. Ability to locate information.
   a. Ability to locate information by using the aid of book parts.
   b. Ability to locate information by using knowledge of alphabetizing.
   c. Ability to locate information by using references.
   d. Ability to use the library and its aids for locating information.
   e. Locate information by using maps, graphs, charts, and pictorial material.
II. Ability to organize information.
   a. Use knowledge of alphabetizing or organizing information.
   b. Construct an outline.
   c. Ability to summarize material.
   d. Ability to take notes.
III. Ability to use and interpret maps, graphs, charts, and other pictorial material.
   a. Use and interpret maps and globes.
   b. Use and interpret graphs, tables, diagrams, and other pictorial matter.
   c. Read and use charts.

The knowledge of this information can appraise teachers of the interrelationships of content areas. The above information may also be used as a checklist of the subparts of each area in order to determine the competency level of students. This process is applicable as a pretest or simply as information necessary to teaching in the various content areas. Critical and creative thinking help children to become active learners rather than passive receivers. They also enable teachers to function as facilitators of learning rather than disseminators of information. Proponents believe that nurturing children's abilities in the area of productive thinking, communication, forecasting, decision making, and planning will improve their academic performance along with their chances for future success.[38] Underlying this approach to critical thinking skills instruction are the following assumptions.

1. People have talents (strengths or preferences) for different thinking processes.
2. Training in the use of these thinking processes can enhance one's potential in various areas of talent and at the same time foster positive feelings about oneself.

3. Training in particular thinking processes can be integrated with knowledge of content in any subject area and can enhance academic achievement.
4. The various thinking processes are also linked to success in the world of work.[39]

APPLYING CRITICAL THINKING SKILLS

According to Fabri and Sloan,[40] efforts have been limited to a discussion of what critical thinking skills are and how valuable they are to the general student population. Such a discussion would be of little value if teacher tested practical applications were not included. Therefore, the information on materials was solicited from practicing teachers, and they are available for use in most classroom situations. Fabri and Sloan also present a list of additional readings in their article.

Marzano et al.[41] present a framework based on general principles of how learning occurs. The "Dimension" framework can be used to plan instruction, coordinate the use of various programs, and select and plan staff development activities.

In the same issue of *Educational Leadership,* Arredondo and Block[42] look at the connections between thinking skills and mastery learning.

ORGANIZING FOR MASTERY LEARNING

A review of basic strategies on the part of the teacher is in order. A resumé of these concepts outlined by Friedman and Rowls[43] fits nicely in the scheme of this review. They review the work of Block for exhibit and use. Moreover, Block[44] described the application of mastery learning strategy to classroom learning. Block summarizes the procedure as follows:

> To apply mastery learning strategy, the teacher defines instructional goals, prepares a final exam to test the achievement of the goals, and establishes a score on the final exam that indicates mastery of the goals much as we have described. In addition, the teacher prepares instructional activities to facilitate the achievement of the goals and a short diagnostic-progress test to be administered at the end of each instructional activity to assess progress toward the goal and to diagnose impediments to student progress. The instructional activities are used initially to produce the desired learning. They can later be used as corrective activities for students who do not show adequate progress on the diagnostic-progress tests.

Further, the authors outline the structure for planning teaching. For more information, the basic outline is in seven steps. Moreover, these steps are very closely related to effective teaching methods espoused by persons interested in clinical supervision. Hence, teachers who organize their lessons in such a fashion can improve their lessons. As stated in Clark and Starr,[45] the role of teaching method is to bring about learning. It includes content and techniques as well as strategies and tactics. The key is to bring about the desired learning in students by selecting the appropriate strategies and tactics and, consequently, the proper content and techniques. They go on to say that subject matter is not all the same and so not all subjects should be taught in the same way. Rather, the teaching approach should vary according to the structure and methods of the disciplines concerned as follows.

Step 1. *Orienting the Student:* The student is informed of what he is going to learn and how he is going to be taught.

To orient the student to the total instructional program, the teacher can distribute the table of specifications to the students and discuss it with them. The table shows what the student has mastered so far and what he is to learn. The teacher can discuss the mastery learning strategy to acquaint students with how they will be taught.

As teachers prepare to move students from a readiness state to a particular desired learning outcome, they can distribute and discuss the relevant goal statement.

This acquaints the students with what they will learn next. To acquaint the students with how they will be taught, teachers can describe the sequence of instructional activities they have planned, as well as the diagnostic-progress tests they will use and when they will be administered.

Step 2. *Administering Instructional Activities:* The instructional activities are administered according to plan.

Step 3. *Administering Diagnostic-Progress Test:* The diagnostic-progress tests are administered at the completion of each activity. In order to coordinate thinking skills, levels of thinking, and measurement, one might consider the *Cognitive Domain Levels According to Bloom* in Table 4.1.

Step 4. *Relating Feedback to Students:* The students are given feedback. The results of the test are discussed with the students privately and their strengths and weaknesses are described. They are also given encouragement.

Step 5. *Moving to the Next Learning Activity:* Students who have made satisfactory progress move on to the next learning activity. Correctives are administered to students who do not make satisfactory progress. If teachers desire to keep the students

TABLE 4.1 Cognitive Domain Levels According to Bloom[46]

If you want to measure:	Use these key words in the exercise:			
Knowledge	list define repeat	fill in what who	describe label name	identify when
Comprehension	paraphrase review discuss	translate how	explain match	interpret why
Application	apply draw sketch	employ predict	construct simulate	restructure how
Analysis	classify distinguish subdivide	contrast separate break down	dissect compare	categorize differentiate
Synthesis	combine collect	integrate put together	relate	assemble
Evaluation	judge assess decide	rate evaluate should	argue appraise defend	debate choose

moving at the same pace, they can have the students who made satisfactory progress tutor the others or involve them in enrichment activities.

Step 6. *Monitoring Corrective Activities:* The teacher monitors the corrective activities to make certain that the students who need correctives get as much guidance as they require in order to get back on the track.

Step 7. *Administering the Final Exam:* The final exam is administered and the teacher certifies mastery for those who score above the mastery cut-off score on the test. If the feedback corrective procedures have been thoughtfully planned and carried out, most of the students will achieve mastery. The few who do not are recycled to an earlier stage of instruction and given more correctives so that they may achieve mastery.[47]

The implications for instructional planning require the teacher to prepare a variety of instructional activities to facilitate a desired learning outcome. Some activities are used in initial instruction and some are used as correctives. The corrective activities should be different from the initial activities. In this manner, a student who does not make acceptable progress as a result of the initial instruction may choose an alternate mode as a corrective. In addition, the teacher gives short tests at the end of each instructional activity. Hence, the teacher uses the tests to provide feedback concerning student progress and reasons for lack of progress. Then, the teacher prescribes corrective activities for students who need to be directed back on the track that leads to the desired learning outcome. Students are given all of the opportunities they need to achieve the desired outcome.

According to Skon, Johnson, and Johnson,[48] teachers need to know what outcomes they hope to achieve in order to teach a unit successfully. An approach that is now being used in many schools and in many subject areas is cooperative learning. Students work in pairs or in small groups in a process that helps to develop the young adolescent's capacity for active, engaged thinking. Hence, a disciplined mind is disposed toward inquiry, discovery, and reasoning across all subjects. Young adolescents need group approaches to learning. Learning often takes place best when students have opportunities to discuss, analyze, express opinions, and receive feedback from peers.

SUMMARY

This chapter focused on basic skill repair and extension. The overall thesis was on basic concepts required in the middle school instructional programs. Specifically, attention was given to basic concepts and instructional strategies for the regular classroom teacher. All teachers in middle schools need to be teachers of reading and study/critical thinking skills regardless of their discipline or assignment.

At the outset, three recent studies were quoted to develop the overall rationale and urgent need for general instructional improvement in the middle schools. The remainder of the chapter provided ideas and concepts in reading, reading in the content fields, language arts, and study/critical thinking skills. Teachers who are serious about improving their instruction may wish to follow these basic ideas and/or turn to additional study by seeking the references used herein. These materials possess many excellent concepts and teaching ideas.

We must remember, as Clark and Starr[49] have pointed out in their book, *Secondary and Middle School Teaching Methods,* that for many years, teachers and scholars have been trying to create a science of teaching. Teaching still is and ought to be, an art as well as a science, however. It requires a large stock of skills, but more importantly, it requires that teachers be able to put these skills together in new forms at the spur of the moment as new situations arise. This is what keeps middle school aged children challenged. New and exciting teaching methods like cooperative learning are the means by which the teachers attempt to bring about desired learning.

ENDNOTES

1. NASSP. 1986. *An agenda for excellence at the middle level.* Reston, Virginia: NASSP.
2. Carnegie Council on Adolescent Development. ''Turning points: Preparing American youth for the twenty-first century: The report of the Task Force on Education of Young Adolescents.'' New York: Carnegie Corporation of New York. June, 1989.
3. See note 1.
4. George, P., and G. Lawrence. 1982. *Handbook for middle school teaching.* Glenview, Illinois: Scott Foresman.
5. See note 2.
6. Eichhorn, D. H. 1980. The school. In *Toward adolescence: The middle school years* (NSSE Series), edited by M. Johnson. Chicago: The University of Chicago Press.
7. See note 6.
8. Toepfer, C. F., Jr., and J. V. Marani. 1980. School based research. *Toward adolescence: The middle school years* (NSSE Series), edited by M. Johnson. Chicago: The University of Chicago Press.
9. Humm, W. M. 1979. ''The junior high school: No person's land of compromise.'' *Thresholds* 5: 8–12. DeKalb, Illinois: College of Education, Northern Illinois University Press.
10. Fabri, L. A., and C. A. Sloan. 1988. A comparison of N.I.C.E. schools with a survey of 116 Illinois middle/junior high schools' developmental skills programs. Northern Illinois Cooperative in Education occasional paper, DeKalb. Photocopy.
11. Sloan, C. A., and J. Walker. A survey of 110 Northern Illinois middle/junior high schools. *Association for Perception.* 1980, Winter.
12. See note 10.
13. Copperman, P. 1978. *The literacy hoax.* New York: Williams, Morrow and Co.
14. Duffy, G. G. 1971. *Reading in the middle schools, perspectives in reading,* #18. Newark, Delaware: International Reading Association.

15. Heilman, A. W. 1977. *Principles and practices of teaching reading.* Columbus, Ohio: Charles E. Merrill Publishing Co.
16. Bond, G. L., and M. A. Tinker. 1967. *Reading difficulties: Their diagnosis and correction.* New York: Appleton-Century-Crofts.
17. Roe, B. D., B. D. Stoodt, and P. C. Burns. 1978. *Reading instruction in the secondary school.* New York: Rand McNally College Publishing Co.
18. Lapp, D., and J. Flood. 1983. *Teaching reading to every child.* 2d ed. New York: Macmillan Publishing Company.
19. See note 14.
20. Smith, R. J., and T. C. Barrett. 1974. *Teaching reading in the middle grades.* Reading, Massachusetts: Addison-Wesley Publishing Co.
21. Gunn, A. M. 1969. *What we know about high school reading: What does research in reading reveal?* National Conference of Research in English, National Council of Teachers of English.
22. See note 14.
23. See note 17.
24. Vacca, J. L., R. T. Vacca, and M. K. Gove. 1987. *Reading and learning to read.* Boston: Brown and Company.
25. Stoodt, B. D. 1981. *Reading instruction in the secondary school.* 3d ed. Boston: Houghton-Mifflin Company.
26. See note 20.
27. Bush, C. L., and M. H. Huebener. 1979. *Strategies for reading in the elementary school.* 2d ed. New York: Macmillan Publishing Co.
28. Burns, P. C. 1974. *Diagnostic teaching of the language arts.* Itasca, Illinois: F. W. Peacock Publishers, Inc.
29. Polley, R. C. 1974. *The teaching of English usage.* Urbana, Illinois: The National Council of Teachers of English.
30. See note 28.
31. Triplett, D. 1980. "A developmental checklist (for language arts)." DeKalb, Illinois: Northern Illinois University. Photocopy.
32. See note 28.
33. Marzano, R. J., D. J. Pickering, and R. S. Brandt. Integrating instructional programs through dimensions of learning. *Educational Leadership* 47, no. 5: (1990) 17–24.
34. Rankin, S. C., and C. S. Hughes. (Feb. 1990) "The Rankin-Hughes framework." *Focus* 2 (1986, Fall).

35. Ennis, R. H. 1985. Goals for a critical thinking curriculum. *Developing minds: A resource for teaching thinking,* edited by A. Costa. Alexandria, Virginia: The Association for Supervision and Curriculum Development (A.S.C.D.).

36. Friedman, M. I., and M. D. Rowls. 1980. *Teaching reading and thinking skills.* New York: Longman, Inc.

37. Van Dongen, R. D. 1967. An analysis of study skills taught by intermediate grade basal readers. M.A. Thesis, University of New Mexico. In *The Reading Process,* edited by M. V. Zintz. 1980. 3d ed. Dubuque, Iowa: Wm. C. Brown.

38. Barbieri, E. L. "Talents unlimited: One school's success story." *Educational Leadership* 45, No. 5. (1988).

39. Schlichter, C. L., D. Hobbs, and W. D. Crump. April, 1988. Extending talents unlimited to secondary schools. *Educational Leadership* 5.

40. See note 10.

41. See note 33.

42. Arrendondo, D. E., and J. H. Block. "Recognizing the connections between thinking skills and mastery learning." *Educational Leadership* 47, no. 5: (1990) 4–10.

43. See note 36.

44. Block, J. H., ed. 1971. *Mastery Learning: Theory and practice.* New York: Holt, Rinehart and Winston.

45. Clark, L. H., and I. S. Starr. 1991. *Secondary and middle school teaching methods.* 6th ed. New York: Macmillan Publishing Co.

46. Bloom, Benjamin S. 1964. *Taxonomy of Educational Objectives: the Classification of Educational Goals.* White Plains, N.Y.: Longman Publishing.

47. See note 45.

48. Skon, L., D. Johnson, and R. Johnson. "Cooperative peer interaction versus individualized competition and individualized efforts: Effects on the acquisition of cognitive reasoning strategies." *Educational Psychology* 73: 1981, 83–92.

49. See note 45.

Multimedia Materials Approach

TWO CLASSROOMS

The teacher is sitting behind his desk, which is located in the front of the classroom, while he is conducting a "discussion." The sixth-graders are at their seats, which are in neat rows. Their textbooks are apparently open at the right page. Two of the youngsters are fast asleep, three are doodling (two on paper and one on the desk), and four seem to have their eyes glued to the clock. As for the rest of the group, they are apparently "listening."

The teacher was saying in a booming voice, "Jefferson was not interested in what happened in Europe. Yes, he wanted to stay out of their hair. In the meantime, Spain had a secret treaty with France . . . they were returning Louisiana to France. All that land would be France's. Jefferson didn't want the French here. He was afraid that they would close New Orleans. We needed New Orleans. . . ." This monologue continued for 11 minutes and the bell rang. The students jumped to their feet and scurried out of the door, except for one boy who was still asleep. His buddy shook him and said, "Let's go, man!"

In another classroom, the seventh-grade teacher was standing before the class reading a story out loud from the literature textbook. The pacing was much too fast to follow, but the reading continued for almost 20 minutes. No discussion was held or questions asked concerning the content of the story. "Now," said the teacher, "John will pass out the literature books and you will read silently the remainder of the story starting on page 115. Tomorrow I will have a mimeographed list of questions for you to answer."

In another classroom, all the students were answering questions on a three page mimeographed item in science. Some of the questions were as follows: Name the nine planets. Which planet does man live on?

Which is the largest planet? Which planet has rings on it? etc. This activity continued for 25 minutes followed by 15 minutes of group correction of these tests.

Are these typical classrooms? Obviously, the sampling is far too small to draw any conclusions. In another report in the sixties,[1] in which shadow studies were completed, it was found that the most prominent classroom strategy was one dominated by the teacher in full direction of the learning. Lectures were common in classes ranging from English to art. In other classrooms, the collecting of homework papers, going over homework, giving the next assignment, introducing new work, and allocating time for starting the homework in class was common. Other instructional practices included (a) lecture-demonstration, (b) read-recitation, and (c) correct-explain-practice. In these classrooms, the need to ''cover'' the material and workbooks was quite evident. Although these activities were found in junior highs thirty years ago they also seem to represent what goes on in many of our middle schools today. A more recent report[2] pointed out that ''sameness'' still characterizes instructional programs. Teachers are currently obsessed with ''staying on task'' and the ''task'' is too often that of the teacher's creation.

These are Middle School Youngsters

The classrooms observed in this study were conducted as though all students were identical mentally and therefore performing at the same level. Data on the development of preadolescents show they are as different as their fingerprints, yet we treat these unequal youngsters as though they are equal. As one person aptly stated, ''There is nothing so unequal as the equal treatment of unequals.''

Wattenburg[3] points out that in a class of 40 sixth-graders made up of 20 girls and 20 boys, there are 2 fully adolescent girls, 8 preadolescent girls, and 10 childish girls. As to the boys, there are no adolescent boys, 4 preadolescent boys, and 16 childish boys. This same wide range is found when we examine the intellectual development of these youngsters. Furthermore, a study of 5 sixth-graders shows that there are often sharp differences *within each student in each instructional area* as shown in Figure 5.1.

In Figure 5.2, the graph shows greatly accelerated growth between grades 6 and 8. In the basic skill areas, we find a range of at least six years in reading, math, and spelling at the sixth-grade level, while at the eighth-grade level, the same class shows an even greater disparity of performances. One could truly call the middle school youngster a juvenile hodgepodge.

What are the implications of these wide variances in the growth characteristics in the middle school student? Frankly, it means that we are going

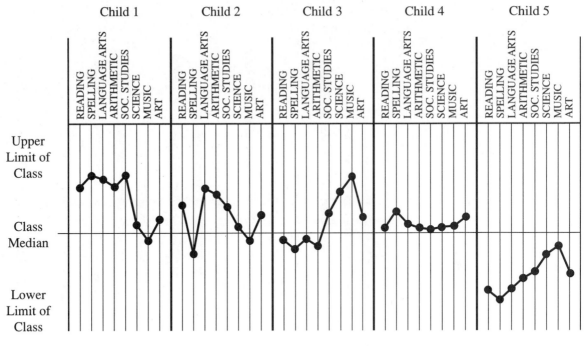

FIGURE 5.1
Individual Performance of Five Children in a Sixth Grade Class.

to have to eliminate some of our traditional practices and to implement those practices which are consistent with what we know about the variances we find in the classrooms. It is unfortunate that we tend to hang on to old practices in education. We are much like the Rhesus monkey. Trappers of these monkeys would take a coconut and cut out a hole large enough for the monkey to put his hand in. Then they would place some delicious food inside the coconut. After the trappers hung this coconut from a tree, the monkey examined the coconut and, seeing the delicious food, placed his hand in and grabbed it. He would try to get his hand out, but with the food in his hand, he was trapped. He could not release the food. He would scream and the trapper would know that he had caught another monkey. We are often very much like the monkey . . . if we would only change, we could be free, too!

THE MULTIMEDIA APPROACH

With the wide range of abilities within the middle school, an approach to teaching and learning is needed to meet the various learning styles of the students. The multimedia approach recognizes that learning, which is always

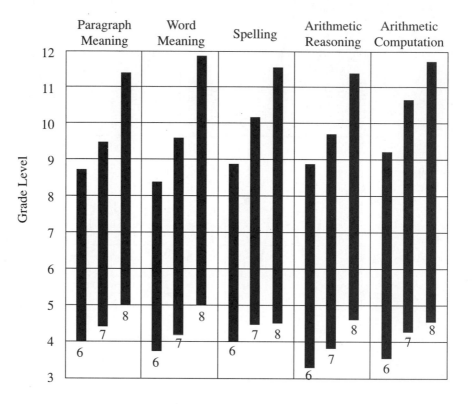

FIGURE 5.2
Range in Achievement by Grades for Same Students in Grades 6 through 8.

complicated, is further complicated when one examines the diversity of talents and interests within a middle school class. Specifically, multimedia refers to the use of various materials of instruction, both hardware and software. They reinforce one another to ensure that we provide the most effective teaching-learning for the mastery of the objectives to be learned.

For example, if the objective to be learned in a unit on meteorology is, "Students should be able to show how the processes of evaporation, condensation, and precipitation are related to weather and the water cycle," the suggested activities to help the student are as follows.

1. Draw and label the water cycle and its various pathways.
2. Observe the film: *What Makes Clouds?* See list of questions for discussion purposes.
3. Read pages 103–118 in *Investigating the Earth.* Be able to describe, in some detail, the processes of evaporation, condensation, and precipitation.
4. Experiment: Follow the directions on how to experience the process of evaporation, condensation, and precipitation. All materials are on the experiment table.

5. Take black-and-white photos of at least seven different cloud formations. Classify them according to a U.S. Weather Bureau cloud
chart. Find out what these various cloud types tell you about the
condition of the atmosphere.

These activities take into consideration the abilities and the learning
styles of the students. In the first activity, students can draw the concept of
the water cycle. They may be especially talented in art and could present a
most interesting chart which could be useful to others in the class. The second activity calls for viewing a film on the topic. A small group or the
whole class could very well see this film. For some students, it would be an
activity for learning this objective while others would use it to reinforce the
learnings gained from another activity. The fourth point calls for a hands-on
activity. An experiment to show evaporation, condensation, and even precipitation can be conducted at the science table. A guide sheet asks the student to take a series of pictures on cloud formations with a camera. The
pictures could be carefully labeled and mounted on the bulletin board to be
shared with others in the class. Each of these activities are directed toward
meeting the objective and, in most instances, they ensure that all students
master this particular objective. It should be pointed out that the choice of
learning activity is left up to the student. Students will usually choose an
activity which they feel they will be successful in accomplishing. Teachers
can then ask them to choose a second activity to reinforce the learning and
to ensure mastery.

Selecting Media for Use

Dale[4] talks about his ''cone of experience'' as a model for media selection.
This model (Figure 5.3) serves as a reminder to teachers of the various kinds
of experiences that are available to learners.

The model may be envisioned as an upside-down ice cream cone,
broad at the base and coming to a narrow point at the top. The purpose of
this model is to show the degree of abstraction in the message presented to
the learner. At the lowest level, we see ''direct, purposeful experiences.''
These experiences involve ''doing'' and are the least abstract types of instruction possible. For example, a class studying ecology could study farming practices such as strip farming. Plans could be made by the group to
visit a model farm where various conservation practices could be observed
on the farm. Besides viewing, the students could don chore clothes and actually take part in various conservation practices—including spreading manure
with the farmer and his manure spreader. This experience would constitute
direct, purposeful experience (Level 1). At the other extreme, or the top of
the cone, the messages are highly abstract and consist of spoken or printed

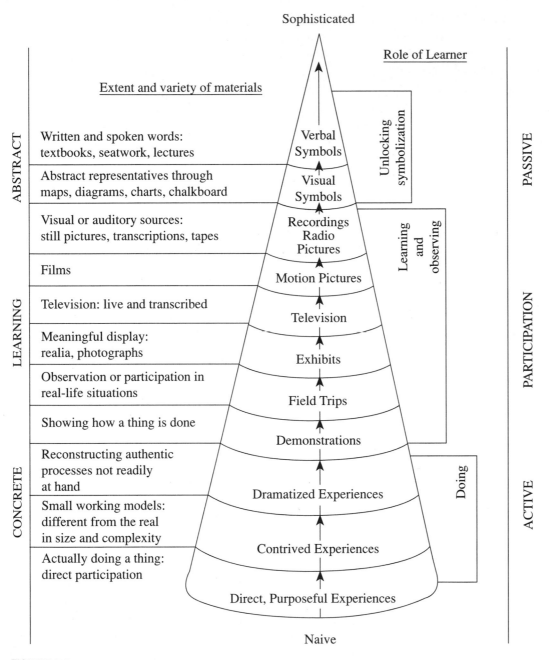

FIGURE 5.3

Dale's Cone of Experience.

From *Audiovisual Methods in Teaching* by Edgar Dale. Copyright © 1969 by The Dryden Press Inc. Reprinted by permission of the Dryden Press Inc.

symbols (words). The student is a passive observer. Between the lowest and the highest level represented on the cone, there are a number of intermediate levels, as shown in Figure 5.3. Each level becomes more abstract than the one below it; that is, students are less actively involved. Thus instruction loses elements of reality found in direct, purposeful experiences. These intermediate levels are represented by some media that carry messages, and in many cases, it is the attributes of these media that determine the degree of abstractness of the message.

Visiting the farm and observing the various conservation practices is reality itself (Level V), but certain elements of reality are lost when these conservation practices are seen in a motion picture (Level VIII). Further loss takes place when still pictures (Level IX) are observed. Another example might be moving from the level of direct, purposeful experience which contains all the elements of the ''real world'' to contrived experiences, where the environment of the learner is simulated. Contrived experiences lack some of the atmosphere of the direct experience. Dale further states that one cannot arbitrarily attach a ''good or bad'' label to the media at any level. Whether the media (or degree of abstraction of the message) are good or bad will depend on many things, including variables related to the learner and the task.

Too often, the teaching-learning situation centers on verbal and visual symbols rather than experiences enumerated in the base of the cone. According to Goodlad and Klein,[5] textbooks and workbooks dominate the teaching-learning process. This is unfortunate when there is a plethora of resources available to teachers to meet the various learning styles of students. This is not to suggest the abandonment of the textbook. The textbook can be a valuable resource if employed for the needs of the students, but it must be questioned if it is the only instructional tool used in the teaching-learning situation. Other stimuli which can be used in conjunction with the textbook are films, filmstrips, records, tapes, transparencies, television, computers, charts, games, field trips, etc. With the use of many stimuli, the classroom does not become a limited learning environment. It can be greatly expanded through various multimedia materials. Greenfield[6] pointed out that a multimedia approach encourages students to develop skills that print alone doesn't. It also enables educators to boost the value of media children are exposed to anyway. Furthermore, the electronic media have strong motivational qualities for children.

The Multimedia Approach Is Effective

Do students learn more of the vocabulary of science units when motion picture films and project still pictures are added to the use of other audiovisual materials? This question was examined by Romano[7] in a study which included students from two fifth, sixth, and seventh-grade groups in the public

FIGURE 5.4

Superiority of Gains in Science Vocabulary by Experimental Groups Using Cross-Media Techniques Over Control Groups.

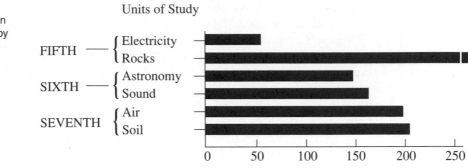

schools of Shorewood and Whitefish Bay, Wisconsin. These groups were rotated so that each served in turn as an experimental and a control group. Blackboards, bulletin boards, charts, models, flat pictures, and field trips were used both in the control and experimental situations, but motion pictures and projected still pictures (Filmstrips, 2x2 slides, and pictures used with the opaque projector) were used only in the experimental situations and served as the experimental factors. Both groups also used a wealth of printed materials. This study, according to Wittich and Schuller,[8] was unique in that the researcher studied students who were already accustomed to a learning environment that their teachers considered unusually enriched.[9]

Significantly greater vocabulary gains were made by the group using projected pictures in a multimedia approach (Figure 5.4).

Results showed that the fifth-grade students in the experimental group learned up to 300 percent more science vocabulary, the sixth-grade group twice the vocabulary, and the seventh-grade group 200 percent more than the control group students learned.

Four years after the completion of this study, Georgiady[10] studied the effect of the 16-mm sound motion picture film and the use of related projected still pictures on vocabulary development and growth in social studies among students in grades 6, 7, and 8. This study closely paralleled Romano's investigation and the results almost matched those of the earlier study. Thus, two careful investigations of the use of films with related audiovisual materials concluded that a multimedia approach enhances learning.

These studies are significant because they did not attempt to determine the effectiveness of a single audiovisual material over other visual materials such as slides, demonstrations, maps, and the like. Nor did they attempt to determine the effectiveness of the more traditional classroom procedures using verbal instruction by means of textbooks or supplementary reading. Instead, they attempted to determine the effectiveness of using numerous audiovisual materials in coordinated fashion over using limited audiovisual materials singly. Dale[11] points out that in previous audiovisual studies, the researcher failed to establish normal classroom procedures. The researcher used a single audiovisual aid such as a filmstrip, film, etc. Good classroom procedures call for a multimedia approach.

These studies have added significance because they showed that an important basic skill, acquisition of vocabulary, can be achieved in a multimedia situation in the middle school.

The reactions of students following the Romano study indicate the inherent value of the multimedia approach to learning.

"We learned more because we could see what was meant instead of reading about it or hearing it alone."

"Astronomy filmstrips are more interesting. They help me to get a better idea of what the book said."

"I'll never forget how the layers of earth folded over. I just couldn't understand that when we talked about it in class, but I got it right away from the film."

Implementing the Multimedia Approach

One of the best techniques to ensure that teachers will use the multimedia approach in the classroom is to develop units of study. The basic idea of a unit is very simple, and all teachers can use it effectively. More importantly, all teachers should have these units available for preplanning purposes prior to teaching. Simply, a unit of study is a collection of objectives, activities, materials, etc., on a specific topic, prepared by a teacher for a specific time, to be used with a particular group of students.[12]

In the development of units of study, a body of research about pupils at this level presents some guidelines for the grade placement of social studies units and for activities within the units. Although these statements are related to social studies, they obviously have implications for other instructional areas.

Keeping in mind the growth characteristics of the middle school students, the selection of topics for units should

1. Be cultural rather than chronological in nature and emphasize how people have adjusted to their environment and adapted it to meet their needs.
2. Deal with man's technical control over his environment and his use of natural resources because of interest in mechanics, science, and natural phenomena.
3. Help students understand themselves, adjust to their immediate physical and social environment, and establish satisfactory personal relationships.
4. Help students understand the likenesses and differences in people and the desirability of cultural plurality of American life and the world community.

5. Include great personages in order to satisfy the inclination toward hero worship.
6. Satisfy their basic drives to be active, to dramatize, to construct and manipulate, to satisfy curiosity, and to communicate, as well as to satisfy their ego-integrative needs.

EXAMPLES OF UNITS

We hope that in the determination of units of study in social studies, science, English, etc., care will be taken so that there is a sequential development of learnings from the elementary grades to the middle school grades. For example, a sequential development in social studies would eliminate unnecessary duplication and ensure, to a certain extent, that important topics are not omitted from the instructional program. Once a sequence of topics is determined, then the next steps include writing the units of study.

Although there are several models to choose from, the format shown in Box 5.1 has been used over a period of several years in a number of middle schools and found to be simple to write and most appropriate to preplanning.

BOX 5.1
Format for a Unit of Study

Title Page: Title of Unit
Grade Level/s
Purpose of the Unit

PreTest

Behavioral Objective	Suggested Activities	Suggested Materials

The title page includes the title of the unit, grade level or levels, and the purpose of the unit. For example:

TITLE: English Colonization in the New World

GRADE LEVEL: 8

PURPOSE: To give the students an understanding of how the English settled thirteen colonies along the Atlantic Coast of North America to become prosperous and progressive, and why they revolted and won their independence to form a new nation, the United States of America.

A pretest should be developed to coincide with the behavioral objectives to be learned in the unit of study. The pretest itself should be the short answer type, such as matching, etc., rather than the essay type at this point. The purpose of this pretest is to assess the student's knowledge of this topic, and then to plan and individualize the instructional program to include only those behavioral objectives which the student does not understand. Other students with the same learning needs can be formed into a small group and can work together. In other words, the teacher has arranged for learning activities which teach *what the student does not know rather than what he already knows.*

Pretest

Mark each of the following either *true* or *false.*

_____ 1. Religious freedom was one reason why people left England and migrated to America.

_____ 2. The "Lost Colony" in Virginia was a group of people who disappeared.

_____ 3. Government by-laws was one democratic ideal reflected by the Mayflower Compact.

_____ 4. An indentured servant could be sold to a new owner.

_____ 5. The Indians taught the colonists to grow corn.

_____ 6. Puritans wanted to break away from the Church of England.

_____ 7. A charter was required before a group could settle in a region in America.

_____ 8. Learning to grow cotton was one reason why the Virginia colony grew and prospered.

_____ 9. The Jamestown colony was started by Sir Walter Raleigh.

Match each of the following people with a role in the early colonies.

_____ (a) John Smith   1. Governor of Massachusetts Bay Colony

_____ (b) Roger Williams   2. Started village of Hartford

_____ (c) Sir Walter Raleigh   3. Leader of Jamestown

_____ (d) John Rolfe   4. King of England when Jamestown was formed

_____ (e) John Winthrop   5. Learned how to grow tobacco from the Indians

_____ (f) King James I   6. Founded colony at Roanoke Island

                                7. Founded colony of Rhode Island

FIGURE 5.5
First Permanent
English Colonies.

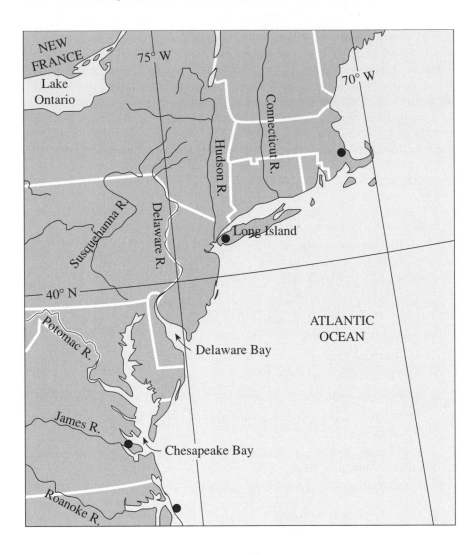

On the map in Figure 5.5 locate the following places:

A. Jamestown   C. Roanoke Island
B. Plymouth   D. New Amsterdam

    The pretest can also be used as the posttest, which is given at the termination of the unit of study to determine mastery of the behavioral objectives. The writers recommend that the posttest may include some objective type questions, but should also include essay type questions. Students should be given an opportunity to learn how to pull together key ideas of the unit of study into coherent, essay type questions.

Clearly Stated Objectives

The writers of the units of study should keep in mind that the behavioral objectives should be written *first,* before writing the pretest. In other words, the pretest should be closely geared to the behavioral objectives because these are to be achieved by the students. Specifically, what are behavioral objectives? They are clearly worded instructional statements which can be measured. Mager[13] states that the most meaningful stated objectives attempt to exclude the greatest number of possible alternatives. Since many words are "loaded" and open to interpretation, he suggests the following which are open to fewer interpretations: to recite, to identify, to differentiate, to solve, to construct, to list, etc. Note that these words describe what the learner will be *doing.* On the other hand, other words are open to many interpretations: for example, to understand, to appreciate, to enjoy, to believe, etc. He further states that to make each objective more specific, one might include the following. (Figure 5.6.)

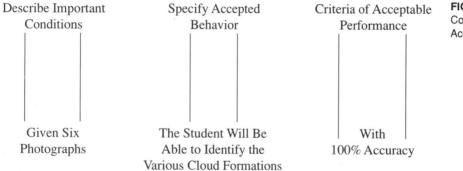

Describe Important Conditions

Given Six Photographs

Specify Accepted Behavior

The Student Will Be Able to Identify the Various Cloud Formations

Criteria of Acceptable Performance

With 100% Accuracy

FIGURE 5.6
Components of Acceptable Objectives.

Suggested Activities

Suggested activities are an important part of a unit which deals specifically with the multimedia approach. In this section, the writer must supply at least five different activities in order for students to achieve a particular activity. If the writer only includes activities which call for reading and writing, then we have limited the options for the students. What about the student who has difficulty reading or lacks an understanding of the printed page? What about the student who learns best through an audiovisual presentation or one who can reinforce the learnings of the printed paper through the film or filmstrip? Or the student who has art talent and can pull together all of the key ideas of the unit into a pictorial presentation, or the construction of a papier-mâché item? Activities should be included which give the student opportunities to achieve the objectives through problem-solving techniques, through skills of inquiry and research, through the use of the basic skills, through dramatic plays, through construction, through art and music, through audiovisual materials, etc. Throughout the unit, every effort should be made to include examples of the various types of activities, such as art experiences, research experiences, construction experiences, etc. Care should be taken so that certain students don't limit themselves to just one type of activity, such as reading only the textbook or viewing only certain audiovisual materials.

Suggested Materials

Once the activities have been defined, then it is a matter of including the materials which are needed for the particular activity. Specificity is important, such as listing the pages in the textbook, the name of the filmstrip and source, the materials and directions for making a papier-mâché model, etc. This keeps the teachers or the students from having to hunt for these materials during the teaching-learning situation.

Let's examine the unit "English Colonization in the New World" to see what it looks like with the behavioral objective, suggested activities, and suggested materials. (See Table 5.1.)

INTERACTIVE MULTIMEDIA

Educators are often criticized because instructional materials have focused largely on the mastery of discrete low-level skills and isolated facts, thus denying opportunities for students to master subject matter in depth, learn more complex problem-solving skills, or apply the skills they do learn.[14] That's why some educators are restructuring educational programs.

Today, we find in a few middle schools an instructional multimedia approach which will change the face of how instructional programs will be delivered to students and how students will respond to classmates. This phenomenon, known as "interactive multimedia" or as it is also called "hypermedia," will streamline multimedia as never before (Trotter, 1989).[15]

Interactive multimedia will drastically change teaching and learning. Today, advances in information storage technology will make available whole libraries of documents, sounds, video, and graphic images to be placed on laser or videodiscs, possible by computer.[16] Information will be available to the students. They will be able to browse through tons of information nonsequentially rather than plow laboriously through from page one to the end of the printed material.

TABLE 5.1 English Colonization in the New World

Behavioral Objective	Suggested Activities	Suggested Materials
The student will be able to explain the role of the Native Americans in the growth of the colonies.	Read textbook pages 77–89 looking for information on how the Native Americans helped the early colonists to survive.	Textbook: *Liberty & Union,* Pages 77–89.
	Discuss the role of the Native Americans in the growth of the colonies. List or chart their efforts. (3 students)	Colored chart paper in the art cabinet.
	Watch film "The Pilgrims" and look for the role of the Native Americans in the survival of the Plymouth Colony.	Film "The Pilgrims" (in Instructional Media Center).
	Role-playing. Have the students play the parts of the Native Americans and the early colonists, making sure to bring out how the Native Americans could help the early colonists. Six students will write and present their role-playing script to the class.	
	Have the students write reports on one of the following: Squanto, Massasoit, or Pocahontas, and the role each played in assisting the colonists.	See list of books about Native Americans on the bulletin board.
	Draw a picture showing how the Native Americans helped the colonists.	Art materials are in the art cabinet.
	Construct a table top scene of the Native Americans and colonists working together.	Plasticene and other art materials are in the art cabinet.

When students use computers for the purpose of learning, they are interacting with the courseware found within the system. A variety of electronic devices, such as laser and videodiscs, will permit students to be interactive with the program provided.

Here is an example of what happens today in the typical teaching-learning situation. A film may be shown to the students and they just listen or watch passively. They do not interact with the film. In the interactive mode, the students can scan the film like a book, which permits them to focus on a particular portion. Furthermore, with interactive multimedia, an educational package can be available not only in schools but also in homes. Therefore, education will no longer take place only in the school environment, but also outside of the walls of the schoolhouse. Although interactive multimedia will be available outside the schoolhouse, it should be pointed out that the classroom has certain qualities of openness, companionship, and discipline which no microcomputer or network could replace.[17] Also, the computer can provide an individualized education which will meet the instructional needs of the slow learner and the fast learner. Students can choose a presentation to meet their needs—a procedure not found in most regular teaching-learning situations. It should be pointed out that interactive multimedia does *not* replace the classroom teacher. The well-planned computer program does release teachers from standing in front of the classroom presenting a lesson so that they have more time to work with individual students. This should provide greater learning for the students without dehumanizing the teaching-learning environment.

Previous teaching-learning environments focused primarily on teacher presentations, textbooks, and workbooks. Products in production today will further revolutionize the classroom environment. One example is the new *Compton's Multimedia Encyclopedia* from Encyclopedia Britannica Educational Corporation. With use of a computer and a special compact disc player, an entire nine million words, 5,000 articles, 63,000 entries, 15,000 photographs and charts, 60 minutes of sound, and 45 animated sequences will be available on a single compact disc to be used at home or at school. The *Merriam-Webster Intermediate Dictionary*[18] will also be available.

Examples of Interactive Multimedia

An example will give the reader an understanding of interactive multimedia. In one classroom, students are asked to prepare a book report. Students read a book and then use the computer, digitize photos, do voice-overs, and put the entire book report on videotape. An added advantage is that students are learning to work together and to show leadership skills.[19]

Another example of an activity which shows the immense value of interactive multimedia is Palenque, an interactive multimedia optical disc research prototype which was developed for home use for 8 to 14-year-old children and their families. In the program, middle school children are introduced to the science of archaeology and the culture of ancient Maya in Mexico's Yucatán peninsula. These materials were produced as a ''real world'' activity to make various scientific concepts understandable to children.

What makes this study of Mayan culture so exciting is that students can use a joystick to take a self-directed, simulated ''walk'' around the ancient Mayan site at Palenque. This program is not a step-by-step instructional sequence. Its data base includes information stored in a variety of formats (graphics, text, sound, narration, slides, and motion video). A student is able to browse through Palenque rather than follow a required procedure. If a student prefers walking through the rain forest surrounding the historical site, he can do so. He might meet a howler monkey. The animal interests him, so he may want to see a motion video of howlers or he may want to hear the monkey howl. Available to the student are slides, sound effects, text, movies, and narration. All information formats include a variety of learning modes.[20]

RELATED STUDIES

A study was conducted comparing the multimedia approach to a single method in the teaching of physics. One group of students used the laboratory method only, a second group used the computer only, and a third group used both the laboratory method and the computer. This study reported that the combination of the laboratory method and the computer was most effective. Students who used both were able to research conclusions more effectively and had the highest examination scores.[21]

Another study is in its second year in a Rochester, New York middle school. Collaborative efforts in this project include the Rochester City Schools, the University of Rochester, the Rochester Museum and Science Center, and the Center for Technology in Education at Bank Street College.

It should be pointed out that this urban community, made up of significant numbers of poor students, became involved in a major restructuring of its middle schools. To break down the large numbers of students in each school, the middle schools were reorganized into houses and further subdivided into grade-level clusters taught by teams of four teachers.

This project, entitled the Discover Rochester Project, included a class of eighth-grade students. The objective of the project was to help students develop thinking and problem-solving skills. The interdisciplinary unit of study included a subject matter curriculum but made extensive use of the community and its resources. Students learned about Rochester Community from various perspectives, namely, historical, mathematical, scientific, cultural, and literary perspectives. Groups of middle school children conducted studies and shared their findings and understanding of the community via a multimedia museum exhibit. This exhibit, entitled ''Discover Rochester,'' is on computer and the efforts of students are presented through text, audio, graphics, music, and maps.

What are the results for students involved in this program? It was found that (1) student absences dropped, (2) students were much more involved in the project, and (3) there was greater participation in class discussions. It was reported that some students gave up their lunchtime to work on the project. Furthermore, teachers found that the quality of students' efforts increased and they learned to use the computer with greater skill.

Other side effects included greater teacher involvement and significant changes in lesson presentation from directive to more facilitative. Also, teachers who were not involved the first time volunteered to be involved in the next phase of this project.[22]

The above examples are just a few of the activities in the teaching-learning situation. The use of interactive multimedia can bring to our classrooms a resource rich environment for our often resource poor classrooms.

Today our society is changing rapidly from an industrial society to one which will focus on the advantages of technology. It is hoped that these great strides in information technologies will provide our future citizenry with the needed skills to meet the challenges of a global market. Not only will it help them meet global market needs, but it will also provide further skills for the development of self-actualized people.

SUMMARY

The multimedia approach is a technique which enables the teacher to coordinate the use of a variety of media, including the textbook, to enable students of various abilities and interests to learn the behavioral objectives in any instructional area. Studies in both science and social studies have shown the effectiveness of the acquisition of vocabulary learnings in these two areas. Because of its proven effectiveness, the multimedia approach should be included in teaching-learning. Furthermore, literature on media in education consistently shows a multimedia approach to a subject can be a more effective way of teaching than a single medium in isolation.[23]

One of the best instructional tools for a range of learners is the unit of study. The unit of study includes behavioral objectives, suggested activities, and suggested materials. It is primarily a preplanning tool for teachers. It enables them to provide learning activities which are consistent with the needs and interests of the middle school student.

The future will provide for more opportunities for middle school children to interact with multimedia in several ways. In this procedure, the computer will be used in a host of ways to enrich learning and to reinforce the printed page. Truly, middle school children will be excited about interactive multimedia. Most of all, it will ensure greater learning.

ENDNOTES

1. Association for Supervision and Curriculum Development. *The Junior High School We Saw: A Day in the Eighth Grade.* 1964.

2. Lounsbury, John H., Jean V. Marani, and Mary F. Compton. *The Middle School Profile: A Day in the Seventh Grade,* National Middle School Association, 1980, 62–63.

3. Wattenburg, William W. "The Junior High School—A Psychologist's View, *MASSP* Bulletin. (April 1, 1965): 34–44.

4. Dale, Edgar, *Audio-Visual Methods in Teaching,* The Dryden Press, Rev. ed., 1954.

5. Goodlad, John, and M. Francis Klein and Associates. *Looking Behind the Classroom Door,* Worthington, Ohio: Charles A. Jones Publishing Co. (1974): 81.

6. Greenfield, Patricia M. "Multi-Media Education: Why Print Isn't Always Best." *American Educator,* (Fall, 1985): 18–21 and 36–38.

7. Romano, Louis. "The Role of 16 mm Motion Pictures and Projected Still Pictures in Science Unit Vocabulary Learning at Grades 5, 6, & 7," unpublished Ph.D. Thesis, University of Wisconsin, 1955.

8. Wittich, Walter A., and Charles F. Schuller. *Audio Visual Materials, Their Nature and Use.* New York: Harper Publishers, 1957.

9. See note 7.

10. Georgiady, Nicholas. "The Role of 16 mm Motion Pictures and Related Projected Still Pictures in Social Studies Unit Vocabulary Learning, Grades 6–8," unpublished Ph.D. Thesis, University of Wisconsin, 1959.

11. See note 4.

12. Nerborvig, Marcella H. *Unit Planning: A Model for Curriculum Development.* Worthington, Ohio: Charles A. Jones Publishing Co. (1970): 12.

13. Mager, Robert F. *Preparing Instructional Objectives.* Palo Alto, California: Fearon Publishers, 1962.

14. National Governors' Association. *Educating America: State Strategies for Achieving the National Educational Goals,* Washington, D.C.: National Governors' Association, 1990.

15. Trotter, Andres. "Schools Gear Up for 'Hypermedia': A Quantum Leap in Electronic Learning." *The American School Board Journal.* (March, 1989): 35–37.

16. See note 15.

17. Porter, Rosemary Lee. *Using Microcomputers for Teaching Reading in the Middle Schools,* Phi Delta Kappa, Fastback 296, 1989, 9–13.

18. Brooks, Robert, and Pearl Barry. "Interactive Technology for Education." *Business Week.* (December 10, 1990).

19. Honore, Sheridan. "Multi-Media Classroom." *Lansing State Journal.* (August 26, 1991).

20. Wilson, Kathleen S. "The Palenque Optical Disc Prototype: Design of Multimedia Experiences for Education and Entertainment in a Nontraditional Learning Context," Technical Report No. 44, Bank Street College of Education, New York, New York, May 1987 (Paper presented at the A.E.R.A.).

21. See note 6.

22. Sheingold, Karen, and Marc S. Tucker. *Restructuring for Learning with Technology,* Bank Street College of Education and National Center on Education and the Economy, December 1990.

23. See note 21.

CHAPTER

6

Creative Exploratory
and Enrichment Activities

THE NATURE OF CREATIVITY

Creativity has been defined in many different terms. For purposes of this book, we will define it as a blending of originality, curiosity, and strong interest in ideas which enable the student to pursue an activity that gives him personal satisfaction and a feeling of accomplishment.

Creativeness is not a single quality but rather consists of a number of different abilities. These will vary in each individual. They may include verbal fluency, nonverbal fluency, unique ideas, a flexibility of mind, and sometimes a complex conceptual capability. Creative students are often independent in thought and action. These students frequently experience pleasure and excitement in dealing with questions and problems which cause them to exercise their creative talents as they seek solutions or answers.

While the quality of creativity is important at any age level, it is particularly important in the middle school years. Previous chapters have dealt with the changing nature of the transescent individual, one who is no longer a child and who is moving into adolescence. The transescent experiences a growing interest in a wider world and a greater curiosity about many things of which he is now becoming conscious. This enlarged view of his world provides him with many more opportunities to exercise his curiosity in his own way and to learn more about those matters that interest and, at times, puzzle him. Unfortunately, many schools fail to recognize the importance of providing opportunities in the school curriculum for the exercise of creativity by students. This is particularly true in the middle school years, where the view often held is that the curriculum must be geared to preparing students academically for the senior high school in a very traditional way. Consequently, experiences leading to the enhancement of creative talents and ability have not been sufficiently present in most middle school curricula.

Another probable reason for the lack of nurture of creative talents in the middle school may be due to the general anxiety of educators about public concerns for standardized test scores. These concerns are based on the assumption that most, if not all, emphasis in the classroom should be on drill and memorization designed to produce better test scores. Yet there is strong feeling by many that creative teaching and learning can also be very valuable in aiding student mastery of basic materials. These two areas do not necessarily have to be mutually exclusive. The creative student pursuing a problem which intrigues him will frequently find it necessary to utilize his basic skills of logic or science or mathematics as well as reading in order to pursue the study he has undertaken. The practice and further refinement of those skills will be even more effective for him since they are being utilized in a task which has great interest for him. They are also far more likely to be retained. Torrance points out that "The development of the creative thinking abilities is at the very heart of the achievement of even the most fundamental educational objectives, even the acquisition of the three R's. It is certainly not a matter of specialization."[1]

THE CREATIVE MIDDLE SCHOOL TEACHER

Anyone familiar with the ever-changing, often puzzling, sometimes frustrating, but usually fascinating nature of the transescent can understand that it takes a very special kind of person to serve as a teacher for these students. Besides possessing a good understanding of the characteristics of middle school students, teachers working with them must not only be patient with their changing moods and behaviors, but must also be innovative and creative in their instructional planning. The middle school student, whether consciously or not, is continually seeking to express individuality and to gain status and recognition. The task of the middle school teacher is to recognize these needs and to provide outlets for creative expression by students.

To develop a setting for creativity, the middle school teacher must do several things.

1. Establish a setting in which creativity can develop and flourish. This involves the physical nature of the setting including room arrangement and other physical facilities, and the operational procedures in the classroom which makes it possible for students to feel free to express creative thinking. It also includes the availability of a wide range of resources both in the classroom and in the building which can be rich sources of information for creative inquiry and thought.

2. Be prepared to use problem-solving approaches for activities that are open-ended and divergent rather than more limited, teacher-dominated conventional and traditional classroom procedures.

3. Help students see and realize the value of using skills in a natural, interrelated way in pursuing problems more creatively.

4. Assist students in learning facts and basic skills in meaningful situations so that their use in problem solving will be more natural and logical.

5. Encourage cooperative learning as a way of enhancing intellectual growth as well as development in interpersonal relations at a time in students' lives when this is so important.

Beyond this, the teacher's task is to provide opportunities for students, whether individually or in groups, to learn and to grow in their understanding of themselves, of others, and of the world in which they live. The teacher must also understand that creativeness cannot be directly and specifically taught. Rather, teachers must realize they need to guide students and create an environment where they may freely express creative thought.

Classes should be organized by the teacher so that students will feel comfortable in making individual contributions, respect the contributions of others, and be willing to participate in making group decisions.

The creative teacher's classroom is also one in which students are sufficiently motivated so that they carry on their studies even in the absence of the teacher.

Creative teachers are ones who are comfortable enough with divergent thinking to encourage it often. They are not threatened by unique results. At times, such teachers are willing to stand aside so that students can plan, discuss, and interact by themselves. Teachers also seek to encourage self-initiated learning by students. While they remain available for consultation and guidance, they do not dominate the student's planning efforts.

A CURRICULUM FOR EXPLORATION

Educators have a golden opportunity to capitalize on the growing curiosity of the transescent. Transescents feel a strong urge to find out about things that arouse their curiosity and to learn more about ideas that capture their interest. The task of the middle school is to recognize this development in students and to provide a curriculum which fits the situation—a curriculum which includes exploratory activities and opportunities for students.

To begin the process, it is necessary to examine the curricula in place in each subject field in turn and to try to identify those activities and studies that fulfill the creative exploratory needs of the students. This evaluation process should begin with the formulation of criteria which will be the basis of the evaluation. What are the activities and studies carried on in the science classes? Do these challenge the students? Do they arouse their curiosity? Are there provisions for the wide range of individual differences in the age group? To what extent do the activities call for initiative or self-reliance on the part of students? What are the kinds of media and materials needed for these activities?

These are some of the kinds of questions which may be asked in an effort to evaluate the science program. Once information is gathered, it will become clearer what changes need to be made in the science curriculum to fit it more closely to the students.

Further examination of the science program can then focus on the actual lesson plans developed by teachers for their classes. Here, too, the kinds of questions asked should seek to determine how much provision there is in the lessons for the exercise of creative exploration by students. Opportunities for both hands-on activities as well as more verbal-oriented kinds of activities should be provided. Involvement on the part of students is extremely important for this age group. Also important is the use of a variety of media and materials for learning. Some students are more comfortable with one kind of material whereas others prefer a different kind of material. Having a range of materials and media will do much to motivate students in their studies, as is pointed out in a previous chapter.

Valuable exploratory experiences for middle school students can be provided in a number of subject areas or programs. One which lends itself well to this is the Unified Arts program which can be defined as a planned combination of Art, Industrial Arts, and Home Economics. Some schools may also include Music, Drama, and Physical Education. Combining these otherwise separate studies almost necessitates the development of an exploratory curriculum in order to capture the inherent value of each subject for the students. This serves to make this clearly a student-centered approach.

The focus of the Unified Arts is to provide students with opportunities to explore a range of different tools, materials, and techniques which can be valuable in self-expression, emotional release, and satisfaction. The self-image of the student can be greatly enhanced as a result of successful interaction with the skills, techniques, and materials in the program. In addition, the laboratory approach used here can offer additional value to student personal growth and development. Such development results from the many opportunities to interact with other students informally in a more casual setting than in a more structured academic classroom setting. This is particularly important in view of the growing awareness of changes in boy-girl interests and relationships during this age.

Further support for the Unified Arts program can be found in the realization that where Art, Industrial Arts, and Home Economics are taught separately, there may well be some duplication in the curricular provisions of each separate subject. By combining these in a meaningful and logical way, this duplication will be avoided. In fact, the interdisciplinary approach, since it makes better use of the time available, will also allow more time for program enrichment and enhancement.

A CURRICULUM FOR ENRICHMENT

Middle school age students enjoy exploring, investigating, and testing. They may encounter certain ideas for the first time. There may be a role in which they see themselves. There may be specific materials or objects they can handle. Curiosity at this age is high as the transescent seeks to arrive at a better understanding of himself and his world.

The effective middle school program recognizes this and seeks to provide opportunities for students to engage in activities which will satisfy them and enrich their young lives. We live in a time in our society when there is great impetus for purely academic accomplishments and course grades along with test scores. Students' lives can be greatly enriched when there are opportunities in school to derive personal satisfaction and gratification from a variety of exciting and challenging activities that are not strictly academic.

In the middle school, activities for enrichment can take many different forms. There may be activities in instrumental music where students who have wondered about playing the violin or blowing a saxophone or touching the keys on a piano keyboard can satisfy that curiosity. Perhaps they will discover a hidden talent worthy of development. The same kinds of opportunities are to be found in choral music as well.

Then there is the act of drawing or working with art materials like clay, wood, plastic, metal, etc., which may fascinate the young individual who seeks to give these substances form.

From a very early age, children are conscious of acting from television or film. Certainly many of them will vicariously take on certain roles in their imaginations. The opportunity to step on a stage or to stand before a camera is one that can hold great interest for them.

Modern science also captures the interest of transescents. Whether it is space travel or earthbound computer technology, there is a great deal of challenge and enrichment for students as they contemplate the exciting possibilities in activities dealing with study of phenomena and even imagine themselves as scientists.

Some middle school programs have recognized the value of enrichment and have developed studies which provide students the personal satisfaction of trying something they've been curious about. Creative middle school teachers can study the curriculum and identify places where enriching activities can be introduced as a means of making their studies more valuable and exciting for students. In the following section, there are some specific suggestions for activities as well as examples from existing middle school programs.

Ideas for Creative Exploratory and Enrichment Activities

The suggestions offered here are only some of the many possibilities. Creative teachers and students can use them as a springboard for their own suggestions.

Drama or Playmaking

Playmaking provides unlimited possibilities for developing and extending academic skills. Creative activities can be designed to provide reinforcement, review, and enrichment of learning components of the middle school curriculum. Perhaps reading is one of the areas in which playmaking has made the greatest impact on skill development. What better way is there to help students discover and remember the moral, sequence, and plot of a story than to allow them to dramatize it? Some other reading skill improvements which playmaking can bring about are: (1) Improvement of oral expression—repeated practice with pronunciation, enunciation, and intonation helps to produce better articulation skills. (2) Improved critical reading and thinking skills—creative activities cause students to be more attentive to what they read, better listeners to what they hear, and therefore able to understand the nature of a character and/or the main event of a story. (3) Improved auditory discrimination—active involvement and participation increases vocabulary development and enhances decoding and encoding training.[2]

Other benefits from playmaking are found in the art work necessary for stage sets along with carpentry, painting, mathematics, electrical lighting, costuming for historical period plays, and many others.

Time for Trying Out and Testing Ideas

With the mounting pressure of state requirements for courses and the growing influence of standardized test scores, many middle schools find it difficult to provide for enriching and exploratory studies. One school which has developed an interesting exploratory studies program is the Hadley Watts Middle School of Centerville, Ohio, which has replaced its general noon recess period with

Exploratory Activities. A 70-minute block of time is divided into half for lunch and the other half for a number of activities. Students sign up for those activities which interest them. The activities provide them with an opportunity to explore without the pressure of grades or fear of failure. They may select from a list which might include: instrumental or choral music; computer labs; MATHCOUNTS (a national competitive program); several gym activities, including volleyball and girls' basketball; photography; drawing activities; Junior Achievement; video club (where videotapes are made for schoolwide use on a local T.V. channel; peer tutors for work with multi-handicapped students; hunting and fishing; and counseling groups and ''talk time'' to discuss ''hot'' topics, anxieties, and concerns of the moment. There are many others on the list, even including study hall, for those who want this quiet, private time, as there are no study halls during the school day. The schedule varies with students as they sign up for activities on a daily basis. The list of activities is drawn up twice during the school year and is based on teacher and pupil interest and suggestion.

Bridging the Age Gap

At the Cooke Middle School in Northville, Michigan, an interesting community oriented program has been developed. Senior citizens are provided transportation to the school by bus, arriving about 4:30 P.M. For the first hour, they are welcomed and an explanation of the middle school and its program of studies is provided. This is illustrated by a videotape. Following that, in the second hour, guests are treated to a spaghetti dinner prepared by students in the life skills class and served by student waiters and waitresses. After dinner, a jazz band from the high school plays dance music and seniors and students dance together as partners.

Young and old alike are enthusiastic about the benefits of this event as a way of making each age group more conscious of the other. It also clearly relates the school to its community.

Community Service

The East Grand Rapids Middle School provides a ''real life'' education experience for students, one which develops a sense of social responsibility for others and enriches them with a better understanding of life, aging, poverty, and handicaps.

The Parent Teacher Student Association works on three projects during the year: (1) United Way and disaster relief, (2) Adopt-A-Family during the winter holiday season, and (3) Kent County Special Olympics for the handicapped.

The school feels that this community service is valuable for these reasons:

Enhances a positive self-concept.

Promotes a ''sense'' of belonging.

Provides a ''real life'' education experience.

Develops organization and leadership skills.

Increases awareness of career opportunities.

Promotes communication between students with different interests and abilities.

Develops a range of skills correlated with being a success in adult life.

Further Suggestions for Creative Expression in the Curriculum

Communities and their populations vary widely in this nation. The opportunities for creative expression are almost unlimited and a wide range of exciting and challenging ideas for expressing creativity can be developed and applied in every middle school. Creative expression can do a great deal to make the curriculum come to life for students. Following are a few of the many possible kinds of activities for doing this.

Science

Use scientific methods and apply them to kitchen chemistry to create edible compounds.

Use drawing skills to teach bone positions in the human skeleton.

Create posters to illustrate lab techniques and safety procedures.

Create a cartoon strip with a science character as star to teach a science concept.

English

Use music to generate creative writing or poetry.

Design original book covers to illustrate stories or books read in class.

Dramatize a story using a modern setting and language.

Create a TV or radio commercial to advertise a story, book, or play.

Create a poster to advertise a story, book, or play.

Create a videotape to illustrate an English principle such as parts of speech.

Write a script, cast and stage a short play.

Social Studies

Create three-dimensional maps of places studied.

Use music, food, costumes, or language from countries studied.

Dress in period costumes or art work showing these.

Present short plays on places or events in history.

Library or Media Center

Poster on library etiquette.

Form a video club to plan and make videos of school events.

Display student artwork and creative writing.

Display materials related to units of study in classrooms.

Cafeteria

Plan a mural to brighten the wall.

Have a contest for the best poster on basic nutrition topics.

Provide a theme meal to parallel a country studied in social studies class.

Hallways and Corridors

Plan a display of artwork by students on a regular basis.

SUMMARY

The nature of middle school age students makes it logical and appropriate to provide them with opportunities for creative exploratory activities and for enrichment through their studies. The creative teacher can establish a setting in which students feel free to engage in exciting and challenging opportunities and reap their rewards.

ENDNOTES

1. Gowan, John C., J. Khatena, and E. P. Torrance. *Creativity: Its Educational Implications,* 2nd edition, Dubuque: Kendall/Hunt Publishing Co., 1981.

2. Muldrew, J. M. ''Focus on Creative Playmaking in the Middle School.'' East Lansing, MI: Michigan Association of Middle School Educators (1989): 2.

Independent Study

THE MEANING OF INDEPENDENT STUDY

Is independent study a myth or a reality in our schools? A more basic question might be whether independent study is something that should be included in the educational environment of the young adolescent learner.

Independent study has been used for many years in a great number of our secondary and elementary schools in one form or another. In fact, in recent years more and more schools have implemented some type of independent study program. In *Middle School: Humanizing Education* (Overly, Kinghorn, and Preston 1972, 105)[1] independent study is referred to in the following manner:

> It has become professionally fashionable to institute some form of independent study. Who can be against either independence or study? Combined, independence and study make an appealing label. However, independent study means different things to different people.

By breaking the concept of independent study into its separate parts, it becomes evident how value laden this concept has become. A look at how teachers vs. students might view independent study supports Overly, Kinghorn, and Preston's statement that ". . . independent study means different things to different people." For example, most middle school teachers would agree that their students are struggling with a newfound desire for independence. Likewise, middle school teachers might say that studying does not have a high priority with these youngsters. Middle school teachers probably would recognize a need for independent study, but would question the degree, commitment, and method of implementation by their students.

Then there is the attitude of the middle school student toward independent study. For the most part, these students see a much greater need for independence than their teachers and usually have much more confidence in their ability to handle such independence. Middle school teachers see a great need for studying while the middle school student sees it as a lesser priority. There is a mixed reaction when the middle school student is asked to define the concept of independent study. Independence, which has a high priority, and studying, which has a somewhat lower priority, are two terms which are often hard to synthesize in the minds of young adolescents.

If these reactions are accurate, it would appear that the teacher and student each has his/her own feelings about independence and studying as separate concepts. However, when the two are combined into one concept there are not only differences of opinions but also confusion as to its meaning and relevance. Before talking about how independent study can be implemented in middle schools, let us examine the question of *why* independent study should be implemented.

Relationship of Independent Study to the Middle School

When combining the two terms, independent and study, middle school teachers would most likely agree that both are important but may not be synonymous when applied to young adolescents. If meeting the developmental needs of the young adolescent is at the core of the middle school philosophy, then middle school educators cannot afford to fall in the age-old trap of accepting an educational innovation such as ''independent study'' without first considering the reason for its inclusion into the curriculum. It becomes extremely important that middle school educators keep in mind that the prime reason for the existence of the middle school is to fit the educational system to the student, not the student to the educational system. The decision to include an independent study program can be no exception to this cardinal rule.

The critical question then becomes: Is independent study a viable means of meeting the needs of young adolescents and what needs will it meet? The answer to these questions helps establish the philosophical foundation for including independent study in a middle school curriculum. We must first accept the fact that early adolescence is indeed a unique and distinct developmental stage. Volumes of books, articles, and research could be cited substantiating this assumption. However, let us focus our attention for the moment on why the needs of these students argue for inclusion of independent study in the middle schools.

Diversity in Growth, Development, and Interest

Many things make the young adolescent different. However, all these differences can be summarized in one word: *change*. At no other time in their lives will these youngsters have to contend with so many personal changes at one time. They are making significant changes in their physical, emotional, and intellectual makeups. To complicate matters even further, these changes do not occur at the same time or at the same rate. At no other time in school are the differences in maturation levels as evident, even though the chronological ages may be the same.

Thus, differences in levels of maturation might be justification enough to warrant an individual approach to instruction. It stands to reason that the diversity found at this age level would demand diverse methods of instruction. The old adage that no two people learn in the same way would certainly apply to young adolescents. For example, a child who is at a concrete stage of thinking might respond much differently than a child who has attained formal operational level, according to Piaget's theory of cognitive development.

Not only do young adolescents find themselves in the midst of physical, social, emotional, and intellectual transition, but they are also in the midst of developing new and diverse interests. Though often short in duration, they nevertheless may be one of the best means a middle school teacher has of accomplishing an educational goal with a student.

On the surface, it would then appear that independent study would have significant implications as a means of meeting the needs of groups of youngsters with such diverse interests. However, to justify independent study for this reason alone would not be altogether accurate. It would be more accurate to justify individualized instruction for the middle school, but not necessarily independent study. Alexander and Hines[2] point out that these two concepts are definitely not synonymous. They further explain that individualizing instruction can be extremely teacher centered, as in tutoring. Independent study, on the other hand, although it may be used as a means of accomplishing individualized instruction, connotes more than a one-to-one mode of instruction. Preferably independent study should nurture some type of self-directed or independent learning on the part of the student.

This by no means diminishes the role of independent study in providing for the individual needs of students. In a survey of 300 schools done by Alexander and Hines, teachers and administrators indicated that the most beneficial aspect of independent study was that it provided for the needs and interests of the individual student.[3]

Meeting the Need for Independence

Although justification of independent study as a means of meeting the diverse needs and interests of young adolescents certainly is important, one must be careful that the essence of the concept is fully realized. One of the most important needs of young adolescents is that of independence. Merely focusing on an individual students' interest and/or abilities does not necessarily mean that their needs for independence will be met. The need for independence might even be stifled.

A teacher may recognize that a student has discernible interests or a particular learning ability (exceptional or remedial). Unless the teacher provides that student with a certain amount of autonomy for making decisions and accepting the responsibility of his/her learning, however, these interests and learning abilities will not have been adequately addressed. Completing questions in a workbook independently of the teacher's directions does not necessarily foster independent learning on the part of the student. Working with a student on a one-to-one basis, where the teacher is the primary source of direction and information, also fails to foster independent learning.

Independent study begins to make even more sense as part of a middle school program when we look at how it can help young adolescents in their struggle to make the needed transition from the dependency of childhood to the relative independence of a mature adult. Margaret Mead points out that this transition is extremely important and that in a technological society, such as ours, adolescence tends to be prolonged. Thus, it becomes a period when the rights and privileges of adulthood are gradually and sometimes reluctantly given to our youth as opposed to other less advanced cultures, which bestow all rights and privileges at the onset of puberty.[4]

A survey of a typical group of middle school youngsters revealed some interesting insights about their feelings of independence.[5] The following questions were asked of 150 youngsters in a sixth through eighth-grade middle school in a suburban community of 60,000 people.

1. I see myself as being:
   (a) dependent on others
   (b) more dependent on others than independent
   (c) more independent of others than dependent
   (d) independent of others.
2. I feel my teachers:
   (a) are too restrictive
   (b) allow me the right amount of independence
   (c) are not restrictive enough.
3. I feel my parents:
   (a) are too restrictive
   (b) allow me the right amount of independence
   (c) are not restrictive enough.
4. I would like to be more independent to make my own decisions.
   (a) agree
   (b) disagree

TABLE 7.1 How Young Adolescents View Themselves
in Relationship to Independence

	6th grade	7th grade	8th grade	Mean
Dependent	5.0%	0%	4.2%	3.1%
More Dependent than Independent	13.0%	4.5%	24.9%	13.9%
More Independent than Dependent	46.1%	67.6%	57.1%	58.0%
Independent	35.9%	27.9%	13.8%	25.0%

This survey tends to affirm the idea that the young adolescents see themselves as being more independent than dependent. Approximately 83 percent of the students who responded saw themselves as being either independent or at least more independent than dependent. On the other hand, a very small percentage (3.1%) of the students saw themselves as being dependent.

The figures in Tables 7.2 and 7.3 would seem to indicate that there is a basic satisfaction with the amount of independence allowed by teachers and parents. However, when comparing the two extremes, it is evident that the students involved in this survey felt that teachers and parents were much more restrictive than nonrestrictive.

The final question of the survey substantiates the notion that independence is an important need of young adolescents. As can be seen in Table 7.4, there was only a small percentage who did not perceive a need for more independence (9.3%). Even though Tables 7.2 and 7.3 did not indicate that there was a great deal of conflict in what the students saw as a need for independence and what teachers and parents permitted, Tables 7.1 and 7.4 indicate that young adolescents see a need for more independence. It would seem logical that if independence is a perceived need for young adolescents, then middle school educators should develop strategies to help them cope with this need.

In this era of the knowledge explosion, it is impossible to know all there is to know about any given subject. In fact, what knowledge we have at our disposal today might not be applicable or even true a few years hence. Thus, to base education entirely around the idea of disseminating knowledge would be an extremely futile, if not impossible, task. Might not a more realistic goal be one of helping students learn how to learn and thus equip them with learning tools to which they can readily adapt the ever changing and expanding knowledge base? However, in order to do this,

TABLE 7.2   How Young Adolescents View Independence with Respect to Their Relationships to Teachers

	6th grade	7th grade	8th grade	Mean
Teachers Are Too Restrictive	13.0%	25.5%	21.2%	20.1%
Teachers Allow About the Right Amount of Independence	84.5%	72.0%	72.3%	75.9%
Teachers Are Not Restrictive Enough	2.5%	2.5%	6.5%	4.0%

TABLE 7.3   How Young Adolescents View Independence with Respect to Their Relationship with Parents

	6th grade	7th grade	8th grade	Mean
Parents Are Too Restrictive	10.0%	27.9%	14.9%	17.7%
Parents Allow About the Right Amount of Independence	85.0%	67.6%	85.1%	79.1%
Parents Are Not Restrictive Enough	5.0%	4.5%	0%	3.2%

TABLE 7.4   The Young Adolescents' Perceptions of Need for More Independence

	6th grade	7th grade	8th grade	Mean
Need for More Independence	97.5%	93.0%	83.0%	90.7%
No Need for More Independence	2.5%	7.0%	17.0%	9.3%

learners must gain some sense of ownership for their learning. How can youngsters assume any type of responsibility for their own learning if they are not given the opportunity to do so?

Middle school students are typically under the constant direction of a teacher who not only determines what they learn, but when and how they learn it. This type of educational environment tends to breed dependent learning rather than independent learning. Dependent learning in turn tends to restrict students' learning rather than move them toward a more adaptive self-directed learning process.

Independent study thus has an important function in providing a meaningful learning environment for young adolescents. It provides a flexible method of meeting the diverse needs, interests, and abilities of young adolescents. It also provides a method by which teachers can facilitate the transition of their students from the dependency of childhood to the independence expected of adulthood.

Implementing an Independent Study Program in a Middle School

Now that we have addressed the basic rationale for the inclusion of an independent study program in the middle school curriculum, let us turn our attention to ways in which such a program can be effectively implemented. It should be stressed that independent study activities are not only for exceptional and gifted students. Unfortunately, some schools have viewed independent study programs as means of expanding the educational horizons of accelerated students. This approach implies that the students with average or below average abilities need more direction and guidance and would not benefit from such a learning situation. In *Independent Study, Bold New Venture,*[6] William Rogge writes:

> The real problem is not to decide who shall be included or excluded in the program but to determine what kinds of adjustments must be made for individual students so that all can be reached and properly challenged.

This statement is particularly applicable to young adolescents. The diversity of maturation and interests plus the need for independence are characteristics found in all young adolescents. Thus, independent study should be viewed in terms of how it meets the needs of each individual student in relationship to personal abilities, interests, maturation level, and cognitive level of thinking.

What about students whom teachers feel cannot be trusted or cannot assume responsibility, even when the learning activity was teacher directed? How can these students be expected to assume responsibilities to learn independently of the teacher? The familiar saying that "practice makes perfect" may have some relevance in this case. If students are never given the opportunity to assume some degree of responsibility for their own learning, how will they develop into independent learners? Certainly teachers have to expect that some students will not readily respond or will even take advantage of such freedom. However, a teacher must also recognize that a majority of the middle school students' behaviors are caused by peer influence. Therefore, some students may seem irresponsible in class but might respond quite differently given the opportunity to work on their own with minimum peer influence.

The success of an independent study program is determined by a variety of factors. Two of the most important, however, are the ability of the teacher to recognize the needs and interests of each student and the willingness of the teacher to commit class time to independent study activities. Independent study activities and learning situations will not happen by accident in the classroom. The teacher must be prepared with ideas, equipment, materials, and class time to aid each student in developing his/her independence in learning to the fullest.

THREE TYPES OF INDEPENDENT STUDY PROGRAMS FOR THE CLASSROOM

Three alternatives for implementing an independent study program in a classroom will be discussed in this section. Perhaps you will find one, or a combination, of these suggestions applicable to your own school.

Independent Project Day

One approach to independent study in a classroom might be through the development of project days for the entire class on a regular basis. On these days, the teacher must be prepared to step aside from the role of an instructor to assume the role of facilitator of student activities. This does not imply that the student is not at the center of the class learning situation every day. It does mean, however, that on project days the students' interests and concerns become the focal point of the day's learning activities instead of the teacher predetermining what will be covered in class.

The regularity of these project days will vary, but for the moment, give consideration to the possible inclusion of a project day once a week. Weekly project time will satisfy several basic needs of a successful independent study program. First, a weekly commitment of time in the classroom emphasizes the importance the teacher places upon students' opportunity to develop personal interests and experiences. Students are quick to respond to teacher enthusiasm toward a program. Weekly independent study time also allows the student to become more deeply involved in appropriate projects with each unit of study, since a project may be developed over several weeks. Such scheduling encourages more in-depth research.

At the beginning of the project day, the teacher should spend a limited amount of time setting the mood for independent study time. This is when the teacher's own enthusiasm for the upcoming activities and commitment to the importance of each student's independence can make or break the program. This is a time also when some student will test the sincerity of the teacher in accepting the right of each student to make choices about an independent project. The activities suggested by the teacher should be just that— a suggestion or starting point. If students independently come up with a research program or activity of their own, this should be readily accepted by the teacher and encouraged. This is the blossoming of independent study and learning.

Once the independent study time has begun, the teacher should assume the role of the resource person for those students who are in need of such help. Perhaps a student has decided to research a related topic of personal interest but has difficulty in using the card catalog in the library. The teacher then needs to help the student develop these skills and locate the needed information. This should be done with the student and teacher as partners only until the student has located the needed information and is clearly capable of pursuing the remaining research independently. At this point, the teacher should move away from the partnership, giving students encouragement to continue the project as they see fit.

Another opportunity which may be developed through project days is peer interest groups. Several students may discover they have interests in the same area and may wish to develop a project as a team. There is no reason why this should be discouraged, as long as the students sincerely work on the project and do not get distracted along the way. Peer enthusiasm and peer teaching can be valuable additions to any classroom and many times are not utilized to the fullest.

Daily Independent Project Time

Another way of implementing independent study time in the classroom might be to devote a certain portion of the class period each day to independent study. This would work extremely well where the teacher has an extended class period in which time is flexible. The type of independent work a student does during this time might vary. However, the majority of the time should be devoted to students working on their own project with limited teacher direction. This time would also enable the student to work on an independent project on a continuous daily basis as opposed to the weekly or periodic project day. However, unless students are given sufficient time to work on their projects, this time will result in just getting started and then having to stop and go on to another class activity. Where daily time is too limited for the task on which the students are working, it might be better to designate an entire day for independent study, such as a project day.

In scheduling independent study time into the classroom on a daily basis, the teacher must not only consider the amount of time but the logistics of providing the proper environment conducive to independent learning. In other words, it would be very difficult for a student to study independently in the back of the room while other students are engaged in a classroom activity in the front. If a teacher is going to attempt to have some students doing independent study while there is another class activity going on, it is best to have the independent study students work at the same time or at least lead the rest of the class in a non-distracting activity.

The one drawback of having some students on independent study while the teacher is working with the rest of the class is the obvious elimination of the teacher as a resource person for the students. This problem is not easily resolved when there is only one teacher in the class. However, in a team teaching situation, multiple classroom activities work very effectively. One teacher can devote time to working with the students on independent study while the other(s) engage in other classroom activities. This type of cooperative teaming lends a dimension of flexibility to the class that allows the student to engage in independent learning activities as well as other more teacher-directed activities.

Independent Project Units

Yet another way of implementing independent study into the classroom is through an independent project unit approach. In such an approach, the teacher makes a commitment that the material covered on a certain topic will be studied by the students on an independent basis. The role of the teacher becomes one of a resource person who helps the students design the manner in which they wish to investigate the topic under study.

A teacher needs to be cautious not to over-use this type of approach. Although some students react very well to this type of independent instruction, most students at this age need to be involved with their peers in class. The need for interaction is not only common among young adolescents, but also essential to their growth and development. Thus, to use the independent project unit exclusively might provide the youngster with the opportunity to develop independent learning skills. At the same time, it might not provide the needed opportunity to interact with peers. The unit approach could be used as a method to study a subject once or twice a year with an entire class. If there was a student who did well with such an approach, he/she could be given the opportunity to pursue other units independently of the rest of the class.

INDEPENDENT STUDY ACTIVITIES FOR A MIDDLE SCHOOL CLASSROOM

Now that we have presented some of the alternatives for implementing independent study into the classroom, let us turn our attention to the types of activities that can be incorporated into these time blocks. This section will describe four types of activities that would lend themselves to independent study periods in a classroom.

Independent Study Projects

Not all material needs to be presented to all students in the same way. In fact, if one accepts the premise that the young adolescent is at a stage of development marked by diversity in ability, interest, and maturation, then to present the same materials the same way to all students is obviously not the most effective way of teaching or learning. To let the students have some degree of determination in the design and implementation of their learning environment is an essential component in helping the students become independent learners.

Independent study projects can be used in two different ways. First, the project can be designed as the principal means by which the individual student learns about the topic under investigation. Second, the student with the help of the teacher can design a project to supplement what is being covered in class. No matter how it is used, there are certain steps which should be followed before a student embarks on such an independent educational adventure.

Prior to the beginning of each unit of study, the teacher should determine possibilities of high-interest projects which could be pursued by the students in the class. In deciding project possibilities, thought must be given to the various modes of learning used by young adolescents and the variety of levels of cognitive thinking present in a class. Suggested activities must cover a wide spectrum so that students have the opportunity to become involved in a learning situation which is appropriate to their individual needs.

One method which works effectively with young adolescents is brainstorming. This is a process of getting students to generate as many ideas as possible in a short amount of time on a particular topic. For example, if a teacher was introducing a unit on current events which focused on great persons in the world today, he/she might divide the class into small groups and have each group brainstorm a list of as many noted people as they could think of in a four or five minute time period. After each group reports their names, they should be assigned the task of dividing these names into categories. The students could then be regrouped and put into a second brainstorming activity to determine possible independent projects based on these personalities. One of the rules of brainstorming is to accept all ideas without making value judgments as to its acceptability or usefulness; thus, the teacher should be receptive to all ideas. From this list of names and activities the students could select who they would like to investigate and what form their projects would take. Once these topics and activities have been determined, the teacher must assemble the materials and equipment needed to complete the projects so that the class time may be spent with the students involved in the learning process and research rather than in a search for needed materials.

The teacher becomes a resource person for each student in the development of projects. The teacher must also be able to recognize students who are having difficulty in completing the tasks they have chosen. If, for example, a project requires students to use the school library and they do not have basic library skills, then it is the responsibility of the teacher to help those students develop the skills necessary to complete the project.

If the intent of the teacher is to use ideas generated by the students as a jumping off point for an independent study unit, then the teacher should allow the majority of class time for completion of projects. However, if the teacher's purpose is to use these ideas to develop independent study projects that would supplement a class unit, then a project day and/or a daily independent study time would be adequate to complete the projects. This would allow the teacher to carry on with the classroom activities planned for this unit.

Independent Study Resources

Besides having different needs, abilities, and interests, young adolescents also have different modalities of learning. Some students may learn better by seeing than hearing. If a teacher recognizes this, he/she may want to establish different modalities of learning. The following summary of a unit in American history dealing with "Causes of the Civil War" is a good example.

The students were given the task of studying the causes of the Civil War. The class was first given some of the major differences between the North and South, such as slavery, tariffs, states rights vs. central government, etc. They were then divided into two smaller groups, one representing the southern point of view and the other the northern. The task was to research this topic from a northern or southern point of view and be prepared to debate that particular topic.

The teacher then set up several different ways in which the students could obtain the material they needed to support their case. Students could select one or a combination of the following to gain the needed information.

1. View videotapes on causes of the Civil War.
2. Read suggested books.
3. Participate in small group discussion focusing on one point of view (North or South) of the Civil War. The discussions would be directed by the teacher.
4. Use computer programs on the Civil War.

Several days were devoted to the task of collecting data. Some students drifted from one station to the next while others stayed with one method of information gathering. They then organized their information and put it immediately to use in their debates.

Allowing the students to select the way in which they feel most comfortable gathering information is a form of independent study. Although the teacher organized and set up all the needed resources, the students were still given the option to select the type of information gathering mode which fit them best. Students most likely did not work strictly on their own. However, with the exception of the small discussion groups, students worked independently of the teacher. This type of independent study, although it does not nurture true independent learning as an independent project might, does provide the student with some independence in how he/she learns.

Independent Learning Labs

A similar approach to independent learning, but on a more permanent basis, is the independent learning lab. Too often teachers expect their students to become independent learners without giving them the time, place, or materials to fulfill this expectation. Learning labs, if established permanently in a classroom and equipped with the proper resources, can provide the place and materials to facilitate independent learning. It is still the teacher's responsibility to give the time. Learning labs may be set up in any classroom, no matter what the content area. These labs should have a designated purpose and should provide the materials needed to accomplish that purpose. They should also be readily available to all students. When the students are given the opportunity to use labs, the exact purpose of each lab should be made very clear to students. Complete directions for the use of the lab and available materials is essential.

Some examples of independent learning labs which might be offered in various academic areas are listed in Table 7.5.

TABLE 7.5 Examples of Independent Learning Labs		
Social Studies	**Math**	**Language Arts**
Reading	Reading	Reading
Use of maps	Math games	Writing
Writing	Basic functions	Word games
Simulations	Geometric design	Poetry
Social studies games	Calculators	Spelling
Listening tapes		Challenges
		Listening tapes

Putting various activities in each lab should enable students to work independently or in small groups. These could be commercially made or teacher made materials such as creative story starters in language arts.

Independent learning labs are usually designed to enhance basic learning skills and skills of particular disciplines, or at least give the students the opportunity to work on them. In some areas, automated equipment such as a listening lab or computer terminal might be used.

Independent Reading

Reading is a good area for a learning lab because it is an important skill which is essential to all content areas. Providing independent study time for reading can certainly have an impact on building reading skills if the lab is equipped with high-interest material.

However, a positive attitude toward reading is just as important at this age as skill development. To develop a positive attitude, students must first have an opportunity to read and second, be given an opportunity to read materials appropriate to their abilities and interests. There have been various attempts to do this on both a schoolwide basis and a classroom basis.

One approach is to set aside a certain time during the day when everyone in school (students, teachers, administrators, custodians, etc.) stops and reads silently for a certain number of minutes. Another such approach is to take a few minutes, preferably at the beginning of each class period, for students to silently read self-selected materials. Once the students get into the habit of bringing their reading materials each day, they tend to come in, sit down, and begin reading. This enables the class to begin with a common activity and also provides a transition period from one class to another.

Using an independent reading time in class in these ways could certainly be classified as a type of independent study. The students are not only working independently of each other and the teacher, but they are also pursuing materials which are of interest and relevance to them.

One of the aforementioned approaches to independent study could be incorporated into the middle school classroom through any of the three methods of implementation described in the previous section. Table 7.6 illustrates some of the possible combinations.

INDEPENDENT STUDY ON A SCHOOLWIDE BASIS

Up to this point, we have investigated the possibilities of implementing independent study in the individual classroom. We have seen that implementation of such a program takes a commitment from the individual teacher. Let us now turn our attention to the implementation of independent study on a schoolwide basis, which demands a much broader commitment from the total teaching staff of a middle school.

If a middle school is to offer the young adolescent learner an opportunity for independent learning during the school day, several key factors must be considered. The most important is the role of the teacher. No longer is the teacher the disseminator of knowledge but rather a resource person who must be able to diagnose individual learning problems and motivate students to become independent learners. Other major factors to consider are scheduling facilities and materials. Various middle schools may choose to institute a schoolwide independent learning program in various ways and to various degrees. Some may decide to design their entire curriculum around the independent learning philosophy, while others may decide to commit only a portion of the school day to such an endeavor. To whatever degree schools devote themselves to the idea of independent learning, the staff must be committed to making it work.

The teacher's role as a resource person during this time would alter the traditional type of student-teacher contact. While working with students on an independent study basis, the teachers might find themselves more in a helping capacity than in a traditional instruction capacity. The teacher must help students identify their own unique interests and abilities and then work with each on developing appropriate activities to enhance each individual's style of learning.

To put the teacher in such a position seems to have some benefit for both the student and the teacher. However, to implement such a program on a schoolwide basis might seem to be more idealistic than realistic. In order for the teacher to be effective in this role, the schedule must be flexible.

TABLE 7.6 Implementation into Classroom

	Project Days	Daily Independent Study Time	Independent Project Units
Independent Study Projects	Devote entire class period to work on project at least once a week.	Devote part of each class period to working on independent project.	Devote each class period during an extended unit to working on an independent project.
	Supplement with teacher-directed class activities between project days.	Sufficient time should be allowed to accomplish certain tasks required to complete project.	Brainstorming may be used to determine possible projects.
	Number of project days determined by project.	Class may be divided so that some are working on independent projects while others are involved in teacher-directed activities.	Options should be available to students both in the process and materials used
Independent Study Resources	Devote one class period per week to allowing different students to use variety of resources to gain information.	Devote part of each class period to allowing students to use a variety of resources to gain needed information.	Devote each class period during an extended unit to providing different independent resource options for collecting needed information on a unit.
	Students would have time to use resources outside the classroom (i.e., library).	Resources would probably need to be available in the classroom because of time limitations.	
Independent Learning Labs	Devote one class period a week to working in independent labs.	Devote part of each class period to having students work on independent labs set up in class.	Independent study labs may be set up to assist students in their projects.
	Each lab should have a specific learning purpose.		
Independent Reading	Devote entire day to letting the students read independently.	Devote part of each period to letting students read independently. First 10 minutes usually works best. Paperback books should be available in classroom.	Students may choose to read and report on certain materials as a project.

Time would have to be available for the teacher to meet with students on a one-to-one basis. At the same time the students must be given time to work independently on projects.

Places within the school must be designated where students have the opportunity to study independently. This does not imply that all students would work completely independently of other students or even other teachers. It does suggest that a variety of places be designated throughout the school where students have the opportunity to work on a variety of independent activities. For example, students might be given the opportunity to go to one of the following areas:

Learning Labs (writing, reading, listening, etc.)

Learning Centers (math, social studies, science, etc.)

Small Group Discussion Areas

Study Centers

Library

A.V. Centers

Interest Centers

Computer Centers

They might also wish to meet with an individual teacher or a resource person within or outside the school.

There is obviously no one plan for implementing an independent study program in a middle school. This would depend on the particular school and its needs. As a rule, most middle schools have chosen not to design their entire curriculum around the philosophy of independent study. Rather, they have chosen to emphasize the idea of independent learning by integrating it into various classes and/or by committing a portion of the school day to a general independent study program. This gives the students some time during the day to engage in some form of independent activity. This is not considered a free period for the teachers or the students. It is instead a period where teachers and students have the opportunity to work together in a more independent learning environment, as opposed to a teacher-directed classroom situation.

Independent study may be scheduled in many different ways. A school may have the entire student body engaged in independent study at one time or it may spread independent study periods throughout the day. Spreading it throughout the day usually has a significant drawback in that not all teachers are available. However, if the independent study time was divided so that each grade level had independent study at the same time, it would minimize this problem because teachers for that grade level would be available. On the other hand, freeing up all students at one time or at least by grade level also frees up the facility. Thus, a student may wish to work on an independent project in science in order to report to the science area where both the materials and resources are available. The classrooms then become independent learning labs where students can take advantage of the resources available in that area. The classroom then serves a dual purpose as an instructional area and also as an independent learning center where students can go during their independent study time.

Overly, Kinghorn, and Preston[7] present an interesting plan to convert a traditional school facility into a facility designed specifically for learning laboratories. Most classrooms serve only as a space where traditional instruction takes place. Their proposal still suggests a single function. However, they think classrooms should function primarily as open laboratories. Their plan first presents a diagram of a section of a traditional school composed of two social studies rooms, two science rooms, two math rooms, and two language arts rooms. They take each of these rooms and reassign the purpose of the rooms to fit a certain learning activity rather than a subject area. The signs on each classroom door might read audiovisual lab, small group learning lab, science lab, large group presentation lab, individual study lab, etc. Each area would be equipped with study tables, round tables, lounge furniture, stage, A.V. equipment, etc., which would be appropriate for that area.

This type of unique learning environment, although it is an extreme departure from a traditional school arrangement, would provide an optimum physical arrangement to enhance independent learning. Using such an arrangement to its fullest potential would depend on many factors (number of students, number of teachers, length of day, etc.). The logistics of developing a schedule is a large task but not an impossible one.

This type of arrangement would definitely be the exception and not the case for most middle schools. If a middle school were to make a schoolwide commitment to an independent study program, it would most likely be on a more limited scale. In many cases, it might be only for a limited number of students for a limited time during the day. This type of program probably benefits those students involved and helps them become independent learners. However, as presented in the first part of this chapter, all young adolescents have a need for independence and thus a much broader approach to include all students might be warranted.

How can this be done? First, a time block during the day must be set aside when all students, or at least all students having the same teachers, can meet on an independent basis. This is probably easier said than done because for most middle schools this would mean that something would be deleted from the curriculum. How and where such a program would fit into a particular middle school would have to be determined by that school. Assuming that at least one period could be found, let us investigate the possibility for implementing learning periods in a typical middle school.

INDEPENDENT ACTIVITY PERIOD: A SCHOOLWIDE APPROACH TO INDEPENDENT STUDY

A schoolwide independent study program needs to have a much broader focus than just as an aspect of the curriculum that was integrated into the school with no distinct and systematic purpose. Such a program not only gives students an opportunity to work independently but also allows students to pursue high-interest activities.

One of the most important prerequisites for a good independent study program is that it allows students time to pursue areas which they find interesting and stimulating. The activities which might be developed for the students during the independent activity period for the most part should be student-generated. These activities are then coupled with a particular teacher's talents. Before the schedule for the independent activity period is developed, the students should be asked to submit suggestions of activities in which they would like to participate or learn more about. This list would then be screened carefully and resource people would be sought to sponsor a workshop on each activity. For the most part, teachers would be the primary source of sponsors. However, parents, teacher aides, school secretaries, the principal, and other resource persons from the community could also be used.

Not all of the ideas generated by the students can be offered in a workshop format. If there are enough students to warrant a workshop in a particular area, then every attempt should be made to offer that workshop. This by no means eliminates those students who marked on their survey an unusual or uncommon interest. Even students who are the only ones choosing a particular area should be encouraged to pursue a project on that topic using independent study. As with any independent study project, there should be unlimited activities for students to choose from to complete their projects.

In addition to participating in various workshops on an independent project, the students would be given a third option, which is participating in intramurals. This means that intramurals become part of the school day rather than an after-school activity. Too often, middle schools find themselves in a position of having to offer intramurals after school. Or if they do offer a program during the school day, they have no options for students who do not wish to participate.

Before examining the logistics involved with an independent activity period, let us first look at each of these options offered to the students. We will look at how they help students pursue independent interests and also become independent learners.

Workshops

Although workshops offer the students the opportunity to pursue high-interest activities, they do not necessarily allow them to pursue these activities on an independent basis. Many of the workshops are planned and directed by the person responsible for them. Thus, the student becomes an active participant in a workshop designed and implemented by another person. However, some workshops have been designed by the students and teacher.

These workshops have many distinct advantages which help foster independent learning on the part of the student. Probably the most significant advantage is the opportunity they give the student to work with a teacher or another resource person on a more informal basis and on a common area of interest. Other school personnel such as the principal, school secretaries, school nurse, and custodians could also offer workshops relative to their own interests. This gives them an opportunity to work with students in a different capacity and at the same time gives the students a chance to get a different perspective of them.

There are a variety of resource people within the community from which to draw. Two that deserve special mention are senior citizens and Boy Scout and Girl Scout troops. The elderly people of the community have both rich backgrounds and unique interests and hobbies. Likewise, the scout organization, of which many middle school students are members, is very willing to have the opportunity to offer workshops on various merit badges. The biggest drawback of using these groups of people is the time commitment required on their part.

Some of the workshops that might be offered during the independent activity period are:

Model rocket building	Creative drama
Backpacking	Golf
Macrame	Leather work
Holiday cooking	Fossils
Needlepoint	Chess
String art	Weight lifting
Creative writing	Judo
Model making	Tall tales
Fly casting	Plant and animal caring

Some of these workshops culminate with an extended field trip. Students in the backpacking workshop, for instance, might go on an overnight backpack trip and students in the golf workshop might go to the public golf courses one afternoon to play a round of golf. Students participating in the weight lifting workshop could take a tour of a local health spa.

Intramurals

Intramurals can be a vital part of the independent activity period. All intramural activities should be designed so that there is equal opportunity for both boys and girls to participate. An effort could also be made to coordinate intramurals with the physical education program. If a unit on basketball is being taught in physical education, time could be devoted to working on the basic skills of the game. The intramural period provides an outlet for playing the game.

Although a variety of sports should be offered, those which require participation by large numbers of students should be emphasized. The following is a list of games which seem to be the most popular with this age level of students: flag football, soccer, basketball, softball, floor hockey, and volleyball. Other games which are also part of the intramural program, but do not have as high a level of participation are: gymnastics, swimming, table tennis, wrestling, and track.

Independent Study

A student may also choose to use the independent activity time to work on an independent project. If this option is chosen, the student will be assigned to work with a teacher. The projects may relate to particular classes and thus teachers of that subject may also decide to do a project which is related to an interest of their own rather than something directly related to a class. This is definitely a viable alternative and a teacher or some type of resource person should be assigned to work with this student.

A student may want to work on an independent project with fellow students. These students should be encouraged to pursue such a project as long as the group size is kept workable. This again would depend on the type of project.

It is essential that each student or group of students be assigned to work with a resource person. This person will usually be a teacher but could be an outside resource person. The teacher's role must be clearly defined as an advisor to the project. The teacher should *help* students clarify the following questions.

1. What type of project do I want to do?
2. What form will the project take?
3. What resources will I need?
4. How much time will it take?

To help the students answer these questions and establish some guidelines for their project, the form in Box 7.1 might be used.

BOX 7.1
Independent Study Project

Name of student(s) working on project: _____

Statement of type of project you intend to complete:

_____

_____

What form will your project take?

_____ written report	_____ drawings	_____ notebook
_____ oral report	_____ maps	_____ diary
_____ audio report	_____ timeline	_____ diorama
_____ videotape	_____ collage	_____ experiment
_____ play or skit	_____ poster	_____ film
_____ other (explain) _____		

What resources will you need to complete your project?

_____ art supplies (list) _____

_____ A.V. equipment (list) _____

_____ records or tapes (list) _____

_____ books (list) _____

_____ magazines (list) _____

_____ others (explain) _____

Develop a timeline for the completion of your project.

Date   Activity

_____   _____

_____   _____

_____   _____

_____   _____

_____

Signature, Supervising Teacher

Once the project has been defined and a procedure for completing it has been identified, the teacher then becomes merely a resource person upon whom the student can rely for assistance. It is important that the teacher give the students a degree of autonomy to develop their own projects. However, it is also important that the teacher be available to support, encourage, and lend assistance when it is needed. Students may need help in getting materials or they may just need someone on whom to try out their ideas.

Logistics

Now that the three components of this program have been briefly presented, let us turn our attention to the logistics of setting up such a program. One of the most important aspects of such a program is the commitment of a certain segment of the day for this purpose. A commitment such as this on the part of the staff assures the availability of the facilities. The various classrooms thus become resource centers where workshops or independent study activities take place. For example, if students wish to work on a science project, they report to the science teacher. Another science room might become an area where a workshop takes place. Once a period of the day has been identified for the implementation of such a program, it then becomes a matter of scheduling teachers and students in a manner that will meet students' needs and utilize teachers' talents.

The students are allowed to sign up for either an independent activity, a workshop, or intramurals every six weeks. The sign-up sheets are then compiled into attendance lists for each teacher for that six weeks. Mr. A., for example, may have fifteen students signed up for his model making workshop while Ms. B. may have four students signed up to work on an independent project. Mr. C. and Mr. D. may have forty students signed up with them for intramural basketball. Teachers who do not have any students signed up for their workshops should be reassigned to help with another workshop or intramural or assigned to work with students on an independent project.

This sign up should be completed before the beginning of each six-week session. On the sign-up sheet, each workshop is listed, plus the intramural activity for that session. In addition, the maximum number of students for each activity, the sponsor, the room, and a short description are also listed. The students are asked to indicate a first and second choice, in case their first choice is full. A typical sign-up sheet might resemble the one in Box 7.2.

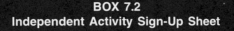

BOX 7.2
Independent Activity Sign-Up Sheet

Student's Name: _____

Workshops

1. _____   **Leather Work** (12 students) Mr. Smith, Shop
Students will be given the opportunity to work with
various leather processing tools to make belts, coin
purses, key cases, etc. Students must provide their own
leather.

2. _____   **Backpacking** (20 students) Mr. Black, Room 204
Students will learn to prepare a pack, techniques of
outdoor cookery, first aid, and how to pitch a tent. The
workshop will culminate with an overnight backpack trip.

3. _____   **Macrame** (15 students) Mrs. Jones, Room 202
Students will work on various macrame knots and make
flower pot holders. String will be provided. The final
product will be used to decorate the various classrooms.

4. _____   **Rocket Building** (20 students) Mrs. White, Room 104
Students will build their own model rockets. The
students will need to provide their own model rocket.
The rockets will be fired on the last day of the
workshop.

Intramurals

_____   **Basketball** (48 students) Mr. Blue and Mr. Green
There will be eight teams of six players each. A
tournament will be established in which each team will
play several games. A traveling trophy will be awarded
the winning team. Teams will be coeducational.

Independent Study

Teachers available to supervise an independent study are:
_____   Mrs. Taylor
_____   Mrs. O'Brien
_____   Mr. Nash
_____   Mrs. Williams

Name of Project: _____

Study Area (upon request) Mr. Lewis, Room 200

_____   Students may sign up for this area for the entire
session or on a one or two day basis if they have work
to make up.

One of the problems that arises in trying to establish any independent study program is that of keeping the student-teacher ratio low for those students on independent study. By offering other options, such as intramurals and workshops, the number of students working on independent study projects is kept to a more workable number.

The independent activity period presented here is only one way in which a schoolwide system might be established to provide the young adolescent an opportunity with which to pursue learning on an independent basis. It not only gives the students an opportunity to engage in independent study but also allows them to pursue high-interest activities. It is hoped that this example might generate ideas by readers as to how independent study periods may be implemented in their schools.

SUMMARY

In this chapter, a rationale for independent study in a middle school was first established. Built on the premise that middle schools are designed to meet the unique needs and characteristics of the young adolescent, the following were recognized as important needs which might be met by an effective independent study program:

1. Meeting the diversity in growth and development of the young adolescent.
2. Helping the young adolescent pursue high-interest activities.
3. Providing an opportunity to move from the dependency of childhood to the independence of adulthood.

Assuming that independent study was a viable means of meeting these important needs, attention was then turned to possible means of implementing such a program into a middle school curriculum. First, different ways and means for including independent study in an individual middle school classroom were mentioned. Second, the institution of a schoolwide independent study program was investigated.

The ideas presented in this chapter are not to be viewed as a panacea for independent study in the middle school. They are rather presented as points of departure. Use them to help stimulate other ideas of how independent study can best be incorporated into your particular middle school to aid students in the process of becoming independent learners.

ENDNOTES

1. Overly, Donald E., Jon R. Kinghorn, and Richard L. Preston. *The Middle School: Humanizing Education for Youth.* Belmont, California: Wadsworth Publishing Company, Inc., 1972, 105.

2. Alexander, William M. and Vynce A. Hines. *Independent Study in Secondary Schools.* New York: Holt, Rinehart, and Winston. 1967, 9–11.

3. See note 2, pp. 92–93.

4. Mead, Margaret. ''Early Adolescence in the United States.'' *NASSP Bulletin,* (April, 1965): 5–10.

5. Swaim, John H. *Young Adolescents' Attitude Toward Independence.* Unpublished research, University of Northern Colorado, 1984.

6. Beggs, Donald W. and Edward G. Buffie, ed. *Independent Study, Bold New Venture.* Bloomington, Indiana: University Press, 1965, 23.

7. See note 1, pp. 105–119.

8

Evaluating Student Progress in the Middle School

PUBLIC CONCERNS ABOUT STUDENT EVALUATION

The topic of accountability in education frequently appears in the media. Examination of reports in newspapers and on television provides ample evidence of public concern for more assurance that educational programs are producing desirable results in terms of learning and growth on the part of students. Concern on the part of the public is prompted by the constantly rising costs of operating our schools and by the painfully visible evidence that students leave our schools lacking the necessary skills of functional literacy needed for employment. Other students are so discouraged by what, to them, appear to be irrelevant programs that they drop out of school prior to high school graduation.

Underlying these conditions is the failure of many schools to provide evidence of the success of their efforts to educate youth. In its statement of evaluative criteria, the National Study of School Evaluation points out that

> evaluation is based on the principle that a school should be judged in terms of what it is striving to achieve (its philosophy and goals) and according to the extent to which it is meeting the needs of the students enrolled and the community it serves.[1]

Indeed, in far too many instances, there is a lack of evidence of *any* kind concerning program effectiveness. For too long schools have operated largely on the basis of inertia, through previous practices without analyzing their effectiveness or justifying it. Study, discussion, and debate regarding the most appropriate role and nature of effective educational evaluation continue.

THE PURPOSES OF EVALUATION

In education, evaluation is the process of collecting and studying data and other information which will indicate growth and other changes in pupils. Consciously or unconsciously, schools and teachers carry on evaluation. Sometimes it is referred to as "feedback." It may be carried on as a combination of testing, examining, and assessing, and it is often expressed in the form of grades or comments as well as other statements. Some of it is formal and some informal. Whatever form it takes, evaluation is necessary in order to determine the next steps to be taken in the educational program. Without evaluation, any planning becomes questionable in terms of its appropriateness. It is an indispensable activity in any educational endeavor. Evaluation is also an indication of how well the goals and objectives of education are being attained. It is an essential part of the educational process and an important activity in the middle and junior high school. Evaluation in any educational program, and certainly no less in the middle school levels, is carried on for several important purposes.

1. Evaluation is conducted for purposes of determining the appropriateness of the curriculum or education plan for the goals that are sought. It should provide information that makes it possible for pupils and teachers to see their objectives more clearly and to relate their learning activities more clearly to these. If the goals are not being met, then part of the problem may very well lie in the curriculum that has been developed. If this is the case, revision of the curriculum becomes necessary to ensure better attainment of the goals sought.

2. Evaluation is also conducted as a means of determining the effectiveness of the teaching that is going on, whether this is by an individual teacher or by a team of teachers. Certainly, the failure to attain goals may very well be due to the inappropriateness and ineffectiveness of the teaching process being carried on. This is not a very flattering prospect for esteemed members of a valued profession, but it is a reality that middle school educators must courageously face.

3. Evaluation is also conducted to determine students' progress in growth and development. This information is essential for the guidance of students. Again, this growth is measured in terms of goals sought by the school program. At the same time it must take

into account the particular and unique capabilities of each individual student. To disregard this essential human characteristic of individuality is to doom any evaluation for its failure to provide for the personal and human qualities so essential to effective education in the middle school.

4. Evaluation should give assurance to teachers, pupils, and parents by providing continuous evidence of growth shown by pupils in school activities. It should also serve to enhance relations between schools and the public by providing desired information to interested and concerned parents and other citizens.

One of the major problems in evaluation of student success in any school program is that there are two major sets of criteria to be considered. One has to do with the relative performance of the student with respect to the rest of his group or class, and the second has to do with the student's performance with respect to his own capabilities and individual goals. Frequently, the means used to evaluate and report pupil progress are confined to the first point. The result, inevitably, is that the less able student suffers since he is inappropriately and unfairly compared to more capable students. The self-image of the individual suffers under the constant pressure of expectations that are inconsistent with his capabilities. In time this takes its toll, and the struggling student becomes discouraged, disillusioned, and disinterested. Failure and retention in the same grade is a frequent outcome.

The crux of the problem may be illustrated with the following exercise. (See Box 8.1.) This can be used by a middle school or junior high school staff as a way to launch the study of evaluating and reporting student progress. Using the traditional A-B-C-D-F grading system familiar to most persons, ask staff members to give each of the three students listed in Box 8.1 a grade based only on the data and other information provided.

Invariably, a range of grades will be given to each student by different individuals. Some teachers even add a plus or minus as a further indicator. The problem of grading students on this basis is further confounded by the student effort as perceived by each teacher. Obviously, evaluation is a complex matter and deserves careful attention. Ongoing discussion about what criteria to use in evaluation, how much weight to give various factors, and how best to use evaluative findings for improving student growth are among important topics for staff members to think and talk about as a continuing concern and activity.

BOX 8.1
Hypothetical Cases—8th-Grade Social Studies

John W.

Age: 13 years 10 months
IQ: 108
Scored 88 out of 100 on a true-false test.
Scored 79 out of 100 on a completion test.
Scored 8 out of 10 on 1st pop quiz.
Scored 9 out of 12 on 2nd pop quiz.
Participated actively in class discussions.
Turned in an 8-page paper on the causes of the Civil War. Paper was
    satisfactory.
Attendance good.
Course grade for 1st term _____ .

Mary D.

Age: 14 years 2 months
IQ: 126
Scored 92 out of 100 on a true-false test.
Scored 87 out of 100 on a completion test.
Scored 9 out of 10 on 1st pop quiz.
Scored 11 out of 12 on 2nd pop quiz.
Participated actively in class discussions.
Turned in a 12-page paper on the causes of the Civil War. Paper was
    outstanding, but parts may have been copied as they were far
    superior to her general work and written at a near-university level.
Attendance good.
Course grade for 1st term _____ .

Bill J.

Age: 15 years 9 months (retained once)
IQ: 91
Scored 72 out of 100 on a true-false test.
Scored 63 out of 100 on a completion test.
Scored 5 out of 10 on 1st pop quiz.
Scored 6 out of 12 on 2nd pop quiz.
Participated in few class discussions.
Turned in a paper with numerous errors and misspelled words.
Absent (sometimes truant) about 25% of the time.
Course grade for 1st term _____ .

**BOX 8.1
(Continued)**

1. Were there differences of opinion on the letter grade for each student? If so, how was each different letter grade justified?
2. Was the IQ a factor in the grade? Should it be a factor? Why or why not?
3. How much, if any, copying of library materials is permissible? What if library research is strongly encouraged by the teacher?
4. Should absence be a factor in the grade? Why or why not? How much absence (percentage) is permissible, if at all?
5. Should any thought be given to effort on the part of the student? What part of a course grade should be due to effort? How should this be shown so that it is clearly understood by all?

There are many other points for discussion. These will undoubtedly be suggested by teachers, parents, and students. Discussion of these ideas can help to bring all concerned to a better understanding of what kind of a grading system is best for that school district.

THE USE OF LETTER GRADES IN EVALUATING AND REPORTING

Pros

1. Grades provide an incentive for learning and studying.

2. This is a competitive world. Students competing for grades are better prepared for the inevitable competition of life.

3. Grades are useful because they are simple, concise, and convenient.

Cons

1. Grades can become so important to students and parents that they become the goals sought.

2. Life depends more on cooperation between people than it does on competition. Therefore, schools should stress development of skills of cooperation rather than those of competition.

3. Grades mean different things to different people. There is no single universal interpretation of letter grades.

BOX 8.1
(Continued)

Pros	Cons
4. Grades are a *realistic* way of evaluating students.	4. Grades are not only arbitrary, but they are often used in a punitive, negative manner. Because of numerous problems of adjustment, students need as much positive reinforcement as possible to develop good self-concepts.
5. Grades provide an index of achievement so that a student knows where he stands in comparison to his peers.	5. Effective evaluation requires measuring individual growth in relation to learning objectives, not to other students.
6. Grades are needed for schools so they can quickly assess the standing of each student.	6. Grades are limited in the information they convey. More can be learned about each student through a variety of information-gathering techniques such as interviews and personal comments by teachers and others.
7. Parents need to know how their children compare to peers. Parents feel they understand grades as an indicator of such class rank or standing.	7. Parents may expect grades but can be reoriented to other, more effective, evaluative procedures. Students don't really need grades to learn better.

RETAINING STUDENTS

It is interesting to note that, while retention in grade or "flunking" students is a common practice in many schools where it is viewed as a solution to the problem of lack of progress, the evidence forthcoming from research in this area does not support this practice. In their investigations, Cheyney and Boyer[2] noted that students exhibiting a lack of readiness for a given kind of schoolwork were not helped to overcome this weakness when they were retained and had to repeat a grade. This is further supported by the investigations of Saunders, who studied the effects of non-promotion on school achievement and reported:

> It may be concluded that non-promotion of pupils in elementary school in order to assure mastery of subject matter does not often accomplish its objective. Children do not appear to learn more by repeating a grade but experience less growth in subject-matter achievement than they do when promoted. Therefore a practice of non-promotion because a pupil does not learn sufficient subject matter in the course of a school year, or for the purpose of learning subject matter, is not justifiable.[3]

Subsequent research evidence continues to question the punitive uses of retention as a way of inducing middle school students to extend greater efforts in the mastery of subject matter. Johnston and Markle[4] report that a review of 49 studies of results of retention was conducted by Jackson, who concluded that "there is no reliable body of evidence to indicate that grade retention is more beneficial than grade promotion for students with serious academic or adjustment difficulties." These authors continue by pointing out that Holmes and Mathews, following a meta-analysis of 44 studies in 1983, concluded that "nonpromotion had a negative effect on the pupils . . . particularly in the areas of language arts, reading, and work-study skills."

This does not mean that such evaluation is to be avoided. In fact, parents as well as teachers, if not the students themselves, want to know how well the student is performing with respect to others in his group. Therefore, it is necessary to determine this and to report it accordingly. One way of doing this is to make use of standardized tests that have been used with large numbers of students. The use of such tests of achievement will provide information as to the standing of each student in his class or with respect to a large population as in the case of nationally standardized achievement tests. It provides parents, teachers, and students with an indication of where the student ranks in his age or grade group. Present national and state trends are moving strongly in this direction.

Another kind of information coming out of the use of standardized tests is the identification of areas of subject matter or skills where the student may show weakness. This information is very useful in making better plans for a program of work for that student.

INDIVIDUALIZING INSTRUCTION AND EVALUATION

One of the important characteristics of the true middle or junior high school described in this book is concerned with the individualization of instruction. There is ample evidence to support the notion that each student is a unique individual, equipped with or characterized by a set of interests, strengths, weaknesses, fears, creative talents, and other traits that make this student different from all other students. Recognizing this, an effective educational plan should take these into account and provide for that student's growth and development. Similarly, expectations of learning outcomes are shaped by the nature of this unique individuality.

One of the earliest and most notable efforts to provide individualized instruction was developed by Burk and Washburn in the Winnetka Plan.[5] The program developed and carried on there for many years, and the model for many similar, later programs in other communities, involved a series of instructional objectives, tests to assess pupil mastery of these instructional materials, individual lesson plans, and steps for checking pupil progress through the sequence. Progress was made by pupils on an individual basis and was self-checked by each pupil, utilizing tests accompanying the work materials. Careful records were kept of each step covered by the pupil, and these were studied by the pupil and teacher in analyzing progress and in making further plans.

Similar, more recent programs that also stress some of the same elements of the Winnetka Plan include Individually Prescribed Instruction (IPI) and Individually Guided Education (IGE). In each of these, as in the Winnetka Plan, the evaluation, like the instructional activities, is carried on individually. There is a wide range of variations as to rate of progress. There is also emphasis on specific learning activities as individually needed.

In any program of individualized instruction, the major function of evaluation is to provide an analysis of pupil performance for use in planning further activities for the individual.

One important aspect is the use of tests which recognize that each student is possessed of a unique set of capabilities. These become the basis for determining his progress. In other words, students set as goals whatever they are capable of achieving, and this is different for each individual. Progress is then determined on the basis of how well they progress toward their own unique sets of goals and objectives. These tests must, of necessity, be individually developed. While this is a demanding task, there is no alternative if the spirit of the middle school is not to be violated.

One effective way of undertaking this task is through the use of behavioral objectives. Educational objectives should be stated in terms that are measurable. To be measurable, objectives should be stated in terms of what the student will be doing when he demonstrates the achievement of an objective. This should be readily observable by the teacher and by the student as well. If he can do what the objective calls for, he has demonstrated mastery of that objective. As an illustration, consider the following objective: A student will be able to write and spell correctly a prescribed list of 20 words in ten minutes with 80 percent accuracy. There is not much question about what is expected of the student, and his readily observed performance either meets or does not meet the criteria of time and accuracy as stated. The author and others have written more extensively on the use of behavioral objectives in evaluation,[6] and this may be referred to for a fuller explanation.

With all evaluation, there must be a beginning point, a point from which progress is measured. As stated earlier, this varies with each individual. One way of determining this is the use of a pretest. This provides benchmark data, a starting point for determining progress toward a goal or objective. After students carry out planned activities in those skills and knowledge which they were not able to demonstrate mastery of on the pretest, there is a posttest which again assesses their status. If successful, the student then moves on to the next unit of study in the sequence. The schematic or flowchart in Figure 8.1 is one way to illustrate this procedure.

Examination of the flowchart leads to the inevitable conclusion that its adoption and implementation can facilitate an individualized program of instruction and evaluation that is consistent with the middle or junior high school concept. One excellent technique along these lines is the use of the student contract for planning the work of each student on an individualized basis. Further, the flowchart fits one of the important characteristics of a good middle or junior high program, the principle of continuous progress. If learning is accepted as being an individual matter, differing with each person as to rate and intensity, then by the same token, progress is also an individual matter. The idea that all students at a given grade level are to be ready for promotion at the end of the school year flies in the face of what we know about human growth and development. In continuous progress, students are not "flunked." Rather, each progresses as well and as rapidly as he can. At the beginning of a new school year in September, the student resumes progress at

FIGURE 8.1

Flowchart for Evaluating the Progress of Pupils in Middle and Junior High Schools.

Hannah Middle School, East Lansing, MI.

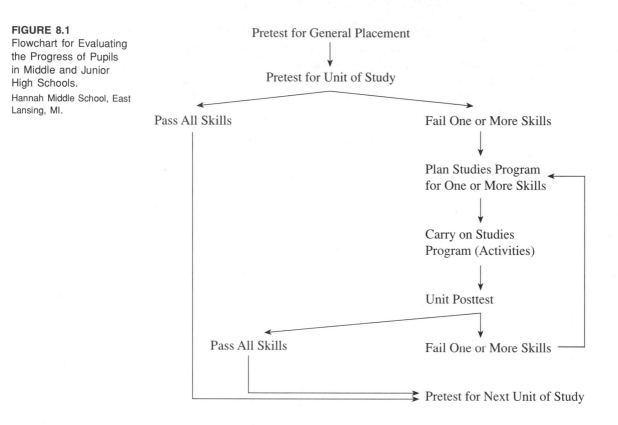

the point where he stopped in June or, rather, at the point where he is ready to resume work. The disastrous blow to the self-image of a student who has not quite made the grade in his school work is avoided, and he is not forced to repeat the entire year's work because he was retained in grade. There is a full discussion of continuous progress in another chapter.

STUDENT EVALUATION AS A TEACHER TEAM EFFORT

Although only a few techniques for evaluation have been discussed, there are many more worthy of our attention. The middle school team of teachers has the responsibility for meeting regularly not only to plan the work of the team, but also to share in the evaluation of the students entrusted to their care. Through the pooling of their respective assessments, a composite picture of the strengths, weaknesses, needs, and accomplishments of each student will develop. The data shared will be gained from a variety of sources, including the use of standardized tests, teacher-made tests (often utilizing behavioral objectives), and from continuous, subjective observation of the students in a variety of situations. In addition, these data may be periodically augmented by input from other staff members, including the principal, guidance counselors, psychologist, remedial teachers, school nurse, etc. The importance of keeping careful records in the process cannot be overstated. A longitudinal file on each student is a necessity for evaluating and effectively planning for that student.

With the present public concern for accountability, the importance of effective evaluation is immediately more evident to educators. Parents are calling for evidence to assure them of the quality of the programs in the schools their children attend. The gathering of data from evaluation is of limited value unless these data are communicated in meaningful, intelligible form to parents. Many parents want to know how well their children are doing with regard to class or group norms. To educators, effective evaluation must be based on individual differences. Both kinds of data cannot be reported by a single set of grades. Therefore, any reports to parents must recognize the inherent differences between these kinds of data as well as their interrelationship. To facilitate dealing with the problem, written reports should include how the student stands in his group and how well he is doing with respect to his own capabilities. In addition, since written reports suffer from inherent shortcomings due to language semantics and other factors, conferences with parents and with students should be held by teachers to facilitate communication. This personal contact not only aids in understanding of evaluation but serves as a powerful public relations asset as well. It also gives added emphasis to the important humanistic dimension of the middle school.

When teachers continue to examine the means for more effective evaluation of middle school students and their programs, they exercise their professional expertise. This can bring added dividends to their professional growth. This will also give a better understanding of themselves as individuals and of their role in society. Parents will be assured that their children are in good hands and that schools are indeed responsive to their concerns and wishes. In all respects, evaluation is an activity that holds great promise for a better future if it is pursued on a logical basis consistent with our knowledge of effective education.

Evaluation is concerned with the total development of the middle school student, with broad personality changes and with the attainment of major objectives of the educational program of the middle school. Included in evaluation are not only subject matter achievement but also attitudes, ideals, interests, ways of thinking and working, and personal and social adaptability. Not only must teachers in the middle school evaluate how well school objectives produce desired behavior on the part of students, but they must also evaluate the learning experiences that best promote and produce these behaviors. Students, too, have an important role to play in evaluation. They ought to evaluate their own progress and growth toward goals that they understand and accept.

STEPS IN THE EVALUATION PROCESS

The general procedure for pursuing a program of evaluation includes several steps as indicated below.

1. *The teacher needs to examine the objectives of a school program and, with these in mind, to establish criteria.* This can begin with a realistic knowledge of what each student needs and what behavior patterns are most logical for him in light of his makeup. This requires a thorough knowledge of the principles of human growth and development and of the psychology of learning. It also requires an accurate knowledge of community expectations of education. One way of preparing such criteria is to express them in terms of abilities expected at each age level, desirable habits that can be attained, and attitudes and understandings that may be achieved. With this knowledge, a better selection of learning experiences can be made. Evaluation of progress becomes clearer as both teacher and student in the middle school become more familiar with what the student actually does.

2. *The teacher proceeds to collect data and information.* The source can be a testing program that supplies objective data on each student. It can also come from observing the behavior of the student in a variety of situations, both formal and informal, providing valuable subjective information.

3. *The teacher studies and analyzes the data, making appropriate interpretations.* How well is the student progressing toward desired objectives? Is behavior constructive and desirable? Is the student's self-evaluation consistent with the teacher's evaluation? In what areas is further progress desired?

4. *Using the information thus gained, the teacher plans a course of action.* Changes in learning activities and materials may be necessary. The assistance of resource persons available to the middle school may be called for by the plan, including guidance counselors, school nurse, the principal, psychologist, or parents, as well as others, including subject matter specialists.

A variety of techniques for learning about the student can aid in building a body of data. Again, some of these are subjective in nature while others are more objective.

1. *An assessment of readiness for contemplated learning activities.* Although a great deal has been written about the matter of readiness, there still remains a great deal more to be learned. Nevertheless, readiness is regarded as essential to successful learning, despite the fact that it is elusive and highly subjective. The training, experience, and intuitive insights of the teacher into the nature of each individual are important to accomplishing this assessment.

2. *Using achievement tests, mental maturity tests, and intelligence tests.* Although there are dangers inherent in relying too heavily upon a single test score as an accurate indicator of a quality, there is value in having such test results to be considered *along with* other information in better understanding the individual student and his makeup. This diagnostic aspect, identifying areas of strength and weakness, is essential in planning learning programs for the individual.

3. *Using the case study approach.* By keeping notes on incidents concerning certain observed behavior on the part of students, it may be possible to identify clues that will assist the teacher in arriving at conclusions and plans for further needed activities. This can be time-consuming, but every teacher makes these observations either formally or informally, consciously or unconsciously. The systematic recording of these incidents can provide much valuable information of great use to the teacher in understanding the uniqueness of individual students.

4. *Using sociometry.* Each individual exists not only as an individual but also as a member of society. Careful study and analysis of how individuals function in a group can also provide valuable information about their true nature. Most teachers have an ongoing knowledge of the social makeup of a class. This may or may not be accurate. Along with this informal approach of observing how the individual functions in a group, widely recognized sociometric instruments can be used to objectify such observations.

5. *Additional techniques may be used.* There are a variety of other techniques for use in evaluation. One of these is the parent-teacher conference. Whereas this may be viewed simply as a technique for verbally reporting pupil progress to parents, it is also a potential source of additional valuable information about the student. In the

conference, there ought to be ample opportunity for the parent to express an opinion on the progress of the student as observed in the home or neighborhood. Such information, added to that the teacher already has, can round out the evaluation of the student and increase the effectiveness of plans made for further progress.

THE PARENT-TEACHER CONFERENCE

Parent interest in schools has never been greater than at present. Parents expect full information about school programs and particularly information about the progress of their children. They are entitled to it. The parent-teacher conference is an important vehicle for communication. It provides for a two-way exchange of information about the student. It may be used as a supplement to the report card, but, because it can do much more than a report card alone, it is increasingly being used. However, to make the best use of this technique requires careful planning on the part of middle school staff. In some schools, the student also participates in the conference, making it a three-way exchange of information.

What Parents Want to Know

1. What subjects the students will study—the curriculum for the year.
2. An explanation of the grading system and how it works.
3. How much emphasis is placed on the basics and on other studies.
4. Pertinent school policies, school rules, and procedures, including discipline.
5. How parents can help students learn.
6. Homework policies.
7. What you, the teacher, expect of the student.
8. How well students get along with others (i.e., are they well liked)?

What Teachers Can Learn from the Conference

1. Information about how the student is treated at home.
2. How the student feels about school, teacher, and other students as reported by parents.
3. Strengths or interests the student has that may not have shown up in school.
4. Any problems regarding homework or study habits that show up at home.

Tips for Better Parent-Teacher Conferences

1. Prepare for the conference! Make an outline covering major points you want to discuss. You might want to send a copy of this brief outline of topics home to parents after they have confirmed the parent-teacher conference date and time. Stick to the outline!
2. Be courteous and cheerful.
3. Give the parents a chance to talk *first* and to share *their* views and their problems.
4. Be a good listener.
5. Be truthful but tactful. Don't forget that a child is a *most* precious possession!
6. Try to avoid prescribing solutions. Offer suggestions and alternatives. Give parents a part in deciding any action to be taken.
7. Begin and end on a positive note.

The value the parent-teacher conference can have is quite apparent when one examines the lists of expectations held by parents and teachers. Both parents and teachers learn more about each student. Teachers learn how the child is treated at home and what bearing, if any, this may have on behavior in school. Parents can learn about the year's work for students, what is expected of students, how the teacher and the school function, and most importantly, that teacher and school are there to help in every way possible. Besides direct benefits for learning by students, the parent-teacher conference has great public relations potential that cannot be overlooked.

EXAMPLES OF EVALUATION REPORTING FORMS

The preceding general discussion of the importance of evaluation in a successful middle or junior high school program provides a backdrop for developing specific measures for accomplishing this task. With the challenges of effective evaluation in mind, the middle school faculty has the task of adapting effective measures to its own school situation. Here is what is needed: consideration for teaching staff members' capabilities as professional educators; consideration for parents' expectations regarding data and information about pupil progress; and consideration for the information that students need in order to use their talents and reach their goals.

For further insight into the nature of effective evaluation, let us examine what several middle schools have done. Following are several evaluative forms developed by middle schools. These forms take the important aspects of evaluation and deal with them in a way that is both understandable and also consistent with the nature of human growth and development. They vary widely in the way in which they perceive their evaluative functions, following the principle of local determination based on local needs and other conditions. Obviously, these samples are offered for analysis and discussion rather than as models for replication.

The Middle School Progress Report

The Middle School Progress Report is designed to inform parents of their youngsters' progress, effort, and overall performance. (See Figure 8.2.)

Progress. In the upper right-hand box, the teacher indicates a student's progress in relation to the expectations for the course. One of three statements regarding progress will be checked for each reporting period:

_____ exceeds expectations for the course

_____ meets expectations for the course

_____ is below expectations for the course

Whenever the teacher checks the statement "exceeds expectations for the course," he is reporting that the child's progress is greater than one would expect from a typical student of similar age enrolled in that course. If the teacher checks "meets expectations for the course," he is reporting that the child's progress is at the pace one would expect of a typical youngster of similar age. If the teacher checks the statement "is below expectations for the course," he is reporting that the child's progress is less than one might expect of a typical student of similar age.

Effort. In the upper left-hand box, the teacher indicates the effort a youngster puts forth in the particular course. One of two statements regarding effort will be checked for each reporting period:

_____ is satisfactory

_____ is unsatisfactory

Whenever the teacher checks the statement "is satisfactory," he is reporting that the student is putting forth a reasonable effort in that course. A student of high ability or aptitude may exceed the expectations for the course without much effort. If the teacher believes that such a student's progress would have been significantly greater with more effort, he will inform the parent that the child's effort "is unsatisfactory" and indicate why in the "Comments" sections. Another student may be putting forth sufficient effort but may be progressing below the expectations for the course. Again, the teacher will so indicate by checking the appropriate statements and also note why the youngster's progress is below the expectations for the course.

Student's Name	Subject	Instructor	Date	Team

Reporting Period   Effort   Reporting Period   Progress
1st 2nd 3rd 4th   1st 2nd 3rd 4th
—   —   —   —   is satisfactory   —   —   —   —   exceeds expectations
                                                                        for the course
—   —   —   —   is unsatisfactory   —   —   —   —   meets expectations
                        (see comments below)   for the course
                                                  —   —   —   —   is below expectations
                                                                        for the course (see
                                                                        comments below)

WRITTEN COMMENTS
1st REPORT
2nd REPORT
3rd REPORT
4th REPORT

OTHER COMMENTS

Items in the following general checklist may indicate areas affecting the student performance and progress. A minus (-) indicates the student needs improvement whereas a plus (+) indicates especially positive behavior. If the box is not marked the student is performing satisfactory.

Reporting Period   Reporting Period
1st 2nd 3rd 4th   1st 2nd 3rd 4th
☐ ☐ ☐ ☐ 1. Is attentive   ☐ ☐ ☐ ☐ 10. Contributes in class
☐ ☐ ☐ ☐ 2. Follows directions   ☐ ☐ ☐ ☐ 11. Demonstrates reasoning abilities
☐ ☐ ☐ ☐ 3. Brings necessary materials   ☐ ☐ ☐ ☐ 12. Consistent in quality of work
                to class   ☐ ☐ ☐ ☐ 13. Practices self-control
☐ ☐ ☐ ☐ 4. Makes use of class time   ☐ ☐ ☐ ☐ 14. Is courteous, respects rights
☐ ☐ ☐ ☐ 5. Completes assignments on time   of others
☐ ☐ ☐ ☐ 6. Cooperates in large and   ☐ ☐ ☐ ☐ 15. Is punctual
                small groups   ☐ ☐ ☐ ☐ 16. Relates with peers
☐ ☐ ☐ ☐ 7. Has a positive attitude   ☐ ☐ ☐ ☐ 17. Displays decision-making ability
☐ ☐ ☐ ☐ 8. Works independently
☐ ☐ ☐ ☐ 9. Takes care of property, his own and others

FIGURE 8.2

East Lansing Middle Schools—Progress Report Form.

East Lansing Public Schools, East Lansing, MI.

Comments. ''The Written Comments'' and ''Other Comments'' sections on the progress report give the teacher an opportunity to sum up a student's overall performance and to indicate areas that may affect his progress. Parents are encouraged to contact the teacher for a conference whenever they have any questions regarding their youngster's progress.

The problem of proper evaluation is closely related to effective communication. Parents are frequently disturbed when they are informed that students are not performing satisfactorily or are actually failing. They are most disturbed when this kind of news reaches them without prior warning. Therefore, *frequent* communication with parents is desirable, particularly when there are problems in performance. Following are some sample forms used in a school program, including a ''sad'' note and a ''glad'' note.

Date _____

Dear Mr. and Mrs. _____ ,

Because we know that you are concerned parents, we wish to inform you that _____

_____ does not have necessary supplies.

_____ is not using class time constructively.

_____ lacks adequate daily preparation.

_____ is often tardy.

_____ exhibits disruptive behavior.

_____ has difficulty in meeting deadlines.

_____ It is necessary that lost time be made up after school on

_____ from _____ to _____ .

- -

Please sign and return this card so we know that you have received this communication.

_____

Not all communications need to be negative. When progress is commendable, call attention to it with praise.

Date _____

Dear _____ ,

While _____ is performing adequately in other areas,

_____ deserves special commendation for:

_____ doing an outstanding job in _____ class.

_____ demonstrating outstanding qualities in citizenship in class.

_____ performing important services for the class.

_____ demonstrating outstanding qualities in athletics.

_____ dramatic improvement in _____ .

_____ other:

Sincerely yours,

Another school has used skills checklists, one list for each academic area for each quarter of the school year. Student evaluation is done with respect to individual ability, that is, indicating whether or not the student is exerting reasonable effort. In addition to the checklist, teachers may also add comments regarding student progress or effort. The listing of skills has previously been worked out by a teacher assigned to each academic area and further defines the objectives sought for that grade level. (See Tables 8.1–8.6.)

TABLE 8.1 Middle School—Social Science Skills Checklist

NAME _____ LEVEL _____ ADVISOR _____

Second Quarter

On the basis of his/her ability, he/she:	Outstanding	Acceptable	Not Acceptable
1. Can describe the destruction caused by the Civil War.			
2. Can locate on a map where major battles took place and other areas important to the Civil War.			
3. Can describe the feelings or attitudes of soldiers involved in the actual fighting of the Civil War.			
4. Can distinguish between the effect the Civil War had on the South from its effect on the North.			
5. Can describe how the Civil War changed farming and the plantation system in the South.			
6. Can describe how the transportation system of the South was affected by the Civil War.			
7. Has demonstrated a responsible degree of effort on the packet series.			

Reading Community Schools, Reading, Ohio.

TABLE 8.2 Middle School—Mathematics Skills Checklist

NAME _____ LEVEL _____ ADVISOR _____

First Quarter

On the basis of his/her ability, he/she:	Outstanding	Acceptable	Not Acceptable
1. Has mastery of addition and subtraction of whole numbers vertically and horizontally.			
2. Can solve multiplication problems with at least 2-digit multipliers.			
3. Can solve division problems with at least 2-digit divisors.			
4. Has a proficient knowledge for use of the least common multiple and greatest common factor of a number.			
5. Can apply an understanding of equivalent of fractions.			
6. Can add and subtract fractions.			
7. Demonstrates the relationship of improper fractions to mixed numbers.			
8. Demonstrates the relationship of mixed numbers to improper fractions.			

Reading Community Schools, Reading, Ohio.

TABLE 8.3 Middle School—Science Skills Checklist

NAME _____ LEVEL _____ ADVISOR _____

Second Quarter

On the basis of his/her ability, he/she:	Outstanding	Acceptable	Not Acceptable
1. Can observe and write reports about experiments.			
2. Shows ability to gather needed background information from the Learning Center through written and/or oral reports.			
3. Shows ability to use Science Vocabulary.			
4. Can collect, classify, evaluate, and report information orally and in writing.			
5. Can write an explanation of magnetism.			
6. Can write or illustrate the law of magnets.			
7. Can list the different kinds of magnets.			
8. Can explain and/or demonstrate the use of a directional compass.			
9. Can write and demonstrate electromagnetism.			
10. Can write an explanation of static electricity.			
11. Can write an explanation of electricity.			
12. Can write an explanation of parallel and series circuits.			
13. Can write an explanation of fuses.			
14. Can write an explanation of insulators.			
15. Can apply the safety rules of electricity.			
16. Can solve problems of measurement in electricity (ohms, amperes, volts, watts, and kilowatts).			
17. Can label the parts of a dry cell.			
18. Can explain the operation of a storage battery.			
19. Can detect the harmful effects of electricity in and out of the home (lightning).			

Reading Community Schools, Reading, Ohio.

TABLE 8.4   Middle School—Language Arts Skills Checklist

NAME _____ LEVEL _____ ADVISOR _____

First Quarter

On the basis of his/her ability, he/she:	Outstanding	Acceptable	Not Acceptable
1. Recognizes a ballad by its basic characteristics.			
2. Reads silently and then writes at least the main idea and the supporting ideas of the poem read.			
3. Writes a newspaper story from the given facts after reading a selection of poetry involving a historical event.			
4. Describes orally the author's point of view on a poem with a specific topic.			
5. Can identify the events in sequence after listening to a poem.			
6. Relates the content of poems to major themes of life.			
7. Can retell in written form a poem he/she has read or heard, changing the ending.			
8. Writes a poem of at least one rhyming couplet.			
9. Can rewrite the story of a poem in prose form in a modern setting.			
10. Reads, uses, and spells words specified in the story of poetry.			
11. Participates in oral discussions using acceptable speech patterns.			
12. Uses correct punctuation and capitalization in written communication.			
13. Is able to use subject-verb agreement in writing sentences.			

Reading Community Schools, Reading, Ohio.

TABLE 8.5 Middle School—Physical Education Skills Checklist

NAME _____ LEVEL _____ ADVISOR _____

Second Quarter

On the basis of his/her ability, he/she:	Outstanding	Acceptable	Not Acceptable
1. Dresses appropriately for physical education activities.			
2. Has coordination in body movements through running, jumping, walking, and other basics.			
3. Has a sense of rhythm in body movements.			
4. Is a good sport and team player.			
5. Has developed skills, habits, and attitudes that will help in his/her social and emotional growth.			
6. Exercises caution in a safety-sense in all activities.			
7. Accepts responsibility of leadership by acting as a squad leader, scorekeeper, and captain.			
8. Accepts physical education as an integral part of his/her school life.			

Reading Community Schools, Reading, Ohio.

TABLE 8.6   Middle School—Unified Arts Skills Checklist

NAME _____ LEVEL _____ ADVISOR _____

Second Quarter

On the basis of his/her ability, he/she:	Outstanding	Acceptable	Not Acceptable
Fine Arts			
1. Identifies the primary colors and mixes the secondary from the primary colors.			
2. Mixes tints and shades of secondary and intermediate colors and uses them in a painting or color project.			
3. Identifies warm and cool colors and differentiates their use in creating a mood in painting.			
4. Demonstrates the use of value as the degree of light and dark in color and in black and white through a charcoal or ink drawing.			
5. Uses value to create form, volume contrast, and movement in a drawing composition.			
6. Points out in reproductions of works of art how value is used to create mood, perspective, and emphasis.			
7. Composes a project using the principles of formal and informal balance in a composition.			
8. Demonstrates the use of rhythm in a repeat pattern design.			
9. Composes a project employing the repetition of line, shape, color, and value.			

TABLE 8.6   (Continued)

On the basis of his/her ability, he/she:	Outstanding	Acceptable	Not Acceptable
Home Arts			
1. Constructs a crocheted and woven woolen scarf.			
2. Constructs a yarn painting on burlap. (Stitchery)			
3. Constructs a yarn painting on cardboard. (Glued)			
4. Constructs an article of clothing.			
5. Constructs a finger woven belt.			
6. Constructs a necklace from handmade paper beads.			
7. Designs and constructs a Bargello tapestry.			
8. Ties a double half hitch and square knot to construct a macrame belt.			
9. Identifies basic abbreviations, equivalents, and procedures used in cooking.			
10. Identifies the essential foods which our bodies need every day.			
11. Participates in a cooking experiment.			
Applied Arts			
1. Researches and completes an oral or written report.			
2. Designs a project.			
3. Completes a sketch of his project.			
4. Constructs his/her project to conform to his sketch.			
5. Participates in a brainstorming session in working out his project idea.			

Reading Community Schools, Reading, Ohio.

SELECTING AN EVALUATION SYSTEM FOR A MIDDLE SCHOOL

The following list of criteria provides an indication of the potential scope and complexity of an evaluation and reporting system.

1. Does the system fit purpose (or purposes) of middle school/junior high school education?
2. Is the system explicit and clear in exactly what qualities are being evaluated?
3. Will the system communicate to the student what he wants or needs to know about himself?
4. Does the system recognize differences in individuals and provide for evaluating progress or growth in terms of each individual's capability?
5. Is the system sensitive to wide variety of capabilities of students (i.e., creativity, diligence, intelligence, independence, interest, articulateness, human relations)?
6. Would the system promote the kind of instruction desired, that is, close interaction between students and teachers?
7. Is the system adaptable to the special needs and requirements of different segments of the community?
    a. Can it deal with the matter of student retention?
    b. Can it deal with the needs of special curricula or courses?
8. Would the system provide maximum encouragement to students (i.e., be stimulating to the unmotivated without stifling the independent or frightening the insecure)?
9. Would the system provide useful information to high schools? Or to other schools for transfer students?
10. Would the system communicate to the parents (a) what they *want* to know and (b) what they *need* to know in order to assist the student?
11. Would the system operate at minimum cost in time and money to the school district?

SUMMARY

Any system of evaluating and reporting student progress requires careful thinking and planning by school staff. There are many questions to be dealt with if the system is to do all that is expected. In planning an evaluation system, planners need to be aware of all aspects and provide for each. To do this properly often requires a variety of forms and activities. There is no simple, limited system, such as many schools now use, that can do this and yet satisfy all the expectations. Continuous reassessment of the effectiveness of evaluation procedures is necessary to ensure its relevance to the people involved and the current conditions.

ENDNOTES

1. *Evaluative Criteria.* Sixth edition. Bloomington, Ind.: National Study of School Evaluation, 1987.
2. Cheyney, W. Walker, and Philip A. Boyer. Division of Educational Research, Philadelphia. Extracts quoted in *Elementary School Journal, 33* (May 1983): 647–651.
3. Saunders, Carleton M. *Promotion or Failure for the Elementary School Pupil?* New York: Bureau of Publications, Teachers College, Columbia University, 1941.
4. Johnston, J. Howard, and Glenn C. Markle. *What Research Says to the Middle Level Practitioner.* Columbus, Ohio: National Middle School Association, 1986.
5. Washburn, Carleton W. "A Program of Individualization," *Adapting the Schools to Individual Differences* (Twenty-Fourth Yearbook of the National Society for the Study of Education, Part II). Bloomington, Ill.: Public School Publishing, 1925, pp. 257–272.
6. Georgiady, Nicholas P. "Behavioral Objectives as an Aid to Evaluation." *The Review,* Oxford, Ohio: School of Education, Miami University (Spring 1972).

REFERENCES

Baughman, M. D. (Ed.). *Pupil evaluation in the junior high school.* Danville, IL: Interstate, 1963.

Carnegie Council on Adolescent Development. *Turning points: preparing youth for the 21st century.* Report of the Task Force on Education of Young Adolescents. New York: Carnegie Corporation of New York, 1989.

Drayer, A. M. *Problems in middle and high school teaching.* Boston: Allyn & Bacon, 1979.

Hamachek, A. L., and L. G. Romano. *Focus on parent-teacher conferences.* East Lansing: Michigan Association of Middle School Educators, Erickson 419, Michigan State University, 1984.

Lewy, A. (Ed.). *Handbook of curriculum evaluation, UNESCO.* New York: Longman, 1977.

Messick, R. G., and K. E. Reynolds. *Middle level curriculum in action.* White Plains, NY: Longman, 1992.

National Study of School Evaluation. *Middle school/junior high school evaluation criteria* (6th ed.). Arlington, VA: National Study of School Evaluation, 1987.

Powell, W. B., and L. G. Romano. *Evaluative criteria for a middle school.* East Lansing, MI: Michigan Association of Middle School Educators, 1990.

Rothney, J. W. M. Evaluating and reporting pupil progress. *What research says to the teacher series, No. 7.* Washington, DC: NEA.

CHAPTER

Physical Activities and Intramurals

THE IMPORTANCE OF A PHYSICAL ACTIVITY PROGRAM

Meeting the physical needs of middle school children is critical to their success as learners and to their social, emotional, and mental development. The central fact of these learners' lives is arguably the dramatic physiological changes which occur during the middle school years. Understanding the changes has implications for these learners' self-concepts, social acceptance, and confidence for acquiring mental skills. Their physical and emotional health are directly related to their intellectual development.

Middle school programs should be developed to help children meet their learning needs—physical, social, emotional, and mental. The four areas are not isolated nor mutually exclusive; they are highly interrelated and interdependent. Though physical needs are the focus of this chapter, other needs cannot be ignored. Physical activity programs at the middle level have implications for the cognitive and affective as well as the cardiovascular well-being of the children they serve.

Physical needs are frequently more important than any others to middle school children. Not only does our society place a high premium on physical ability, personal appearance, size, and good health, but the developmental changes that occur in this age group heighten and intensify the anxiety to fit the perceived societal norms. The dilemma of the transescent youth is how to deal with a body that stubbornly refuses to grow rapidly enough, or how to manage a body that grows suddenly and dramatically. The degree to which children's physical needs can be met often influences their social acceptance, self-concept, and confidence for acquiring mental skills.

169

Frequently, physical needs are ignored in school programs and are, at best, generally assumed to be met. A partial physical education program, an interscholastic program, and some minor intramural activities are the extent of any real attention to providing equal physical opportunities for every child.

A clearly defined goal in middle school programming must be to focus on the physical concerns of transescent youngsters. The implementation of that goal must include as priorities: (1) a sound physical education program with special emphasis on helping participants develop a healthy lifestyle; (2) a thoroughly developed intramural program; and (3) directed attention to physical needs in every classroom, program, and activity related to the middle school.

THE PHYSICAL NEEDS OF
MIDDLE SCHOOL CHILDREN

The needs of middle school children are not easily categorized or compartmentalized. The children vary in every conceivable way. The life of a middle school child is filled with change of such constancy and intensity that many recall the ages of 10 to 14 as the most difficult in their lives.

Some physical needs which can be identified and that seem to be common in the development of middle school youngsters are:

1. To have a nutritious diet to accommodate the rapid growth taking place.
2. To engage in regular physical activity for the high energy level that exists between growth spurts, for fitness, for periodic stages of high restlessness, and for rapidly developing muscle groups.
3. To have regular rest for mind and body because middle school children often tire easily and may have a tendency to overexert.
4. To be in physical proximity to peers. The approval of peers is critical and nearness is often a prelude to, or a factor in gaining acceptance in a group. Group membership is highly sought.
5. To have physical differences accepted. The middle school student needs to feel that differences in appearance and ability are natural and will not interfere with acceptance.
6. To have some ''time alone,'' almost totally free from others, especially adults.
7. To have relationships with the opposite sex. Sex characteristics and needs are developing. Appropriate interaction with the opposite sex is important to test out new behaviors and gain acceptance.

8. To have a safe and secure environment. Even though students are seeking independence, there is still a need to return to the physical safety and security of the home and the adult world.
9. To know, understand, and manage feelings about the rapid physical changes or lack thereof. Perceptions and feelings are generally more important than the changes themselves.
10. To have skill activities appropriate for their level of development. The opportunity to succeed and to avoid frustration is maximized when students are able to work at their rate of readiness level.

In middle school students, actual physical growth tends to be well ahead of muscular strength. However, rapid skeletal growth spurts begin during this period and coordination may decrease for a time as muscle growth catches up and bone growth continues.

Girls are often taller and more developed than boys. Many girls begin to menstruate, although irregularly, and this causes them some anxiety. Secondary sexual characteristics are also developing and personal appearance becomes a concern as rapid growth may bring poor posture, acne, and longer arms and legs.

Competitiveness begins to increase with the middle school years, and worry about winning and losing can be a critical factor in self-concept development. Experiences must be provided in which the student can both compete and succeed.

SOME REMINDERS ABOUT LEARNING

Learning occurs when experiences are need-fulfilling, relevant to values, and analogous to past experiences. As the individual interacts with his environment, he learns. Learning has the potential for positive or negative changes in the individual.

Students learn most effectively when they can identify present and future use for the learning. Learning also has a much greater chance of being used in the future if it is utilized immediately. Children, like adults, also tend to remember information which confirms previously held attitudes much better than information which runs contrary to them.

There are variations among students regarding: 1) readiness for any learning; and 2) the time it takes to learn a given skill or idea. Readiness and speed of learning are products of many variables: physical maturation; prior learning experiences; the student's value system; the student's beliefs about the relevance of the learning; and his feelings about self, home, school, and teachers.

Learning is likely to be supported by the learner if he or she feels a sense of choice or participation in selecting the learning activity. When a person is not involved in determining those things which are to be learned, the commitment to the learning is minimized. In addition, there does not appear to be any subject in school which is superior to others in strengthening a person's learning skill.

The theory of multiple intelligences posited by Howard Gardner suggests that greater attention be paid to the different ways individuals apprehend and engage the world. Of particular importance to this discussion is his notion of bodily-kinesthetic intelligence. Those who have this particular intelligence need opportunities to maximize its development and to explore the possibility that its development might provide an avenue for the education of other intelligences.

HOW MIDDLE SCHOOL CHILDREN BEHAVE

The behaviors of middle school students are clear evidence of the growing-up process. It is important to recognize that one command element in describing the behavior of middle school students is diversity. The behavior of an individual can be erratic and often found at opposite extremes within a short period of time. The behavior of a group of students regularly shows that same diversity and extremes. Behavior reflects the wide range in maturation levels among middle school youngsters. The behaviors which individuals exhibit in the transescent years coincide with their needs. Middle school students will usually attempt to satisfy their social, emotional, and physical needs before attending to their mental needs.

The literature regarding physical activities provides some generalizations to consider in developing sound programs for middle school students.

Much of the psychological development and socialization which occurs within the transescent is a result of the entry he makes into a peer group culture. Adult intervention in children's games has questionable positive effect on the growth of children. On the contrary, there is a distinct possibility that adult interference (which is frequently most intense in interscholastic athletics) may damage the natural process of growing up.

Transescents are not physically mature adults. Adult activities are frequently too strenuous for the normal development of middle school age individuals. In addition, there are great differences in physical development at this age. Chronological age, certainly, is not an accurate indicator of physiological age. Determining the level of physical development is extremely difficult. Thus, adults take great risks in providing highly competitive and strenuous activity for children who may not be physically mature in bone development and muscle strength.

Interscholastic athletics may, in fact, actually reduce the opportunity for students to participate. The exclusive nature of interscholastic activity is one factor. The high degree of imposed structure, when the child's involvement is directed by others, also reduces participation for the individual.

When the middle school age youngster is exposed to experiences in which he cannot be successful simply because of his lack of physical or emotional maturity, success is minimized. Desire for further positive physical activity is often diminished, too.

Intense competition for many students of middle school age may cause severe emotional damage. When the student is not emotionally or physically ready, being thrust into the competition of making the team or of being on the first team will frequently end in failure and may cause permanent damage. Many individuals are not ready emotionally and/or physically until they are 15 years old or older.

Late maturing individuals often have more difficulty establishing positive self-concepts. Frequently, they feel more inadequate, rejected, and dependent on adults. Thus, increased adult sensitivity to the needs of both the late and early maturer is critical.

WHY MIDDLE SCHOOL INTERSCHOLASTIC SPORTS ARE INAPPROPRIATE

Interscholastic athletics are not appropriate at the middle school level. They are exclusive in nature, incompatible with the developmental levels of 10 to 14 year olds, consume an inordinate number of resources that could be better utilized in programs for all students, and are mostly adult-oriented and adult-directed activities.

Schools which are attempting to implement the middle school concept often find it difficult to drop an existing interscholastic program. Some schools have had success modifying the usual interscholastic format. They take into account the developmental differences of middle school students and diminish the emphasis on individual or group superiority. Even if such a program can supplant an existing interscholastic program or provide a transition to an intramural format, the ideal remains a middle school without interscholastic sports.

MAKING THE SCHOOL ENVIRONMENT
MEET PHYSICAL NEEDS

The total school learning environment must be developed in a manner which takes the physical needs of middle school age students into consideration. The school must provide an environment where they can feel physically safe and secure so that other needs can also be addressed and met.

Every program and learning experience should be constructed to include both active and sedentary activities. It is also important to provide time for rest and relaxation. The physical activity which is planned should be frequent but not based primarily on complex motor skills.

There are times when activities may need to be different for boys than girls, based on their developmental levels. Opportunity must be available for individuals to choose those activities in which they will participate. Therefore, there must be ample and varied options from which they can choose. Required activities for all students will be effective only when they fit the particular developmental level and interest of all participants.

In addition to opportunities for rest and a break in the day, there should be time to get a nutritional snack at a time other than lunch. High energy levels necessitate adequate diets to cope with the demands of a long school day.

Time must be provided in many programs for students to study and discuss their personal growth and development as well as their health, nutrition, and personal care.

A comprehensive guidance program should be easily accessible to assist students in understanding and coping with their intense and changing physical needs, and the problems which result. In addition, guidance staff must provide for all parents to learn and understand about the physical needs of their children. Parents often feel puzzled, helpless, and frustrated by the rapid and drastic changes taking place in their children. They usually welcome the chance to obtain information and discuss mutual concerns with teaching staff and other parents.

All programs need to have accessible materials from which students can learn about being a transescent. In particular, the media center should be adequately supplied with appropriate growth and development related materials. It is important that students have easy access to these materials so that they are not embarrassed when they attempt to use them. Both fiction and nonfiction materials are available and appropriate.

Sufficient opportunity must be provided for middle school students to learn about posture and grooming. In addition, every individual should have the opportunity to learn and develop first aid skills.

The chance for middle school students to meet physical needs is often greatest when activities take place outside the walls of the school. Outdoor education, resident camping, survival activities, and community service often provide students new avenues for successful physical endeavors.

School activities should stress the importance of leisure time utilization and the role physical activity can play. All activities should stress the ancient Greek concept of being sound in mind and body. It is interesting to note that this notion of sound mind and sound body is echoed in literature regarding Japanese education. The integration of physical activity with other forms of learning is more complete in Japanese than in Western school curricula. The emphasis is on exercise, which puts children in an energetic and positive frame of mind. It also teaches them how to push themselves and develop unity with others. Sixth-grade students, for instance, go out in all kinds of weather to do calisthenics, led by classroom teachers who regularly wear exercise clothes and warm-up suits in the classroom.

Since many American school districts have begun wellness programs to promote healthier life-styles among staff members, it is time to consider integrating staff wellness with student wellness. Though physical education instructors should continue to provide the leadership and most of the direct instruction for student physical skill building, physical activity need not be solely their domain. If all adults show concern for healthy physical activity, there can be big dividends for both teachers and students.

PHYSICAL EDUCATION PROGRAM COMPONENTS

Physical education for all middle school students is a high priority. Resources should be allocated to insure that a quality program can be provided. Facilities, equipment, materials, time, and staff must be available to provide for both individual and team activities. Students should have access to activities and resources necessary for developing the basic skills and positive attitudes necessary for effective use of leisure time, lifelong physical activity, and sound physical health.

Facilities. Physical education activities can be held in many settings. Gyms, stages, cafeterias, playfields, classrooms, bowling alleys, sidewalks, woods, fields, and swimming pools are some places which creative physical education staff members utilize. Intramural programs should have the highest priority for facility use after regular school hours. Other school activities should generally be scheduled after intramurals have been completed.

Equipment and materials must include much more than balls and bats. Racquets, bows and arrows, gymnastic equipment, field hockey equipment, and Ping-Pong tables are examples of other equipment that can be used in a physical education program. Video equipment is also a valuable tool for helping students view their performance and identify ways to improve their skills. Physical education and intramural staff can cooperate in the use of materials and equipment for more efficient utilization.

Time may be the most important resource to obtain. Middle school students should have physical education on a daily basis, with time equal to other required school programs. The practice of using a nine-week block for physical education alternating with a nine-week block without physical education is inadvisable. It interrupts the continuity of learning and neglects the students' often urgent daily needs for physical activity.

Staff members in physical education should be fully certified and qualified. The teacher must have mastery of the specific competencies involved in teaching physical education along with awareness of the physical, mental, emotional, and social needs of the middle school student. The teacher has the responsibility to help students develop the skills, master the knowledge, and acquire the attitudes and social qualities that will help them become all that they are capable of becoming. Physical education staff members share the responsibilities for program planning, evaluation, testing, counseling, and caring for equipment and facilities.

TOTAL SCHOOL STAFF INVOLVEMENT

In addition, the physical education teacher has the responsibility to provide in-service training for the rest of the staff regarding the importance of physical education as an integral part of the student's lifelong learning.

To ensure full use of resources, it is recommended that teachers operate as a team in planning and presenting the physical education program. Teams allow effective use of teacher strengths, facilitate flexible group sizes, and present opportunities for diverse offerings. Class sizes should be similar to those throughout the school. A proper pupil-teacher ratio which allows for individualized instruction is as important in physical education as in any other program of the school.

Processes for student evaluation and measurement should be diagnostic in nature and designed to build upon the strengths of each individual. Individual goal setting and evaluation with guidance from staff is critical for the transescent. Letter grades are not necessary. However, individual progress reports and planned parent conferences are key parts of the program.

IMPORTANCE OF A WRITTEN PLAN

A written instructional program should exist for physical education. Included should be clearly defined goals, objectives, program descriptions, and plans for ongoing program evaluation. The program should provide students with opportunities:

1. For success.
2. For individuals to progress at their own rate and ability level.
3. For directing some of their own activities and making choices regarding their program.
4. For individual interests to be pursued.
5. For multiaged and coeducational learning activities.
6. For play.
7. For participation without fear of put-down or reprisal due to different developmental levels or abilities.
8. For developing physical fitness habits.
9. For learning leisure time skills.
10. For team activity.
11. For individual efforts.
12. For competition which is primarily focused on one's self but also provides for team effort.
13. For working with adults who model sound concepts of physical fitness through activity and appearance.
14. For learning about one's bodily capabilities.
15. For experiencing some form of leadership.

Since physiological functioning affects middle school students' capacity to learn, it is important that the school become a health promoting organization. Statistics clearly indicate that the current generation of young people is less physically fit and more prone to obesity than the young people of two and three decades ago. This less active generation poses special problems in the classroom because many children who have opted for sedentary pursuits lose learning opportunities naturally encountered in active play. The importance of physical activity in the development of motor skills and neural functioning necessary for school success continues to be investigated.

However, preliminary findings indicate that a clearly defined and comprehensive physical education program, including both health-related and skill-related instruction, may pay cognitive dividends.

INTRAMURAL PROGRAM COMPONENTS

An intramural program draws its strength from a strong physical education program. The materials and resources used in developing physical education programs naturally carry over to successful intramural programs. But as important as materials and resources are, the real success of intramurals lies in a school's philosophy, its desire to meet the needs of the students, its understanding of student behavior, and the commitment of personnel involved in the program.

Offerings should be geared to the interest of the students and provide a variety of activities geared to those interests. Frequently, these activities can take place away from the school. Canoeing, fishing, bowling, horseback riding, cycling, and roller skating are some examples. In-school activities could include wide participation in leagues, tournaments, ladder challenges, skateboard contests, Ping-Pong, and dance.

Often intramural activities can be effectively planned with other schools. If the activity is low-key and informal and participation is not limited, students can gain much from interaction with students from other schools.

The times intramural activities are offered must be chosen carefully to assure maximum opportunity for participation. Students should be able to participate in one or more activities each week and have an opportunity to be exposed to individual, dual, and team activities.

An intramural program should have a designated director to assure the planning, scheduling, and organization vital to its success. Staff members involved in an intramural program should be paid at rates equivalent to those paid for other extracurricular activities. Many staff members can be involved on a short-term basis to supervise specific activities in which they have interest and expertise. Frequently, persons from the community can become key members of an intramural program as well.

Since the success of the intramural program depends on the beliefs which drive it, it may be useful to examine a typical belief system and objectives. The following belief system and objectives were developed by the Forest Hills Public Schools of Grand Rapids, Michigan, for their middle school intramural program.

Belief Statement

The purpose of the intramural program is to provide a positive recreational and athletic experience for middle school students through a planned activity program which supplements and expands upon the regular physical education program.

Emphasis in the intramural program will include:

1. Program planning which generates participation of the greatest number of students.
2. Equal opportunity for boys and girls to participate.
3. Development of interest and skills in athletic activities which carry over into high school athletics and/or leisure time activities.
4. Instruction and supervision by qualified personnel.
5. Providing individual, team, and recreational sports.
6. Providing equal participation time for all players in a team situation as opposed to stressing a win-loss record.

Since the scope of the intramural program is intended to be comprehensive, student and parent input will be sought through a needs assessment survey. An Intramural Advisory Board, made up of students and parents, will also be developed.

Objectives

1. The intramural program will provide an opportunity for interested students to explore a variety of team, individual, and recreational activities which extend beyond those offered through the physical education classes.
2. Skills taught in the physical education program will be assessed and upgraded when necessary as a regular part of the intramural program.
3. The intramural staff will try to provide an environment where students feel more secure in participating because no one can be cut or dropped.
4. More students will be encouraged to participate because the emphasis will be on participation. In some instances, students may even be referred to the physical education teacher or some other resource for specific skill instruction.
5. Field Trips: Groups of students may attend special athletic tournaments and exhibitions by amateur and professional athletes.

Once the beliefs and objectives of the program have been established, students' interests should be carefully surveyed. A variety of activities should be considered to encourage the participation of as many students as possible. Here is a list of possibilities taken from a survey used at the Kinawa Middle School in Okemos, Michigan:

Archery	Kickball
Backgammon	Kite Flying Contest
Badminton	Mile Run
Basketball	Obstacle Course
BB Gun Shooting	Open Gym
Bowling	Open Swim
Canoe Racing	Pinball Bombardment
Checkers	Physical Fitness
Cheerleading	President's Physical Fitness Award
Chess	Racquetball
Cross Country Skiing	Roller Skating
Cycle Riding Club	Skateboard Derby
Dancing	Skeet Shooting
Diving	Self-Defense
Fishing Derby	Soccer
Fly Tying	Snowshoeing
Floor Hockey	Softball
Frisbee	Swimming Tournament
Golfing	Table Tennis
Group Gym Activities	Tennis
(Parachute, Cageball, etc).	Tobogganing
Gymnastics	Track Meet
Horseback Riding	Water Polo
Horseshoe Pitching	Whiffleball
Horse Show and Competition	Water Volleyball
Ice Fishing	Volleyball
Activities with other Schools	Father/Student Night
Boat Safety	Mother/Student Night
Snowmobile Safety	Hunter Safety
Ice Skating	Punt, Pass, and Kick

Devising a program from diverse interests requires the coordinating skills of a director of intramurals. Without strong leadership and coordination, intramural programs are difficult to maintain and improve. Successful intramural programs have clearly stated belief systems and objectives, a variety of activities based on student interests, and the steady coordination and leadership of an intramural director.

SUMMARY

The physical needs of middle school children are intense. They must be provided for in the development of instructional programs. In order to provide effectively for physical needs, teachers, administrators, and board of education members must understand basic human needs and be knowledgeable about how children learn. Physical needs can and must be addressed: (1) in the entire school program, including every classroom and school activity; (2) through activities in a well-planned physical education program; and (3) in an intramural program for all children.

Planning instructional activities which provide opportunities for transescents to meet their physical needs is an exciting challenge which must be met if they are to realize all of their human potential.

REFERENCES

Bain, L. L. Curriculum for critical reflection in physical education. In R. S. Brandt (Ed.), *Content of the curriculum* (pp. 133–145) (Association for Curriculum and Development Yearbook). Alexandria, VA: ASCD, 1986.

Blom, F. S., A. Kinsinger, and G. A. Gerard. *A middle school belief system.* East Lansing: Michigan Association of Middle School Educators. Erickson 419, Michigan State University, 1974.

Caine, R. N., and G. Caine. *Making connections: Teaching and the human brain.* Alexandria, VA: ASCD, 1991.

California State Department of Education. *Caught in the middle: Educational reform for young adolescents in California public schools,* 1987.

Carnegie Council on Adolescent Development. *Turning points: Preparing youth for the 21st century.* New York: Carnegie Corporation, June, 1989.

Gardner, H. *Frames of mind: The theory of multiple intelligences.* New York: Basic Books, 1985.

Gerard, G. K., R. Schwenter, and F. Watters. *Focus on physical education, intramurals and interscholastics.* East Lansing: Michigan Association of Middle School Educators, Erickson 419, Michigan State University, 1978.

Graham, G. M. Developmentally appropriate physical education for children. *Streamlined Seminar.* National Association of Elementary School Principals, September, 1991.

Healy, J. M. *Endangered minds: Why our children don't think.* New York: Simon & Schuster, 1990.

Kirkpatrick, B. "Ultra physical education in middle schools." *Journal of Physical Education and Dance,* (August 1987): 46–49.

Riemcke, C. "All must play—The only way for middle school athletics." *Journal of Physical Education and Dance,* (March, 1988): 82–84.

Romano, L. G., and N. Timmer. "Middle school athletics: Intramurals or interscholastics?" *Middle School Journal.* (May, 1987).

Walters, J. M., and H. Gardner. The development and education of intelligences. In F. R. Link (Ed.), *Essays on the intellect* (pp. 1–21). Alexandria, VA: ASCD, 1985.

White, M. *The Japanese educational challenge: A commitment to children.* Tokyo: Kodansha International, 1987.

Class Organization for Instruction

PART III

Chapter Ten discusses several middle school organizational patterns. Team planning and teaching is identified as a key element for a successful middle school. They make use of the combined resources and thinking of teacher members of a team, rather than teachers planning singly and apart from each other. The more effective use of time through block time periods and the advantages in flexibility for teachers in their use of such larger blocks of time are also discussed.

Chapter Eleven analyzes some of the many possible arrangements of class schedules designed to fit the needs of a classroom or school. Advantages of certain arrangements and problems which may be encountered are pointed out as well.

Chapter Twelve discusses the all too common practice of having all students proceed through learning activities at the same rate. It shows how increasingly unworkable and unfair this becomes in a middle school. Instead, the idea of continuous progress on an individual student basis is offered as a logical and defensible alternative, one which is consistent with the increasingly wider range of growth in achievement among these students.

CHAPTER

Middle School Organizational Patterns

SEARCHING FOR THE BEST ORGANIZATIONAL PATTERN

One of the most pressing issues facing the development of a middle school program is the one that deals with the organizational pattern of the students and teaching teams. Inherent in the research on middle school students is the fundamental assumption that the pre-adolescents involved are functioning socially, emotionally, and cognitively very differently from their elementary or high school cousins. This difference is great enough to demand unique programs and strategies for the middle school students. Added to this vital student concern is a similar concern for the teachers working in the program.

Since their inception in the 1960s, middle schools have used creative and innovative organizational patterns. In each and every pattern it was important to consider the developmental levels of both the students and the staff. To some degree, these developmental concerns influenced the program, the curriculum, and the teaching techniques utilized. In addition, some of the programs attempted to integrate and overlap the content areas.

Schools still struggle to find the right organizational pattern to meet all these demands. Added to these concerns, today's middle schools must reach students whose world outside the classroom often appears to be of more interest and benefit to them than their world inside the classroom. For students, the middle school of today has to connect the relevance between the basic skills that are a necessity for future development with the increased curiosity and exploratory nature of this age student. At the same time, it must prepare students for their entrance into the world of work and into a world where change is ubiquitous.

First generation models of middle schools attempted to reach these varied needs by focusing on the sorting and selecting of students. Unfortunately, many of these designs reflected high school curriculum and therefore did not meet the criteria of an appropriately developed program for young adolescents (ASCD 1975).[1] Fortunately, new research such as that done by Lezotte and Edmonds (1989),[2] has identified the characteristics that make an effective school. This research coupled with Beane's (1990)[3] work on effective middle school curriculum continues to support the notion of integration, cooperation, and exploration.

The design of an effective middle school pattern should reflect the needs and characteristics of the middle school child. Georgiady, Riegle, and Romano (1973),[4] identified 18 characteristics of an effective middle school. Unfortunately, while many people accepted the characteristics and instituted those that they could, they often left out some of the key characteristics. One of those was the implementation of a team teaching approach. It should be pointed out that excellent teaming is not ordinarily accomplished quickly. Many researchers who have spent a considerable amount of time studying effective schools, as well as noting ineffective schools, have suggested that educational programs will only improve if teachers work together in teams. One of these noted researchers, Goodlad (1984),[5] strongly states the need for a more flexible approach to meet student needs. In addition, he recommends more diversified teaching, flexible scheduling, multiage grouping of students, and mastery learning. He proposes that these strategies can succeed through an interdisciplinary team organizational pattern. In addition, Boyer (1983),[6] after a two-and-a-half year study of American secondary schools, recommends explicitly that teachers work in teams with shared space and block schedules. This eliminates the technique of teaching by the clock and institutes the technique of teaching to the student. In addition, the incorporation of team teaching provides students a needed chance for interaction with adults. In fact, when properly executed, team teaching provides the students time to develop positive relationships with various adult resource persons. Therefore, the organizational pattern that best meets the varied needs of the entire middle school program is a team teaching approach. One writer points out that team teaching is "The keystone of effective schools." (Epstein)[7]

TRUE TEAM TEACHING

A multitude of definitions for team teaching has been developed over the past several years. Research shows that one of the most essential elements is cooperation. An effective team is identified as a combination of teachers that is able to accomplish cooperatively, better than individually, the task of meeting the needs of its students. However, the basic philosophy of the middle school requires that team teaching be more than merely a cooperative gesture among the teaching staff. It is not intended to be "turn teaching." Turn teaching is simply a method of instruction that is convenient for teachers. It takes place when two or more teachers decide to bring their students together and conveniently take turns teaching. For example, one teacher teaches math while the other teaches science. An arrangement of this nature is generally considered ineffective and is nothing more than departmentalized teaching, but with large groups. This ineffectiveness is created because of lack of collaboration on lessons, strategies, student needs, and authentic assessment for both the students and the staff. Team planning is the heart of any team effort. Team teaching must not be considered as just an occasional combining or swapping of classes by teachers as the mood strikes them.

A faculty and administration truly committed to teaming will guard against any approaches that are nothing more than a disguise for departmentalized teaching. Team members and the administration must really organize for team planning and teaching. Team teaching's very existence is designed to provide opportunities for a new utilization of the varied talents and strengths of the teaching staff. Team teaching represents a cooperative opportunity for teachers to demonstrate professionally their united strengths and abilities for the direct benefit of their students. According to Erb and Doda (1989),[8] team organization is a way of organizing teachers and students into small communities for teaching and learning. Teams may be comprised of two or more teachers. These teachers practice team planning, collaborate constantly, and have no major problems in being able to communicate with one another. They express sincere interest in the team concept and the many things it allows them to do for their students in classroom-sized groups and small groups, or when providing instruction on an individual basis. Whatever grouping or presentation format is being used, it must be cooperatively planned and evaluated. The cooperative planning component has great potential for enhancing instruction in the middle school. Teachers who plan instruction together for the same group of students can provide those students with many meaningful contexts in which effective instruction can occur (Irvin, 1990).[9] An integrated approach to instruction promotes more relevance and meaning. It also helps students connect concepts so that transfer of information with new learning can occur. As these students are moving toward becoming more abstract thinkers, the interdisciplinary approach helps them make sense of ideas that span many subject areas.

THE COMMON ELEMENTS OF TEAM TEACHING

Critical elements that need to be present to implement team teaching include common planning time, common sets of students, and common space. It is also important to pay special attention to composing the teams of students and staff.

Planning Time

Epstein[10] states that teams should be allowed two hours per week of common planning time. Our recommendation is that teams who want to be successful have a common period every day, with the principal attending one or more meetings, to assist in any way with problems shared by the team teachers. Team teaching requires commitment on the part of team members and *all* supporting staff to the concept. This joint planning time should be used to look at students' strengths and weaknesses, integrate curriculum areas, assess students' academic success, monitor student progress, plan student groupings for instruction, evaluate teacher practices, plan special programs, meet with specialists, set common and agreed upon policies and procedures, and hold parent and student conferences.

This planning time should be a common time for all team members. However, only about 30 percent (Epstein)[11] of the schools that organize interdisciplinary teams provide this time for teachers to meet. Without this common planning time, many teachers try to meet together before or after school or during a lunch break, but team effectiveness in handling the many coordinated efforts is severely hampered. In addition, teachers begin to feel resentful about using all their individual time. They may not be as effective without having the necessary personal breaks needed to keep one's body and mind in optimum working order. If teaming is considered to be a critical attribute of a middle school program, then it appears that school personnel need to work harder to provide the necessary planning time. Without it, a team cannot accomplish all the various tasks that produce a high quality and effective program for early adolescents and their teachers.

Space

When planning activities and instruction for students, space needs to be a consideration. Flexible use of space is a necessity. When teams of teachers work together, the instructional space needs to vary to fit the given learning environment needed for the outcome. For instance, a small group of students may be working in a cooperative learning small group setting while another group of students may be working on an enrichment activity with one of the team teachers. At the same time, the larger group of students may be working with one of the other team members, who may be showing a video or presenting some basic information in a large group setting. The goal here is to provide the necessary space for the teaching, rather than having the space control the type of activities offered.

Sets of Students

Pre-adolescent youngsters face a tumultuous time in their life. Students at this level go through profound changes physically, emotionally, intellectually, and socially (Kaminski and Dornbor, 1991).[12] Having a group of students and teachers with whom these adolescents can build a relationship helps them meet these challenges. In "Caught in the Middle," a 1987 report[13] by the California Superintendent's Middle Grade Task Force, State Superintendent Bill Honig states: "For many students, the middle grades represent the last chance to develop a sense of academic purpose and personal commitment to educational goals." Students should be heterogeneously grouped. Student groups can be multiaged as well if deemed appropriate by the instructional team of teachers. Of critical importance is the development of rapport between the students and the teachers. This rapport, according to Epstein and MacIver,[14] is the driving force behind the improved student attitude and sense of well-being that occurs when all involved work together as a team. It is important, then, that each student be assigned to a teacher who can help guide and build that rapport and relationship throughout the year. This relationship nurtures a positive self-image for the adolescent. In addition, this relationship helps develop the sense of community in students, along with a feeling of security and belonging.

TEAMING STRUCTURES FOR A MIDDLE SCHOOL[15]

Two Teachers/Two Subjects

Under this system, two teachers who teach different subjects get together. This can be done during the two periods assigned to these subjects. The most common subject matter combinations for this variety are language arts/social studies and math/science. These cognitive areas are certainly complementary, but other combinations may be successful. Each teacher may be responsible for developing the plans for one particular instructional area, but they share the plans with each other and both of them teach all of the material.

This teaming necessitates coordination and a different quality of planning. Since one of the goals is to integrate the content areas and show how they impact each other, this variety starts to break down the traditional

FIGURE 10.1
Two Teachers/
Two Subjects.

C. William Brubaker,
Perkins and Wills
Architects, Chicago, IL.

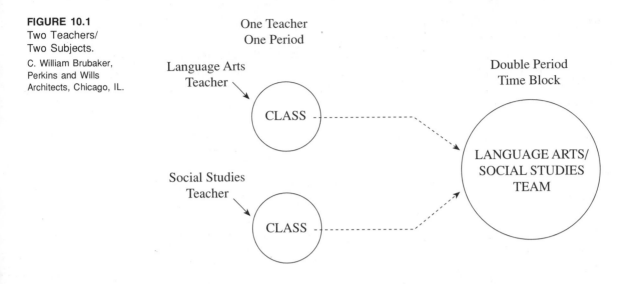

boxes and barriers of education. Students can be helped to understand that English skills are necessary in everything we do and will do, and not just important in a 45-minute English class period. This same opportunity exists in the remaining varieties of teaming.

Both teachers will meet with one group of students for English and social studies ($45 \times 2 = 90$ minutes). They will meet with a second group of students for these subjects for 90 minutes. (Figure 10.1.)

Two Teachers/Multiple Subjects

A more complex organizational structure may involve a four-period time block with two groups of students. One teacher may be designated, on paper, as the language arts/social studies person. The other may be the math/science teacher. (Figure 10.2.) The time blocks can be arranged so that reading can be an extension of the elementary reading program. In planning, the first staff member will plan the units of study in the social studies/language arts instructional program. The other staff member will plan for math and science. The plans are shared, and both of them teach all of the subjects.

In this team teaching plan, the two teachers may plan to use the thematic approach, that is, they may decide upon a unit of study on Ecology. It will include the important concepts related to math, science, social studies, and English. This plan calls for time to write the units of study. This can be accomplished by hiring the teachers to spend time writing during the summer months. This activity is imperative for the success of team teaching.

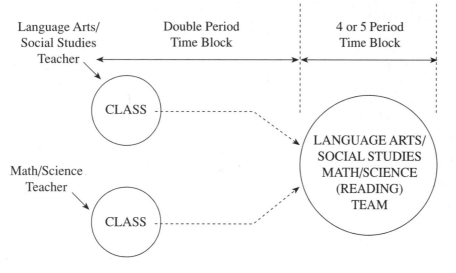

FIGURE 10.2
Two Teachers/
Multi-Subjects.
C. William Brubaker,
Perkins and Wills
Architects, Chicago, IL.

Multi-Teachers/Multi-Subjects

This is an extension of the two teachers/two subjects approach with an even greater range of possibilities. (Figure 10.3.) The presence of more adults and children gives geometrically broader possibilities because of the increased number of resources and their attendant strengths. It may be impossible to incorporate other teachers and subject areas such as music and art into your team, but surely you will be able to correlate these four subjects with art, music, and possibly physical education.

This approach is the most complex one organizationally and interpersonally. Certainly there is increased possibility for conflict, but there are also more numerous learning possibilities. An understanding of how students interact as well as a commitment to adult cooperation is essential. Group process skills are critical.

Interdisciplinary Team Teaching

One of the most difficult and yet rewarding types of team teaching is interdisciplinary team teaching. The interdisciplinary approach calls for the integration of subject matter through focusing on meaningful themes. This approach requires careful planning on the part of the participating team teachers in the subjects of Social Studies, Science, Language Arts, and Mathematics. Through careful planning, each of these instructional areas will provide important concepts related to the thematic unit of study.

FIGURE 10.3
Multi-Teachers/
Multi-Subjects.

C. William Brubaker,
Perkins and Wills
Architects, Chicago, IL.

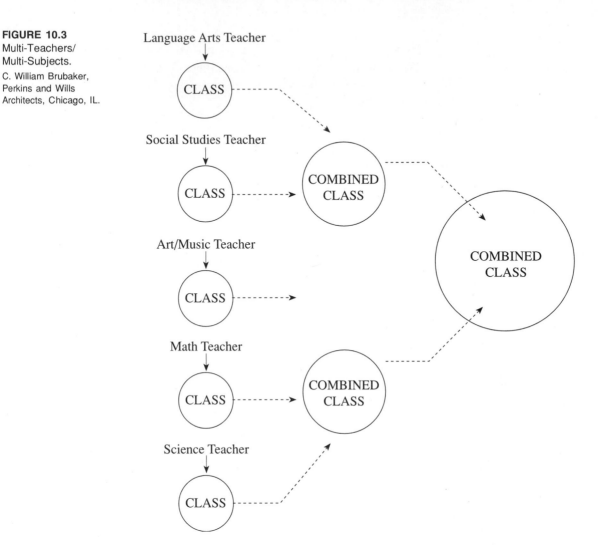

Ample time each day should be provided in the schedule for planning activities. Without this planning time, it will be impossible for an interdisciplinary team to be successful. In the planning sessions, the team members can brainstorm on the thematic units to be covered. Students may be included in the determination of units to be covered. Once a unit is agreed upon, one staff member can proceed in writing the concepts which bring out important learnings for the various instructional areas. After the unit has been written, it is then submitted to the team members for input. At this stage, each subject teacher will insure that the important concepts in that specialized area are included in the unit. It should be pointed out that the written unit will include the following: (1) the important objectives or concepts, (2) at least five activities to meet the various learning styles of the students to accompany each objective, and (3) a list of materials for each activity. Furthermore, the team members may decide to write a pretest and a posttest. The pretest will be given prior to beginning the thematic unit. The staff can then use various grouping techniques and use what the students do not know. This team decided to use cooperative learning techniques.

All of the teachers were involved in the planning. Therefore, knowing the concepts to be taught, each teacher teaches all of the material—regardless of who planned it. At the termination of the study, a posttest is administered. If all the students score at the ninetieth percentile level, then the team proceeds to the next unit of study. If several students score below the accepted level, however, then the team may decide to provide further learning activities for them to insure that all students are successful in gaining the concepts in the interdisciplinary unit.

It should be stressed that interdisciplinary teaming is not "turn teaching" or having teachers take turns teaching their subject matter to the entire group of students. This procedure can be avoided through writing the thematic units of study cooperatively.

Another word of caution. It is very important that the parents of students in the interdisciplinary team are informed as to the program activities of the team. An evening meeting should be planned in which the teaming concept is explained to the parents, insuring them that their children will gain the needed knowledge and skills. One school included several parents in the team planning sessions and a few parents served as paraprofessionals during the instructional period. A meeting was also planned after the completion of the first thematic unit so that parents who served as paraprofessionals could allay any fears other parents had about interdisciplinary teams.

BENEFITS OF TEAM TEACHING

In the discussion so far we mentioned and implied many advantages of team teaching. It may be helpful to highlight some of its major benefits:

- Teaming provides students with a model for sharing and cooperating that can often do more to help them grow than any cognitive material you try to impart.
- A team provides a home base/security group for students. Middle schoolers need to belong. They need that sense of security and consistency that a team can provide. It's their school "family." It understands their behavior and helps to meet their needs.

- Flexibility is tremendous. The team can decide the composition of groups and the frequency of changing them. Class size and pupil-teacher ratio can be changed to fit the particular learning activities.
- Teachers have a greater chance of providing meaningful learning activities for students because they're working with others in the planning. They're pooling their resources and sharing information about what each individual and group needs most. Each team member brings fresh ideas into a team brainstorming session. This fresh, open approach usually leads to better activities and units.
- There is a built-in support system. Not only are teaching peers there to help each other through difficult problems, but in a real team sense, so are the students. With adequate support, a team teacher will be more likely to take risks and try new instructional approaches.
- With a variety of teacher strengths and personalities, students in the team are more likely to find someone with whom they can identify. Few, if any, teachers relate well to all students, and vice-versa. In a team, teachers can focus on meeting the needs of students with whom they are most effective. Students, too, can learn from the successes of other students.
- With the interdisciplinary approach, the number of different students a teacher will see each day can be reduced. This helps teachers know students better, so that they are able to provide more meaningful individualized instruction.
- Teaming provides continual professional growth and in-service for teachers. Working with other teachers provides an opportunity to observe and learn from each other's strengths. Teachers can get new insight into techniques that are effective, and by sharing perceptions with the team, each member can profit and grow tremendously in teaching effectiveness. Teaming also allows an opportunity to teach in some areas that have long interested one, but that have not previously been part of one's teaching assignment.
- The team determines the length of a class period. When students are greatly interested in what they are doing, why should the period end at 45 minutes? If the students are working on writing a play, then more time can be devoted to this activity.
- With our concern today for empowerment of teachers, teaming allows teachers to make all decisions related to the program of learnings. Teachers are directly concerned both with problems related to the instructional program and with maximizing learning for the students; therefore, they should make these decisions.

- Student evaluations and parent-teacher-student conferences can be improved immensely. Each teacher sees a particular child in different situations. So when teachers pool their information and share it with the staff member who is to confer with a parent, conferences are more meaningful.
- New students and teachers can be more easily and quickly socialized to a new school and environment because nobody is out there alone. Everyone is part of a group with members that are working to help each other. Each child is more likely to find someone with whom to identify and make friends. Having a buddy or two in your group every day can make a lot of difference.
- Because of time and scheduling flexibility, teams can more easily adapt to special events such as speakers, field trips, and assemblies.
- Independent study and other learning options, such as using the library/media center, can easily be worked into the unit activities.
- Integration of subject matter is more easily accomplished.
- Learning activities can be more creative and meaningful since they've been planned by the team. The kind of brainstorming discussed earlier is fertile ground for fresh new ideas.
- More can be said about the value of teaming. Team teaching may meet the intellectual, social, emotional, and physical needs of students and teachers better than any other organizational structure. It leads to more individualized activities and programs for children. The increased understanding that teachers develop leads to more personal individualization, too. This is one of the primary purposes of middle schools. Teaming also provides more choices and opportunities to make decisions. Middle schools must be rewarding places for adults, too.

POTENTIAL PROBLEMS

Although team teaching is a practice which has many distinct advantages for students and teachers, there are some potential problems which need to be addressed. (See Figure 10.4.)

- At times it may be necessary to put in extra time, especially in planning instructional units and in developing certain activities. Common planning time is an imperative, and as already stated, should occupy at least one period each day. Without this commitment, the team operation will not succeed.

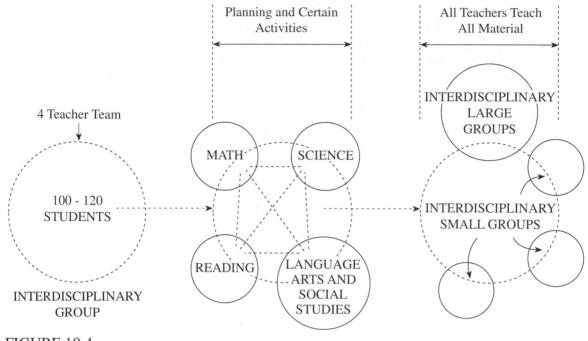

FIGURE 10.4
Interdisciplinary Teaming.

- There will be times when a large room will be needed for the total group, but it should be emphasized that large group sessions should be kept to a minimum. For example, if a resource person is coming to school to talk to a team, then a large room is needed. Many schools make use of the cafeteria, gymnasium, or the auditorium for the purpose.
- It is imperative that the team structure has the complete support of a principal who knows what his or her role is, and is prepared to fulfill this role completely. Principals can be most helpful in making teaming a wonderful experience for students and teachers.
- It is also imperative that parents be informed of the new arrangements. They should also have an opportunity to observe a team in action, followed by a discussion with the team teachers and even several of the students. Remember, parents often evaluate what's going on in school based on their own experiences when they were

in junior high school. Informed parents can be a great help to a team through such ways as accompanying the group on a field trip, planning social events with the team, and providing materials which are available to them that the team could use.

• Some teachers may be threatened by team teaching. Their behavior in the teaching-learning situation can be observed by other members of the team and can cause insecurity for the particular staff member. It behooves the team members to talk about their feelings and about what can be done to improve the situation. When one teacher feels insecure, the other teachers need to be aware of this so that they can function in a nonthreatening way.

TEAM TEACHING IS NOT FOR ALL TEACHERS

Even though team teaching is advocated herein, one must keep in mind that some effective teachers rightly belong in a self-contained or departmental classroom situation. Teachers should not be forced into teaming. Individuals should be permitted to teach in the situation of their strength. Many effective classroom teachers are often collaborating and planning with their colleagues, thereby gaining some of the advantages that a teaming organizational pattern provides. It is hoped that within a short time, these teachers will volunteer to try team teaching.

Block Time

Some staffs are reluctant to do team teaching because it calls for cooperation between staff and exposes one's teaching abilities. Therefore another strategy is suggested. This arrangement was first introduced by Faunce and Bossing (1958)[16] to cut down the number of different students that meet teachers. In the traditional departmentalized arrangement, a student might meet four different teachers, while in the block time arrangement, only two teachers will meet the same student. Teacher A will teach math and science while teacher B will teach social studies and English. The subjects can be taught traditionally, that is, teacher A will teach math for 45 minutes and science for 45 minutes. Then the same teacher will meet another group of students, and will teach math for 45 minutes, and science for 45 minutes. The same schedule is used by the social studies and English teacher. In that way, each teacher meets only two groups of students for four class periods. Each student has only two teachers, rather than four teachers, for the four periods.

A Word About Self-Contained Classrooms

One psychologist examined a class of 40 sixth-graders, 20 boys and 20 girls. He examined them to determine if they were in the child, preadolescent, or adolescent stage. He found the following:

20 boys	0 adolescent	4 preadolescent	16 children
20 girls	2 adolescent	8 preadolescent	10 children

It seems from these data that sixth-grade children need the security of one teacher. Therefore sixth-grade teachers might consider keeping a self-contained classroom, but certainly not a departmentalized arrangement. Furthermore, seventh and eighth-grade teachers might consider a self-contained classroom as an alternative arrangement for students who need the security of one teacher.

SUMMARY

Whatever the blueprint of organization, team teaching in the middle school must provide teachers with the opportunity to better meet the needs of the students. The availability of a variety of techniques of teaching and learning are necessary. Good education takes place when it is implemented according to the needs of the students. A secure and professional atmosphere cultivates the freedom that teams of teachers need to innovate and create. When administrators and teachers work together in a happy and secure middle school program, the same satisfaction and security is passed on to the most important team member, the student.

ENDNOTES

1. ASCD. *Working Group on the Emerging Adolescent Learner, The Middle School We Need.* Washington, D.C., 1975.
2. Edmonds, R. and L. Lezotte. *The Correlates of School Effectiveness.* Unpublished Paper. Institute for Research on Teaching, Michigan State University, January 1989.
3. Beane, J. *A Middle School Curriculum: From Rhetoric to Reality.* Columbus, Ohio: National Middle School Association, 1990.
4. Georgiady, N. P., J. D. Riegle, and L. G. Romano. *What are the characteristics of the Middle School?* in Romano, L. G., N. P. Georgiady, and J. E. Heald. *The Middle School: Selected Readings on an Emerging School Program.* Chicago, IL: Nelson Hall, Co., 1973.

5. Goodlad, J. I. *A Place Called School: Prospects for the Future.* New York: Harper & Row, 1984.

6. Boyer, E. I. *High School: A Report on Secondary Education in America.* New York: Harper & Row, 1983.

7. Epstein, J. L. and D. J. MacIver. *Education in the Middle Grades: Practices and Trends.* Columbus, Ohio: National Middle School Association, 1990.

8. Erb, T. O. and N. M. Doda. *Team Organization: Promise—Practices and Possibilities.* Washington, D.C.: National Education Association, 1989.

9. Irvin, J. L. *Reading and the Middle School Student.* Boston: Allyn and Bacon, 1990.

10. See note 7.

11. See note 7.

12. Kaminski, L. G. and K. L. Dornbor. *Focus on Curriculum Design for Middle Schools Programs.* Michigan Association of Middle School Educators, Michigan State University, East Lansing, Michigan, 1991.

13. ''Caught in the Middle—Educational Reform for Young Adolescents in California Schools''. Sacramento, CA: California State Department of Education, 1987.

14. See note 7.

15. Adapted from Cross, Robert and Sue Cross, *Focus on Team Teaching.* Michigan Association of Middle School Educators, Michigan State University, East Lansing, Michigan, 1983.

16. Faunce, Roland C., and N. Bossing. *Developing the Core Curriculum.* New York: Prentice Hall, 1958.

Flexible Scheduling

PURPOSES OF SCHEDULING

Scheduling of any type is effective only to the extent that it helps support the mission and objectives of the school in which it occurs. It is a means to accomplish the division of instructional time to serve the student. Some administrators might say that scheduling objectives desired by teachers can not be accomplished because they do not "fit in" to the schedule. That should never be the case. The schedule must fit and serve the program rather than the program fit and serve the schedule.

Flexible scheduling, that is, scheduling that fits the program, will often be difficult to accomplish; however, with the availability of computers and many different software programs designed for scheduling, almost any variety of activities is possible. Schools of small enrollment, as well as those with large enrollments, can benefit from computer scheduling. When done properly and with the assistance of a computer, the principal has a wide variety of available by-products such as class lists, sex balance within the classroom, period balance across the program, grade reporting packages, and a host of support information and data.

SCHEDULING PRACTICES

In examining the various kinds of scheduling practices used by middle schools, a recent study[1] among 672 schools showed the following practices:

Type of Schedule	Percentages
Daily Periods of Equal Length	66%
Blocks of Time Combining Periods	7%
Daily Periods of Varying Length	5%
Combination of Block Time and Equal Time Periods	19%
No Response	3%

The large number (66 percent) indicates that equal amounts of time for all subjects is not giving fair consideration to the need of individual, different subjects. It seems highly unlikely, given a menu of subjects, that each subject would require an equal amount of time annually to accomplish the goals. Such a program is obviously driven by fitting a subject into a fixed time period rather than budgeting the amount of time needed to achieve the goals of the subject.

HOW TO BEGIN

An administrator who does not have the experience of scheduling often begins with an attempt to organize the time element. This common error leads to a great deal of wasted time and misses the point of flexible scheduling. In any scheduling endeavor, one should consider the following steps:

1. Prepare a list of courses in the program as well as special events or assembly groups.
2. Determine the number of students selecting each course or special event.
3. Determine the number of sections desired for each course. This depends on the staff available and number of sections desired.
4. Consider what space is available in the building.
5. Determine how frequently each section will meet.
6. Consider the sequence of meeting time and the size of each section. For example: Does the section meet every other day? Does the section meet Tuesday and Thursday only?
7. Consider the length of time each section will meet.

As can be seen, the greater the number of variables, the more difficult it is to schedule. That is why many administrators follow a fixed, rigid schedule. Once the input data is organized, the administrator must fit these variables into available space. The following should be considered:

1. What staff is available to operate the program?
2. How many classrooms or other spaces are available and at what time?
3. What is the enrollment and how is it distributed across the building? What are special needs such as special education, gifted education, sex balance, or physical plant considerations such as gym, lunchroom, science rooms, or library?
4. Start with those courses or activities that meet least frequently and have the fewest sections.

KEEPING THE SCHEDULE FLEXIBLE

After assembling the information, determine how to best meet the needs of the students and keep the schedule most flexible.

1. Will this schedule allow for varied time segments, and will it meet the teachers' needs? Can there be long as well as short periods of time as needed?
2. Can the program fit the space? Are sufficient labs and gyms available when needed?
3. Is this an efficient schedule? Are the class sizes appropriate?
4. Can electives be scheduled as chosen, or must we force choice?

There may be other questions that could be asked, but by now one is aware of the considerations that need to be examined prior to any change in scheduling practices. A degree of security for the administrator and the teacher exists in the traditional six or eight period schedule. The repetitious nature of this type of schedule gives students a predictable day.

These security factors together with a natural anxiety toward the unknown frequently lead educators to resist more flexible schedules. They thus miss the opportunity for enrichment, varied learning sessions, audiovisual experiences, and productive time sessions. Usually educators say they resist scheduling changes because they don't want to meddle with the traditional classroom experience.

CONTRAST OF TRADITIONAL AND FLEXIBLE SCHEDULES

It may be helpful to contrast some of the scheduling elements between a traditional schedule and an effective flexible schedule. (See Table 11.1.)

The examples in Table 11.1 show that an educational experience can be provided by either schedule. However, time becomes the master in the traditional schedule. All elements of the educational process must become subservient to the time plan. This leads to reduced learning opportunities for students and to frustration for teachers. The masters of any truly effective schedule are the educational needs of the students.

This treatment of the problems of time utilization is by necessity brief, since time utilization is not the major justification for flexible schedules. Improved educational experiences for boys and girls must result from the change in scheduling or no change should be undertaken. It serves no

TABLE 11.1 Contrast of Traditional and Flexible Schedules

	Traditional	Flexible
Time	Class meets for 45 minutes daily.	Class meets for any part of 90 minutes or more as needed.
	Class ends when 45 minutes is up.	Class ends when learning value of experience starts to drop.
	Class meets daily all semester or all year.	Class meets as planned by teaching team within broad guidelines.
Space	Science room is available 45 minutes daily.	Science room is scheduled for time needed to do activity planned.
	Gym class is daily, 45 minutes per day minus two changing times.	Gym is required as part of a total learning. It meets irregularly but for extended times if needed.
	Lunch is 45 minutes for everybody.	Lunch fits a flexible schedule that only limits the total flow of students.
Staff	I teach science six periods a day.	As a member of the science team, I plan my time to be the most effective student helper.
	I teach my students and you teach yours. My classes vary in size but never exceed contract limits of 30.	I am part of a team of teachers that determines class size based upon the type of activity.

purpose to spend time examining any of the many failures resulting from supposedly well intended scheduling. A schedule will, of necessity, be a living, changing, open-ended document or it will be only a control device. A program planned around student outcomes will determine the proper allocation of time.

THE COMPUTER AS AN AID TO SCHEDULING

A computer can be of assistance if there is on-line capability. "Batch type" schedules are unacceptable. A batch operation exists when material is sent to a computer center, a printout is received, conflicts are corrected, and another set of materials is sent to continue the process. Any changes in the original "flexible" schedule are time consuming and very difficult to make.

On-line computer scheduling exists when there is a terminal in a building. It is possible to communicate data to the computer via telephone and get immediate return information on a monitor screen. This has greater possibilities for scheduling. It certainly has value in rapidly determining conflicts in schedules and in testing possible alternative solutions to conflicts.

A NEW WAY OF THINKING

To administer a flexible schedule requires a great deal of trust and confidence in a school faculty. The administrator must be willing to share decision making with the other professionals on the team.

Prior to the move to flexible schedules, broadly based acceptance of the following concepts is needed:

1. It is not necessary for every class or any class to meet daily or at the same time every day.
2. Other teachers could add to the value of an individual's teaching if staff worked together.
3. There is no optimum pupil-teacher ratio that makes one class size ideal for all types of educational experiences.
4. All subjects do not need approximately equal time to be effectively presented. Some subjects would benefit with longer sessions while others could best be presented in shorter sessions.
5. Teachers are the very best people to decide the final time utilization schedule.

Once the faculty accepts these concepts, it is time to address the rigid part of the flexible schedule.

TABLE 11.2 Traditional Schedule Based upon a Fixed Time Module and a Daily Cycle

	Monday	Tuesday	Wednesday	Thursday	Friday
Period 1	Science	Science	Science	Science	Science
Period 2	Art	Art	Art	Art	Art
Period 3	Math	Math	Math	Math	Math
Period 4	Lunch	Lunch	Lunch	Lunch	Lunch
Period 5	Language Arts	Language Arts	Language Arts	Language Arts	Language Arts
Period 6	Social Studies	Social Studies	Social Studies	Social Studies	Social Studies
Period 7	Physical Education	Physical Education	Physical Education	Physical Education	Physical Education

BASIC CYCLES

All schedules are designed to repeat on some regular cycle. The most rigid basic cycle would be the daily cycle, where every day basically repeats the schedule of the previous day. Table 11.2 presents a daily cycle based upon a fixed time module.

Characteristics of the traditional scheduling model are:

1. Classes meet the same time every day throughout the week.
2. Every week is the same for teachers and students.
3. All periods are equal in length, requiring teachers to adopt instructional strategies that are workable within a fixed time slot.
4. Combining several same-subject classes into a large group is more difficult because related classes do not necessarily coincide.
5. If lunch is served during one or two of the instructional periods, student traffic is simple to manage and relatively constant from day to day.
6. Part-time faculty and specialized teaching assignments can be accommodated readily.

Table 11.3 presents a possible weekly schedule for a student based upon a fixed time module and a weekly cycle.

The modifications included in Table 11.3 do not allow for flexible use of time. The added time for math and science on Monday or the reduced time for social studies are manipulations intended to avoid time constraints. Double sessions and alternating classes are similar, well intended attempts to provide flexibility in the basic schedules, but all fall short of this goal.

TABLE 11.3 Traditional Schedule Based upon a Fixed Time Module and a Weekly Cycle

	Monday	Tuesday	Wednesday	Thursday	Friday
Period 1	Physical Education	Art	Physical Education	Art	Physical Education
Period 2	Language Arts	Art	Language Arts	Art	Language Arts
Period 3	Math	Language Arts	Math	Language Arts	Math
Period 4	Math	Social Studies	Social Studies	Social Studies	Social Studies
Period 5	Lunch	Lunch	Lunch	Lunch	Lunch
Period 6	Science	Science	Science	Science	Science
Period 7	Science	Life Skills	Life Skills	Life Skills	Life Skills

Utilizing the weekly cycle and the fixed time module, the next step is to examine a rather simple application of block time scheduling. Team teaching is added to provide possible variations.

This student schedule opens some opportunities for teachers to plan daily time usage between two subject areas. The principal has blocked out a 90-minute time and scheduled a group of students with a team of teachers who are responsible for instruction in two areas. A similar circumstance could exist in other subjects, as scheduled in this example.

Flexible schedules are basically extensions of the changes reflected in Table 11.4. The choice of a basic time module is usually an arbitrary decision. It is difficult to defend realistically the merits of a 30-minute, 40-minute, 50-minute, or similar module as opposed to other options. Flexibility is the key factor.

The merits of different cycles need to be considered. The weekly cycle for scheduling may be preferred because it can be easily explained to students, teachers, parents, and other interested parties. The ''even'' or ''odd'' day calendar has also been successful. Students handle it quite well.

BLOCK TIME SCHEDULING

Block time scheduling provides a group of students (60–120), a team of teachers (two to four), and a period of time (two to four class periods) varying from 45 to 60 minutes each. The team usually becomes responsible for instruction in math, science, social studies, and language arts. Teacher teams have been successfully using the block time schedule for many years.

TABLE 11.4 Block Scheduling with Team Teaching

Time	Monday	Tuesday	Wednesday	Thursday	Friday
8:30–9:15 9:20–10:05	Language Arts and Social Studies	Language Arts and Social Studies	Language Arts and Social Studies	Language Arts and Social Studies	Language Arts and Social Studies
10:10–10:55	Physical Education	Vocal Music	Physical Education	Vocal Music	Physical Education
11:00–11:45	Lunch	Lunch	Lunch	Lunch	Lunch
11:50–1:25	Math and Science	Math and Science	Math and Science	Math and Science	Math and Science
1:30–2:15	Unified Arts	Speech Health	Unified Arts	Speech Health	Unified Arts

The interdisciplinary block time team organization frees teachers to allocate time to meet the needs of the adolescent student as well as to accommodate the curriculum.

Several possible options provide maximum flexibility. The team has the option of large group instructional time, one less period per day, with either heterogenous grouping or high-ability groups. High-ability grouping should not be misunderstood for tracking or across-the-board ability grouping, which is not recommended.[2] Rather, it is grouping students who have a high interest or ability in a specific subject. With a block time interdisciplinary schedule, uneven periods can be created, allowing longer time in specific subjects or for special events or assemblies. These longer periods also allow for assessment. A special schedule might have a longer period, followed by several shorter periods.

In some cases, a team member can be released from the team to do research or other team related duties. This can be accomplished with a four-subject team by creating three subjects (or periods) with a redistribution of the students. This schedule "frees up" one of the team members for the day. Class size increases for each of the other classes, but one teacher is available to work with individual students, plan a team unit, or work toward a team project.[3]

Figure 11.1 illustrates the schedule. Cocurricular courses are elective or required courses such as art, physical education, life skills, technology, music, or other courses that the school has in its curriculum. These electives provide a varied and interesting program for most transescents. Other interests

Grade 6

Periods	1	2	3	4		5	6
	Reading	Cocurricular Courses	Block Time ⟶	L U N C H	⟵	⟵————— Block Time ————⟶	

Grade 7

Periods	1	2	3	4		5	6
	⟵————————— Block Time —————⟶				L U N C H	Cocurricular Courses	

Grade 8

Periods	1	2	3	4		5	6
	⟵————— Block Time ————⟶		Cocurricular Courses	L U N C H	Co-curricular Courses	⟵————— Block Time ————⟶	

Periods 1, 2, 3, 5, and 6 are each 60 minutes.
Period 4 is 90 minutes.
Lunch is 30 minutes.

FIGURE 11.1
A Block Time Schedule.

of a greater scope might then be met in a mini-course program. The cocurricular activities program may be divided into four quarters consisting of ten weeks each. The program may be scheduled on even and odd calendar days. Students are classified as either "music" or "nonmusic" based on whether or not they elect to take vocal or instrumental music. Sixth-grade students receive one hour, while seventh and eighth-grade students receive two hours per day of cocurricular courses. (See Figure 11.2.)

Grade 6

Music Students

	10 Weeks	10 Weeks	10 Weeks	10 Weeks
Even Days	Music	Music	Music	Music
Odd Days	Phys. Ed.	Phys. Ed.	Technology Ed.	Life Skills

Nonmusic Students

	10 Weeks	10 Weeks	10 Weeks	10 Weeks
Even Days	Phys. Ed.	Phys. Ed.	Arts	Arts
Odd Days	Technology Ed.	Life Skills	Arts	Arts

FIGURE 11.2
Schedule for Cocurricular Courses.

ORGANIZING INSTRUCTION

Many middle schools are moving toward a combination block time schedule with daily periods of varying length. Using this plan of organization facilitates interdisciplinary teaching. That concept may be the driving force in rearranging a schedule. Interdisciplinary teaching with a team of teachers and a block of time is a very convenient way to arrange teachers, students, and time. It is becoming more popular even at the high school level. This type of scheduling does not present many of the difficulties in the flexible modular schedule attempted in the late seventies.

Where interdisciplinary teaching is done, it most often involves an English/social studies or a math/science combination. It should also be noted that interdisciplinary teaching also provides for joint planning time so that teachers can be most effective.

SUMMARY

There are as many different ways to schedule students at a middle school as there are different ways to create the instructional program. The most important consideration is that the instructional program drive the schedule rather than have the schedule drive the instructional program. Responsible schedule variations make it possible for schools to be better organized to meet the needs of adolescent students. If a schedule change or adjustment is determined to be good for students, it should be implemented. It is important to have an open mind to all options and be flexible. Only then are we truly meeting the needs of adolescents in our middle schools.

ENDNOTES

1. Cawelti, G., "Middle Schools A Better Match with Early Adolescent Needs, ASCD Survey Finds," *Curriculum Update,* p. 1, November 1988, Association for Supervision and Curriculum Development, Alexandria, VA.
2. O'Neil, J., "On Tracking & Individual Differences; A Conversation with Jeannie Oakes," *Educational Leadership* 50, No. 2, 18–21, October 1992.
3. *Schools in the Middle.* National Association of Secondary School Principals, Reston, VA, Fall 1992.

CHAPTER

Continuous Progress

MEETING THE REAL NEEDS OF STUDENTS

As has been described in the initial chapter, one of the cornerstones of the middle school philosophy is to meet more adequately the physical, social, emotional, and intellectual needs of the transescent. The purposes of this chapter are to review some of the characteristics of the transescent, to examine the continuous progress movement, and to indicate advantages and disadvantages of implementing continuous progress. The chapter closes with guidelines for launching a continuous progress program.

BEHAVIORAL CHARACTERISTICS OF THE MIDDLE SCHOOL STUDENT

The rapid physiological changes which take place in transescents result in certain behavioral characteristics typical to the middle school student.

1. Awkwardness in bodily movements due to bone growth preceding muscle growth.
2. Concern with irregularities in physical development such as obesity, scars, acne, and much attention to physical appearance.
3. Conformity to popular styles in clothing and hair.
4. Talkativeness.
5. A great need to release physical energy as denoted by extreme restlessness.
6. Willingness to respond to a variety of nonstructured and leisure activities.

213

With their concern for appearance and popular styles, yet with a need to be themselves, students of middle school age exhibit certain social behaviors and attitudes.

1. They have a desire to conform to peer standards while being aware of adult standards of acceptable behavior.
2. Concern for "right" and "wrong"; stirrings of active altruism and worries about those less fortunate than themselves.
3. A strong need to belong to a peer group.
4. A desire for opportunities to exercise choices in food, recreation, and friendship selections, with frequent changes in friendships.

Enmeshed in their uncertainties and conflicts, middle school students have a tendency to:

1. Act impulsively in terms of language usage and in tasks; are impatient to get things done in a hurry.
2. Want to become independent, yet desire limits to be set.
3. Desire approval and acceptance from adults.
4. Need frequent success and recognition for personal efforts and achievements.
5. Exhibit instability in moods: anxious, then confident; calm, then boisterous.
6. Often delay action on suggestions by adults.
7. Be easily offended and sensitive to criticism.
8. Be anxious about their intellectual and physical development, social relationships, and adult authority.

In terms of their intellectual and physical development, middle school age students:

1. Are interested in both concrete and abstract exercises and are better able to deal with abstractions than formerly.
2. Desire opportunities to participate in practical problem-solving situations.
3. Are interested in making fuller use of basic skills learned in elementary school.
4. Display an interest in cultures and races other than their own.
5. Are curious and inquisitive.
6. Prefer an active to a passive role in learning activities.
7. Have short-term goals, and rarely sustain intense interests in various pursuits.
8. Prefer interaction with peers during learning activities.
9. Desire opportunities to express originality.
10. Want to evaluate their personal capabilities in terms of their attributes and limitations.

These are generalizations only. Individual students of the pre- and early adolescent years vary to some degree from these descriptions. Planners for a continuous progress program, however, must keep these generalizations in mind as they build programs to meet the general and individual needs of the middle school students.

Given these characteristics and needs, what kind of program might best meet them? To begin with, it is obvious that the program should provide optimum individualization of instruction for a population characterized by such wide variability. The program should feature continuing development with a curriculum which provides for (a) sequential concept development in general education areas, (b) major emphasis on learning how to learn (skills for continued learning), (c) balancing exploratory experiences with activities and services for personal development, and (d) values development. The program should also promote continuous progress.

CONTINUOUS PROGRESS EDUCATION

In 1963, Robert Anderson and John Goodlad published *The Nongraded Elementary School,* ushering in more than two decades of debate and writing on continuous education.[1] Their thesis was that rigidly enforced age-grade school organization inhibited learning of pupils, regardless of considerations of ability and interest.

Research in the behavioral sciences has continued to emphasize the uniqueness of the individual while educators have stressed the need for greater individualization of instruction. The philosophical basis of individualized instruction rests on the following assumptions.

1. Schools ought to be accountable for the maximum development of each individual.
2. Individuals have their own learning styles and rates.
3. Each person selects, from the learning environment, those experiences best utilized in the learning process.
4. Active participation in learning processes enhances learning effectiveness.

As most great movements are, the continuous progress movement is a complex set of ideas. Goodlad and Anderson are the first to admit that the movement toward continuous progress education is stalled because of a lack of understanding. Part of the problem stems from inadequate and incomplete conceptualizations. Not enough attention has been paid to how the components of schooling are affected when continuous progress values are applied.

Properly implemented, continuous progress can result in significant improvement in a school's potential for fostering desirable cognitive, affective, and psychomotor growth in children and youth.

A valid continuous progress program in a middle school must grow out of the needs and characteristics of middle school age students. It should be based on a belief in a commitment to the following.

1. Success in school is based on progress in learning rather than on attainment of prescribed standards of achievement within a prescribed length of time. Within this definition, almost all students can be successful in school.
2. The school's program, in terms of methods, materials, and extracurricular activities, must be designed to encourage, support, and reward progress in learning at whatever pace a student can sustain.
3. Learning objectives must be stated with enough flexibility so that all students can achieve them at a level sufficient to maintain self respect.
4. Specific behavioral objectives must be defined in such a way that progress can be visible to both student and teacher.
5. Continuous progress requires that evaluation by teacher and student be continuous in order that the student's needs be defined and prescriptions made.[2]

The continuous progress idea is not new to American education. The one-room rural school was a place where the idea was actually lived. But with urbanization and population increase, schools became larger and continuous progress education, once facilitated by a low pupil-teacher ratio, gave way to larger group instruction. Children were separated into age levels with a high pupil-teacher ratio.

Recent studies of the learner, of our culture, and of organized knowledge have renewed questions concerning the purposes of schools and their relations to the larger rapidly changing society. Goodlad emphasized that developing the learner as an individual and as a member of society is the primary function of the schools.[3] *Mastery by all learners of a specific body of knowledge or a set of skills is not the intent of these schools. Rather, knowledge and skills are valuable as a means by which individuals develop into fully participating members of society.*

The continuous progress movement has its roots in the nongraded movement, a movement which was relatively short-lived, yet useful in that it stimulated discussion and debate about the rigidities of the lockstep approaches which are built into the age-graded, self-contained model. The term ''nongraded'' is giving way to the term ''continuous progress,'' which suggests a broader concept of education. Included in this broader concept are prescriptive approaches to teaching; vertical growth; and horizontal approaches, defined as cooperative or collaborative endeavors among the teaching staff.

Advantages of Continuous Progress Education

1. Better teaching and learning opportunities occur when learning skill sequences are operationally defined to meet the needs of the learner.
2. Students are taught skills in learning sequences which range from readiness to competency or mastery; skill development is fostered.
3. The elimination of passing or failing does away with much of the threat that brings unhappiness in school.
4. Learners can move at their own pace without penalty of being failed simply because they haven't covered as much in a given year as is usually defined by ''grade.'' Faster students are not held back by their classmates. When multiaging is used in skill development programs, older students tend to become leaders when working with slower or younger children.
5. Multiaging frees students to make more contributions in relevant problem-solving work.
6. Repetition of material is avoided since the student begins the new year or term where he left off.
7. Gaps in instruction are avoided since there are no grades to skip.
8. Teamwork among faculty members is facilitated; collaborative planning allows faculty to evaluate and treat needs of individual students.
9. The greater flexibility in grouping procedures allows for more appropriate placement of youth for instructional and counseling purposes.
10. Since continuous progress programs focus more on the learning needs, the social needs, and the emotional needs of the students, the programs are problem solving in nature and result in a substantial reduction in behavior problems.
11. There is greater awareness of student individuality since meeting the individual needs of students is at the heart of the continuous progress program.
12. Where team teaching is used, there are greater opportunities for sharing insights on learner needs and progress.
13. There is no limit for the learning aspirations of students in a continuous progress program.

14. There is no fear of encroachment on materials supposedly reserved for another grade.
15. The "norm" in the continuous progress program is the individual student. Pressures for meeting end-of-term goals normally found in the age-graded programs are avoided. The placement of the student depends upon his readiness, capacity, competence, and social/emotional needs.[4]

Disadvantages of Continuous Progress Education

As with any program, there are disadvantages. The disadvantages are not cited by those engaging in continuous progress education but are enumerated by those who have a stake in maintaining the status quo. Those who have been involved in continuous progress programs are more likely to view difficulties in innovative programs as problems to be overcome. As the reader surveys the disadvantages listed below, it should be remembered that such disadvantages can be overcome by adequate leadership in the central administration and at the local school level.

1. Parents and teachers have been brought up in a graded atmosphere and have a bias for a grading system.
2. Establishing continuous progress programs requires development of new curricula or the programs will develop into mini-grades called levels.
3. There is a greater need for program articulation in such a design; otherwise, the student could suffer discontinuity as a result of going from an open system to a closed one.
4. School curricula are still organized around graded textbooks and topics. The effort required to create curriculum material based on a continuum of skills and concepts is excessive.
5. The teaching in a continuous progress program is demanding and difficult.
6. Special teacher preparation is required, including development of in-service programs.
7. Continuous progress requires greater staff diversity in order to be successful.
8. Continuous progress requires new record keeping and reporting practices since the traditional marking systems are no longer consistent with the aims of continuous progress education. These new developments take additional time. Record keeping and reporting practices are sensitive areas.[5]

This list of disadvantages contains pitfalls to be avoided. It is certainly true, for example, that the lay public and many of the professional educators have "grown up" on the age-graded mode of organization. The graded organization has been with us for over 100 years. Its continued viability rests on its simplicity. It is easier to administer a staff of 40 or more if the staff members are separated (divided) into single classrooms, and given separate teaching supplies and textbooks which can be bought for a cut rate in high volume. Easier and cheaper are equated with better.

Administrators who are saying continuous progress is too difficult may be saying that they don't believe teachers and administrators are dedicated enough to make it work. But is the age-graded school, begun at Boston's Quincy Grammar School in 1848, really the appropriate organization for schools of the 1990s? Playing one teacher or department off against the other, a common practice in age-graded schools, stifles professional and program development. Further, the age-graded model has no research basis whatever. It continues because it is easier, and its continued presence is a manifestation of culture lag. This condition can be overcome by a conscious, long-term public education effort, in-service programs for the professional staff, and hiring policies which have continuous progress programs in mind.

Making Continuous Progress a Reality

Before starting, the school leader needs to realize that the movement toward continuous progress education will be a time-consuming one. The message conveyed by school principals and supporting staff in central offices is basically the same; "It takes *years* to develop the staff and adapt curricular models and school organization to reach the continuous progress level of functioning."

Daniel Purdom in *Exploring the Nongraded School*[6] has set forth a list of propositions for the conceptual model of the continuous progress school.

1. The school assists each learner in developing his potential to the maximum.
2. The curriculum emphasizes the development of the broad structural concepts and modes of inquiry in the disciplines.
3. Learning opportunities are provided on the basis of individual needs, interests, and abilities.
4. All phases of human growth are considered when making decisions about how to work effectively with a learner.

5. Learning opportunities are paced so that each child can progress in relation to his own rate of development in each area of the curriculum.
6. An evaluation of all phases of human growth is made for each individual.
7. Evaluation of each learner's progress is carried on almost constantly.
8. The adequacy of each child's progress is an individual matter determined by appraising his attainments in relation to estimates of his potential.
9. The school is organized to facilitate continuous and cumulative learning for each learner throughout his schooling.
10. The school is so structured that there are alternate learning environments available to the individual and alternate opportunities within their environments to progress at different rates and work at different levels in each area of the curriculum.[7]
11. Each learner uses his own interests and needs to help establish the objectives he will pursue.

These propositions about the continuous progress school are excellent descriptions of an ideal, but how does a staff begin to approximate these functions?

Implementing the Continuous Progress Program

Assessing the current status of the school program is a necessary first step. It would be reasonable to assume that a given school would be strong in some areas, perhaps approaching the ideal, and traditional in other areas, closer to the age-graded model.

The extent to which a school is approximating continuous progress functions can be assessed by using an instrument created by Donald Purdom.[8] The information derived would do much to clarify whether a school is approximating the ideal or only claiming to be.

The best way to ensure that the school will function this way is to hire staff who accept this definition of school purpose and who will work to implement such a program. Without such acceptance of purpose, much conflict and little success will result.

The most crucial factor in making an innovation function at the instructional level is staff reeducation, and the kind of program called for in this instance is one carried on intensely and continuously over a period of time, such as two or three years.

Preparatory to launching the change program, local school leadership must gain a fundamental understanding of school purpose, defined as helping the learner fully develop his potential. The following sources should be examined carefully.

1. Bond, David, *Developing Student Autonomy in Learning,* London: Kogan Page, New York: Nichols Publishing Co., 1988.
2. Goodlad, John and Robert Anderson, *The Non-graded Elementary School.* New York: Harcourt Brace and Javonovich, (Revised, 1963); and New York: Teachers College Press (Revised, 1987).
3. Jay, M. Ellen, *Designing Instruction for Diverse Abilities and the Library Media Teacher's Role,* Hamden, Conn.: Shoe String Press, 1991.
4. Jeter, Jan, *Approaches to Individualized Education,* Alexandria, Va.: Association for Supervision and Curriculum Development, 1980.
5. Strickland, Bonnie B., *Developing and Implementing Individualized Education Programs,* Columbus, Ohio: Merrill, 1990.
6. Wang, Margaret C. and Herbert J. Walberg, *Adapting Instruction to Individual Differences,* Berkeley, Calif.: McCutchan Publishing Corp., 1985.

DEVELOPING AN UNDERSTANDING OF THE CURRICULUM

Next, the school staff must develop the broad conceptual framework for the curriculum. An understanding of the nature of key concepts and discipline structure can be gleaned from the following sources.

1. Brandt, Ronald S., ed., *Content of the Curriculum.* Yearbook of the Association for Supervision and Curriculum Development, 1988.
2. Glatthorn, Allan A., *Curriculum Leadership,* Glenview, Illinois: Scott, Foresman and Company, 1987.
3. Schubert, William H., *Curriculum, Perspective, Paradigm and Possibility,* New York: MacMillan Publishing Company, 1986.

The curriculum planner will need to use several techniques in identifying the broad concepts and inquiry modes in the various disciplines. These include consultation with subject matter specialists, investigating new curricular projects and materials developed by educators, and surveying publication of organizations such as the Association for Supervision and Curriculum (ASCD).

In order to be able to diagnose learner problems and prescribe appropriate instructional procedures and materials, attention must be given to developing a greater range of instructional resources.

The following considerations are essential.

1. Study budgeting and purchasing procedures with an eye toward reallocation of resources. Textbook money might be used to purchase trade books, some textbooks, audiovisual aids, and special reference materials, rather than numerous copies of the same textbook.
2. Establish a central resource area in order to reduce duplication and make a wider range of resources available.
3. Identify community resources, such as places to visit and people with special skills.
4. Purchase self-teaching materials to enhance the self-pacing aim of continuous progress programs. Programmed learning materials seem most likely examples, with special map skills, study skills, and reading kit materials now on the market which have self-checking features. Computer-assisted instruction looms on the horizon as breakthrough in this area. Although costs are currently high for total application, more schools are taking this route.

Record Keeping

Establishing an adequate record keeping system which can record all phases of human growth is essential if such data are to be used in working with the learner and in reporting to parents and other staff members. For example, data on social development, intelligence, aptitude, peer relationships, teacher observation, interest inventories, and attitudes ought to be included.

The prime consideration in development of a record keeping system for continuous progress education is *simplicity*. The system must be simple enough for students to enter and leave learning activities, whether these be short units, learning centers, laboratory areas, or learning packages without the need to reorganize whole classes or roomfuls of students. The advantages provided by computerizing these records are obvious.

Figure 12.1 is an example of such simplicity in terms of student progress individualized learning pacs. There are two main components to this simple system: a wall chart and a notebook using a single sheet for each pupil. Both wall chart and notebook students are to be added or deleted as movement occurs. Note that the wall chart has the students listed alphabetically on the left, with the pac titles listed at the top of the chart. As

STUDENT NAMES	PAC TITLES					
	Supply and Demand	Money and Banking	Where Our Food Comes From	Pond Life	Oxford General Store	Modern Farming
Andrea Apple						
Betty Barnes						
Clothilda Clark						
Dennis Dank						
Everetta Embezzler						
Fanny Frame						
Gerald Gibb						
Harry Hemp						

FIGURE 12.1
Wall Chart.

McLean, Harvard W. and David L. Killian. *How to Construct Individualized Learning Pacs.* Dubuque, IA: Kendall/Hunt Publishing Co., 1973, p. 50.

the student completes the package, his square under the appropriate pac is marked in some way, indicating that it is completed. In the teacher's notebooks (or on spreadsheets), the individual student's progress on a given pac is duly recorded.

Some records should be kept by the students themselves; others by teachers. In preparing the record keeping system, the teacher must ask two questions. (1) "What must I know about the student?" and (2) "How often do I need to know this?" The answers to these two questions will enable the teacher to design different kinds of record keeping devices for the students and the teacher. Instructional pacs which take several days to complete require an evaluation record keeping system which contains the following:

1. Evaluation devices which diagnose and record weaknesses.
2. Evaluation devices which provide feedback on progress.
3. Evaluation devices which determine and record the degree of mastery achieved.

Pupil-Kept Records

Record forms used by the students should be simplified enough for students to maintain them independently of the teacher. It is probable that students will need some training in the use of the system, yet the initial time investment should pay off handsomely in the eventual saving of teachers from some record keeping chores.

The records should be economically kept in terms of pupil time and clear enough to quickly show the teacher or aide what students have accomplished and what they are currently doing. When projects are to be done in sequence, use of the sign-up or check sheets can be maintained easily by the student: The student merely checks off the learning tasks completed. In a different kind of program, where students have the option to select activities in any order, a control sheet or card can be used. The activity titles are listed and students circle the titles they are currently working on. Later, upon finishing the activity, the student may place an X through the circle as shown in Figure 12.2.

Figure 12.2 illustrates the individual student's control card. The teacher (or aide) can tell at a glance what the student has done and is currently working on.

Missing from these examples are indicators as to whether objectives have been met and to what extent pupils are experiencing success. Bar graphs are an excellent means of showing scores on activity post assessments. If the teacher and pupil think it desirable (and the best forms of evaluation grow out of cooperative processes), the student's control card could be altered to show post-assessment scores. As shown in Figure 12.3, the filled in bar graph would indicate completion of the activity and the level of success on the post assessment.

The best forms of evaluation assess the extent to which established goals and objectives have been met. Assuming the objectives can be assessed via pencil and paper, the response items on the post-assessment instrument could be grouped by objectives so that the teacher and student

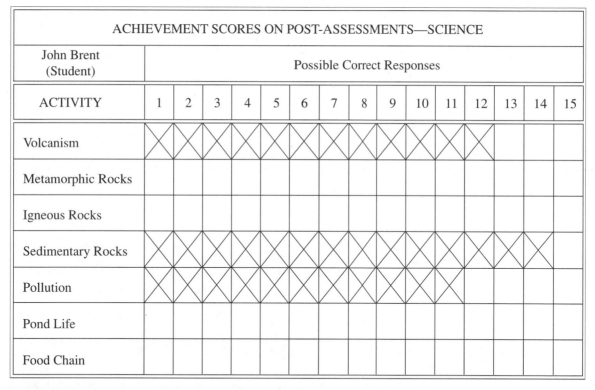

FIGURE 12.2
Student's Control Sheet.
McLean, Harvard W. and
David L. Killian. *How to
Construct Individualized
Learning Pacs.* Dubuque, IA:
Kendall/Hunt Publishing Co.,
1973, p. 51.

CONTINUOUS PROGRESS — Science

John Brent
(Name)

Pollution	Food Chain	Volcanism
Oceans	Ice Age	Pond Life
Metamorphic Rocks	Galileo	Tycho Brahe

ACHIEVEMENT SCORES ON POST-ASSESSMENTS—SCIENCE															
John Brent (Student)	Possible Correct Responses														
ACTIVITY	1	2	3	4	5	6	7	8	9	10	11	12	13	14	15
Volcanism	☒	☒	☒	☒	☒	☒	☒	☒	☒	☒	☒				
Metamorphic Rocks															
Igneous Rocks															
Sedimentary Rocks	☒	☒	☒	☒	☒	☒	☒	☒	☒	☒	☒	☒	☒		
Pollution	☒	☒	☒	☒	☒	☒	☒	☒	☒						
Pond Life															
Food Chain															

FIGURE 12.3
Individualized Student's Control Card.

McLean, Harvard W. and David L. Killian. *How to Construct Individualized Learning Pacs.* Dubuque, IA: Kendall/Hunt Publishing Co.,
1973, p. 52.

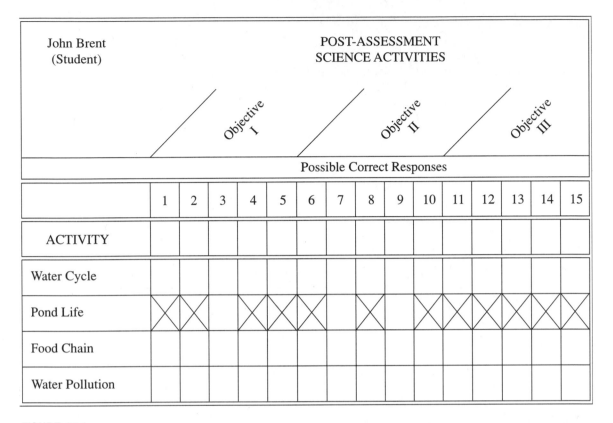

FIGURE 12.4
Student Achievement Card.

McLean, Harvard W. and David L. Killian. *How to Construct Individualized Learning Pacs.* Dubuque, IA: Kendall/Hunt Publishing Co., 1973.

could readily tell which objectives have been met and which ones may require "recycling." Figure 12.4 illustrates a chart showing this kind of feedback.

By grouping response items by objective and charting them as in Figure 12.4, both student and teacher can quickly ascertain that Objectives I and III were attained, but Objective II, with only three out of five correct responses, was not.

The types of records kept by the pupil can also include subjective rating scales whereby the student can evaluate his own work and check whether he thinks it is "Very Good," "Satisfactory", or "Needs Improvement."

Teacher-Kept Records

Carefully designed teacher-kept records are an absolute necessity if teachers are to successfully implement continuous progress education. Such records enable the teacher to plan the individual student's program. The design which a specific record will take depends on the purpose for which it is intended.

The individual student's profile assists the teacher in determining the student's academic achievements, describing strengths and weaknesses, and indicating social and study habits. Such information is necessary before learning can be set and appropriate learning activities selected.

Another type of record the teacher will want to keep is the checklist of student behaviors pertaining to successive approximations of a learning objective. For example, the objective might be: "Pupils will use the learning materials center on a voluntary basis in order to complete projects and side studies." The assessment technique is observation by the teacher. The assessment device is a checklist. The behaviors to be observed could be as follows:

1. Attendance at the learning materials center.
2. Use of the catalogue system in order to locate materials.
3. Use of a variety of learning materials to complete a project.
4. Voluntarily going to the learning materials center when time is available.

Figure 12.5 illustrates the type of checklist which would be useful in recording progress on this objective.

In managing a system of records for groups and for individuals, the teacher still must keep a perspective on the overall progress of the class. For this purpose, a class profile sheet is indispensable in each academic area for the core team in the middle school. The matter is simplified for the secondary school subject matter specialist. The profile sheet can be in the form of a chart based on the teacher's class list and provide spaces for subject matter data. These data could be depicted as checklists, graphs, a series of scores, or a tally. The class profile sheet can assist the teacher in planning the grouping of students with specific learning needs.

FACULTY TEAMS

Organizing the faculty into teams facilitates planning. With provisions made for a common planning time, members of the team can discuss the student's performances in all areas and develop instructional units which meet the needs and interests assigned to the team. The area of team teaching is so crucial that a separate chapter is devoted to this topic.

DATES	Attendance	Catalog System	Variety of Materials	Goes Voluntarily	Observer Comments
BEHAVIORS					
January 5				(Assigned by Teacher)	
January 12				(Assigned by Teacher)	Needed Assistance from Librarian
January 17				(Assigned by Study Group)	Used Catalog Well
February 3				(Assigned by Study Group)	No Reluctance— Worked Readily
February 10					

X = participation

Observer summary: Excellent progress over a five-week period. Growth in independent use of materials. Last attendance was for individual study.

FIGURE 12.5
Student Achievement Card.
McLean, Harvard W. and David L. Killian. *How to Construct Individualized Learning Pacs.* Dubuque, IA: Kendall/Hunt Publishing Co., 1973, p. 54.

EVALUATION

Although evaluation is also a separate chapter, a few ideas concerning this topic will be presented here. A teacher needs to have knowledge about the status of the learner such as abilities, current needs, and interests, all of which are derived from the evaluative process.

If all phases of human growth are to be considered in creating learning environments, evaluation will have to be carried on continuously, and a variety of assessment settings and instruments will need to be identified.

Use of *The Mental Measurement Yearbook*[9] and *Tests in Print*[10] are a good beginning point in searching for a variety of commercially prepared assessment instruments. Specialists in various forms of evaluation can be contacted, such as the reading specialist from the area university who can suggest the most effective diagnostic instruments for comprehension or word-attack skills.

There are areas for which instruments are not readily available. In such cases, other plans must be made. Assessment of emotional maturity could be an example. It is likely that the development of questionnaires, interviews, and observation checklists would allow staff to *infer* emotional maturity.

Once the necessary tools and procedures have been identified for the evaluation system, an in-service program must be undertaken to assure that the staff will be able to use the tools and procedures.

Because of the continuity of the evaluation task in the continuous progress school, it is important that as many self-assessing instructional materials and instruments be purchased as possible. This promotes implementation of the evaluation program and self-reliance as well.

VARIATIONS OF LEARNING ENVIRONMENTS

Given the tremendous variability among the students of middle school age, it should be obvious that no one learning environment would be sufficient. Seeking variations in learning environments is one of the most important tasks of the school leader and his staff. Several approaches can be used to inject alternatives into the learning program.

1. Manipulate the peer group through multiaging via creation of age ranges in instructional groups of two or three years. A talented 12-year-old may not have sufficient challenge if he is placed only with other 12-year-olds. Other approaches in alteration of the peer groups include placing the learner with a group of more socially mature learners, or less (or more) academically mature learners.
2. Alternate the modes of instruction. Instruction can be provided through use of machines, teachers, or use of independent study materials, and in a variety of groupings. Some learners need to have a teacher present; others learn best in peer groups which are allowed to interact. Some students prefer printed matter; others audiovisual materials.

3. Vary the expected performance levels for the learners. Given the fact that learners *within themselves* vary in their ability to perform in different curricular and extracurricular functions, it is clear that numerous levels of proficiency must be provided for. Some students will pursue a given academic area with vigor and to a sophisticated extent with highly specialized materials; others will not have such a capability and will need middle or low-level demands on their capacities.

4. Organize the students into units which span several years and which represent a fairly wide range of instructions.[11] A learner could go outside the unit for special instruction if necessary. The units could operate on a continuous basis and students could move from unit to unit according to need. The change from one unit to the next could be based on needs for different peer groups, for a different teacher, for a change in instructional mode, or special academic subject need.

SUMMARY

The concept of continuous progress is not new. In fact, it preceded the graded organization of schools. Many of the developmental characteristics of transescents, or students of middle school age, require careful consideration in instructional planning and in the selection of learning activities. A singular teaching approach focused on large group instruction—with all students expected to make similar progress—simply fails to provide the individualization needed by this age group.

The increasingly wide range of variability of needs and interests of these students calls for optimal individualization of instruction and a curriculum which provides for continuous concept development in general areas. It also calls for a strong emphasis on development of skills for continuous learning, a blend of exploratory activities with suitable experiences for personal development, and an emphasis on values development.

This high degree of individualization of instruction requires considerable planning time and extensive record keeping by both teacher and student. The development and use of simple but systematic record forms can greatly facilitate evaluation and planning by those involved.

ENDNOTES

1. Goodlad, John I., and Robert H. Anderson. *The Nongraded Elementary School.* New York: Teachers College Press, 1987. (Reprinted)

2. Watson, Carlos M., Vanita Gibbs, and Ralph H. Jones. "Continuous Progress: An Idea, a Method, an Organization." *Contemporary Education* 42 (1971).

3. Goodlad, John I. *Teachers for Our Nation's Schools.* San Francisco: Jossey-Bass, 1990.

4. Hillson, Maurie, and Ronald T. Hyman, eds. Excerpts from *Change and Innovation in Elementary and Secondary Organization.* 2nd edition. Chicago: Holt, Rinehart and Winston, Inc., 1971. Reprinted by permission of the publisher.

5. Ibid.

6. Purdom, Daniel M. *Exploring the Nongraded School.* Dayton, Ohio: Institute for the Development of Educational Activities, 1970.

7. Ibid.

8. Purdom, Daniel M. "A Conceptual Model of the Nongraded School." (Unpublished Ed. D. dissertation, University of California at Los Angeles, 1968.)

9. Conoley, Jane-Close ed. *The Mental Measurement Yearbook.* Lincoln: University of Nebraska Press, 1989.

10. Mitchell, J. V., Jr. ed. *Tests in Print III* Lincoln: University of Nebraska Press, 1983.

11. Purdom, Daniel M. *Exploring the Nongraded School,* p. 35.

REFERENCES

Bond, David. *Developing Student Autonomy in Learning.* London: Kogan Page and New York: Nichols Publishing Company, 1988.

Brandt, Ronald S., ed. *Content of the Curriculum.* Yearbook of the Association for Supervision and Curriculum Development, 1988.

Conoley, Jane-Close, ed. *The Mental Measurement Yearbook.* Lincoln, Nebr.: University of Nebraska Press, 1989.

Glatthorn, Allan A. *Curriculum Leadership.* Glenview, Ill.: Scott, Foresman and Company, 1987.

Goodlad, John I. *Teachers for Our Nation's Schools.* San Francisco: Jossey-Bass Publishers, 1990.

Goodlad, John I., and Robert H. Anderson. *The Nongraded Elementary School.* New York: Teachers College Press (Reprinted), 1987.

Hillson, Maurie, and Ronald T. Hyman. eds. *Change and Innovation in Elementary and Secondary Organization,* 2nd edition. Chicago: Holt, Rinehart and Winston, Inc., 1971.

Jay, M. Ellen. *Designing Instruction for Diverse Abilities and the Library Media Teacher's Role.* Hamden, Conn.: Shoe String Press, 1991.

Jeter, Jan. *Approaches to Individualized Education.* Alexandria, VA.: Association for Supervision and Curriculum Development, 1980.

McLean, Harvard W., and David L. Killian. *How to Construct Individualized Learning Pacs.* Dubuque, Iowa: Kendall/Hunt Publishing Company, 1973.

Mitchell, J.V., Jr., ed. *Tests in Print III.* Lincoln, Nebr.: The University of Nebraska Press, 1983.

Purdom, Daniel M. *A Conceptual Model of the Nongraded School.* Unpublished Ed. D. Dissertation. U.C.L.A., 1988.

————. *Exploring the Nongraded School.* Dayton, Ohio: Institute for the Development of Educational Activities, Inc., 1970.

Schubert, William H. *Curriculum: Perspective, Paradigm and Possibility.* New York: Macmillan Publishing Company, 1986.

Strickland, Bonnie B. *Developing and Implementing Individualized Education Programs.* Columbus: Merrill, 1990.

Wang, Margaret C., and Herbert J. Walberg. *Adapting Instruction to Individualized Differences.* Berkeley: McCutchan Publishing Corporation, 1985.

Watson, Carlos M., Vanita Gibbs, and Ralph H. Jones. *"Continuous Progress: An Idea, a Method, an Organization."* Contemporary Education, 42 (1971).

PART IV

Chapter Thirteen discusses the increased range and number of problems of a personal and social nature, along with academic difficulties, of students in this age group. This calls for a guidance program that involves all of the middle school's professional personnel in helping students make the transition from the self-contained elementary classroom to the highly departmentalized high school. Guidance is also seen as a function which occurs not only in a formal advisory setting but also goes on throughout the school day in a variety of situations.

Chapter Fourteen deals with the changing social needs of the transescent that require programs of social activity which are appropriate in terms of their match with the maturity levels of the students. The kinds of programs with wholesome social contacts which satisfy these student needs and which fit the maturity of the students are discussed. A variety of possible activities are suggested.

Guidance for the Middle School

INTRODUCTION

There is little doubt that today's middle school children lead complex lives that are impacted by a myriad of pressures and demands from a variety of sources. Educators seek to provide a total middle school experience that enables children to progress through school and develop the ability to face the demands of everyday life—as much as possible—with security, confidence, and freedom from anxiety. How should these educational experiences be implemented to maximize cognitive, affective, and psychomotor skills growth? Finally, from what vantage point can accomplishment be best determined? Many of these concerns for the success of middle school children can be effectively resolved by those who are most responsible for child guidance.

It should be pointed out that guidance is not synonymous with counseling as it is applied to middle school aged children. Counseling is a component of guidance in much the same way that teaching is related to instruction. As with instruction, guidance should be viewed as an integral part of the middle school child's total learning experiences.

The child is the central focus in the middle school program. Educational components such as guidance are brought to bear as needed upon the child's development. Cole states that, "A middle school guidance program must be based on a thorough understanding of what is normal growth and development for youngsters at this stage of life."[1] This also serves to broaden the experiential environment of the child. In the case of *guidance*, these resources are as varied as the lives of individual children. Therefore, it becomes a goal of the middle school program to help the child through the use of all the components of guidance.

KEY COMPONENTS

The key guidance components for the middle school child are the parents, the teachers, the school administrator, and the school counselor. While it would be expected that any one of these could exert greater influence than another, it is nonetheless important to recognize that in varying degrees, each makes a valuable contribution to guidance. The typical middle school child receives guidance from all four persons listed above, usually in proportion to the amount of interaction the child has with each. Each component has specific characteristics and elements which, when appropriately utilized, enables each to function in a most effective manner.

Parents

Generally, those adults who have the greatest impact upon the development of children are their parents. Parents provide a home environment that in many ways precludes all other efforts to influence the youngster through non-parental guidance measures. Their guidance actions, deliberate or unintentional, vastly shape the direction of attitude and self-concept.

The role of parents in middle school guidance must be carefully examined and appropriate methodologies utilized to integrate their efforts into a program which effectively meets the needs of the child. Claire Cole emphasizes that, ''Parents and other community members can extend the guidance program beyond the school walls. Group sessions with parents can often be held outside the school building, focusing on how transescents develop, how to assist with career exploration, how to encourage academic achievement, and other topics of interest to parents.''[2]

To insure that parents are making effective contributions to guidance for the middle school, these factors need to be examined.

1. Are the parents providing a home environment that will enable the child to fit into society? It is most imperative that parents understand the extent of their influence upon their children. All children desperately need consistency, particularly in establishing a positive value system. If a child arrives at school with a confused or negative self-concept, it behooves the middle school to work with both the youngster as well as his parents to develop more appropriate modes of coping.

2. As guidance facilitators, many parents need to receive specific training at parenting. Consequently, the middle school should establish a program for parent education. Parents should not be

asked to meet their responsibilities alone; the middle school should actively seek a partner relationship with parents through the availability of guidance services.

3. Every middle school should make its guidance services and expertise known to the home. Whereas there may be an excellent program in the school, its usefulness is restricted when the parents are unaware of its existence.

4. All members of the middle school staff should make a very deliberate effort to work with parents. John Meyers in his research finds that, ''Relations between home and school, as well as between the school and the community, improve as parents become involved. What goes on in school is no longer a name.''[3] Not only is this a prerequisite in keeping the home informed, it is also most necessary in maintaining a dialog between these two guidance entities.

5. Parents should feel favorably inclined toward their child's utilization of the guidance services within the middle school. To insure parents' support for the schools' guidance efforts, they should be encouraged to visit the school to openly discuss any fears or concerns they may have about the guidance process. Emotional irrationality on the part of parents is no excuse for child underdevelopment.

6. Parents need to be strongly aware that they can provide invaluable guidance for their children by setting appropriate standards of expectation. Unlike ''making demands,'' setting appropriate standards offers worthwhile motivational targets that are achievable. Indeed, most children want to please their parents whether it be in academic accomplishment, discipline, or in becoming integral members of society.

School Administrator

As the middle school expands its guidance function, administrative leadership should be at the forefront in the role of change agent. It is not sufficient for the administrator to merely provide information regarding the availability of services—the current thrust of this leadership position becomes one of inspiring and insuring planning, implementation, coordination, evaluation, and revision for utilizing the various components of the guidance program. Claire Cole emphasizes that the principal, ''As the instructional leader of the school, is the person who allocates resources; time, space, equipment, supplies, and perhaps personnel. Along with provisions of adequate space, staff, and materials, enthusiasm for the kind of innovation that is desirable in a middle school guidance program is an administrative imperative.''[4]

To a large extent, then, the middle school guidance program will succeed or fail on the actions or inactions of the school administrator. The achievement of those tasks that are most essential for success are included in the following.

1. It is vital for the school principal to be knowledgeable in the field of guidance. The principal's applied knowledge of guidance becomes one of the pivots upon which this whole effort hinges.

2. The principal must look for those outside of his office for meaningful contributions toward this effort. The most effective educational programs—including middle school guidance programs—are those with input by all who have a stake in its outcome. Such a flow of information and exchange of ideas can only serve to enhance the guidance program's chances of success.

3. In seeking to include others in developing an exemplary guidance program, the principal must make it clear that this process will be made on a democratic, interactive basis. Since the eventual guidance program will be a *tool* for everyone affiliated with the school, it is important that these individuals have an opportunity to make meaningful contributions to the program consistent with their collective knowledge, beliefs, and attitudes.

4. A comprehensive training component should be established to enable the staff to fully unitize the guidance functions of the school. Such in-service would certainly vary with the needs and personalities of the staff. However, it is suggested that sequentially phased in-service be provided to permit greater or lesser training for staff members, depending upon their existing knowledge of middle school guidance and/or anticipated needs in this area.

5. Once training has been completed, the school principal should encourage the full utilization of the guidance program. Above all, the principal must set the tone toward maintaining growth in sound guidance efforts.

6. The school principal should seek to broaden internal and external acceptance of the middle school's guidance program. One highly favorable avenue toward gaining support is through continuous, positive publicity. The leadership role of the principal can be used to overcome any "pockets of resistance" to the school's guidance program as well as to maintain or increase support for its continued development. Like all matters of interest to the school, the guidance program must be constantly promoted as a viable part of the process of education if public support is to remain in force.

Teachers

From both an organizational and application construct, it is the teachers who form the first level of guidance for the middle school child. As these trained personnel interact with their students, they assist young people with personal and social growth along with the day-to-day academics. In his volume, *The Middle School*, Donald Eichhorn states that, ". . . the fundamental core of counselors in the middle school should be the instructional staff. Boys and girls encountering emotional problems due to atypical growth patterns should be aided in meeting these concerns first and foremost by the school personnel with whom they are most intimately associated."[5]

This interaction of the affective domain with the cognitive and psycho-motor is of crucial importance since many potential school problems can be alleviated through the teacher's efforts. Elliot Merenbloom states that, "Teachers must play a major role in the guidance and counseling program of the middle school. With a background in each adolescent development and in some subject, the teacher must be committed to meeting the guidance needs of students through the medium of the particular subject."[6]

In particular, the following teacher contributions are most important in the development of middle school guidance.

1. To be well prepared, the teachers must be aware of the nature and needs of the transescent child. Ideally, they see as "typical" the middle school youngster who possesses a unique complexity of socio-emotional intellectuality. The teachers understand that middle school children's unpredictability is itself predictable.

2. The teacher must have a strong willingness to actively participate on various committees and teams that serve the holistic needs of the child within the school. In essence, guidance committees or teams in which the classroom professional should become involved may be highly defined or loosely structured, but they are nonetheless a viable means for coordinating the child's total school program.

3. The teacher should also be able and willing to become seriously committed as a teacher-advisor to students. One such device is aptly named the "advisor-advisee" program. In this framework, every student is assigned to a teacher who functions as the student's immediate resource person. In the publication "*This We Believe*," the National Middle School Association states the following: "Each transescent learner needs an adult who teaches him or her well and is in a position to give individual attention.

Therefore, the middle school should be organized so that every youngster has such an adult, one who has a special responsibility for the individual's academic and personal welfare."[7]

4. If teachers are to be effective contributors to the development of a strong middle school guidance program, they must be able to interpret and apply appropriate testing data for the purpose of assisting students. These skills are especially important in helping the child with academic decision making along with career exploration and planning. Parents can also benefit from the teacher's explanation of such data.

5. The middle school teacher must be able to recognize *atypical* student behavior such as abrupt changes in moods, attitudes, and/or work habits. Once it has been determined that a child needs special help for correcting personal-social maladjustment, such as emotional instability or chronic physical illness, the teacher must be willing to take the time and effort to construct an informed, factual referral and see it through to completion.

6. The teacher should also be willing to continue training in the affective area. Improved effectiveness in this domain can come from the acquisition of improved skills. The teacher should be willing to attend in-service activities or take additional graduate level classes to attain a higher level of proficiency.

7. The teacher can contribute a great deal of guidance through maintaining a continuous, caring, and accepting attitude toward students. When children feel good about themselves, the realization of expectations is more easily accomplished. William Purkey emphasizes the need for sending positive, inviting messages to students. He states that, "The belief system of teachers, communicated in their inviting or disinviting messages, has a significant impact on student attitudes and behavior."[8]

Teachers must remember that their role as the front line of contacts with students should not be minimized. The role of the classroom instructor is of primary importance in the guidance area. In a recent publication about the teacher-advisor program, the authors, Robert and Linda Myrick, conclude that, "It is clear that counselors, or other specialists, cannot accept total responsibility for guidance and counseling. Good teaching is still, and always will be, the heart of good school guidance."[9]

Counselors

The counselor in the middle school plays an important and pivotal role in guidance. This person assists parents in carrying out the humanistic responsibilities of the home, advises the school principal in matters relating to the school's overall affective program, confers with teachers concerning the performance of their guidance efforts, and meets with students to help them with difficulties or needs of a personal nature. It is within these distinct relationships with parents, administrators, teachers, and students that the primary task of the counselor is synthesized; to provide direction and support for the efforts of others in their involvement with the guidance process.

The counselor must be able to "wear many hats." This person functions as a consultant, advisor, confidant, and friend. Special skills must be utilized in applying programs, integrating curriculum, and providing leadership to student development. It becomes apparent, then, that the success of the counselor is greatly dependent upon this person's interactions with other faculty members. The counselor must be able to support the various personalities in the guidance network, and they, too, must be able to support the counselor.

The counselor's most vital role is that of providing support for the students in their caseloads. The impact that a counselor can make on students is immense, but this is not always the situation that actually takes place. In looking at research conducted with middle school students, James Beane states that, "In our research we have asked transescents to tell us who influences their thinking about themselves or, in other words, who are the 'significant others' in their lives. As it turns out, none has ever mentioned a guidance counselor in this role. This does not mean that no guidance counselor has ever helped a transescent; rather that young people in our studies have not perceived such professionals as significant influences."[10] Obviously then, counselors must exhibit and implement meaningful practices to reverse this perception.

Those areas of responsibility most common to a middle school counselor are as follows.

1. The initial requirement of middle school counselors is the ability to construct an appropriate guidance program. Their energies are applied to assisting directly in the planning, organizing, implementing, and evaluation of a broad-based affective program for

the school. They realize that their knowledge and expertise can be utilized in helping others to help children, rather than trying to "go it alone."

2. In sharing guidance knowledge and expertise with others, the counselor must remain acutely aware of the *fishbowl* syndrome. It is important that other personnel in the building, as well as the parents, view with favor and appreciation the contributions of the counselor.

3. Counselors should be high visibility affective leaders. They should not wait for problems to come to their doorsteps; rather, they should seek out matters in need of attention—before they become crises.

4. As part of guidance development in the middle school, counselors must be able and willing to demonstrate professional/affective competency. In this effort, the counselor should seek to help individual faculty members as well as parents in their guidance roles. Cole emphasizes that, "The consultation role of working with parents and teachers, which has been central to elementary counseling, is essential preparation for the middle grades professional."[11]

5. In addition to concern for his own professional self-improvement, the counselor must also encourage the continuous training and retraining of school personnel to meet the needs of the transescent. Carefully planned periodic school in-service activities can be used to both inform and recharge the school personnel's awareness and enthusiasm toward the affective process.

6. The middle school counselor must be willing to participate in a multitude of student-related conferences. These meetings may involve a variety of interested others such as parents, administrators, teachers, and specialized personnel, along with perhaps the students themselves. Attendance at these meetings will not only keep the counselor informed, but will also give this person the opportunity to have input into the direction of the development of students.

7. The most obvious counselor role—although not the only important one—is that of guidance counselor for the students. Here, the counselor should engage in individual and/or group developmental strategies in which the student is given assistance in solving problems and/or fulfilling needs. To be both affective and effective, the counselor must be perceived by students as one who accepts them for who they are, regardless of circumstances. Consequently, the counselor should not be required to deal with student discipline.

Other Components

There are several other components that also impact the effectiveness of a comprehensive middle school guidance program. These components vary from district to district in terms of availability and resources. Cole lists the following as some of the additional components which may enhance those that are already in place.[12]

1. Division level staff.
2. Agency personnel and other professionals.
3. University professors.
4. State Department of Education.
5. Paraprofessionals and clerical assistants.

When each of the aforementioned components is integrated into an effective whole that works together for the benefit of the middle school student, guidance takes on meaning and relevance. To a large degree, the destiny of effective middle schools is largely within the grasp of meaningful guidance practices. Each component is of vital importance. It is only when all components are integrated into middle school guidance and applied to its child-centered philosophy, however, that their usefulness can be fully appreciated.

STRUCTURING THE CHANGE PROCESS

To be sure, there are numerous and varied ways in which to initiate change in just about any human endeavor. For the change process to be effectively applied to a middle school guidance program, an atmosphere of interactivity, understanding, and support is essential. Here, the probability of acceptance is greater because all those who share in its involvement are given appropriate information and encouragement to participate in its implementation.

Schools today are encouraged to participate in and implement the "School Improvement Process" to bring about meaningful and lasting change. The formation of a School Improvement Team should include counselor representatives and parents who can interact with the other participants to evaluate, study, and recommend changes that can include numerous facets of the guidance and counseling program. Guidance is but one facet of the total school program, but its importance should not be minimized in the overall School Improvement Process.

Out of the priorities of the School Improvement Process may come the need for further subcommittee work in the area of guidance. This would result in a more detailed analysis of the guidance program that will culminate in appropriate changes.

THE SECURITY FACTOR

The typical middle school youngster is a child of many fears. To varying degrees, fears harm the educational development of a middle school student. A fearful child is frequently a slower developing child, because fears have a way of interfering with learning. A fearful child cannot learn with a maximum efficiency and effectiveness. At their minimum, fears cause distractions; at their maximum, total learning blockage. It remains, then, as one of the primary guidance tasks of the middle school to deal with students' fears and anxieties. If student-centeredness is truly the philosophical core of the middle school, it follows that any student need, including those associated with fear, should be met.

What actually is meant by security for the middle school? It is not locks on the classroom doors nor the removal of all bullies from the educational environment. Nor should there be even a hint that security creates a Utopian haven where youngsters can enter, leaving all fears behind. But if these are what security is not, what is it? Perhaps, put in a brief, simple form, security is attitudinal. It describes feelings about the environment within which the individual exists and functions.

In a recent publication from the NASSP, Sherrel Bergman states that, "The need for security and affection, which creates a feeling of being wanted and a sense of belonging," is one of the four needs related to early adolescent's emotions.[13] Provisions in the comprehensive guidance programs of middle schools should then be ready to meet such needs.

To achieve an atmosphere of security for students, the efforts of the staff must be realistically conceived, properly planned, thoughtfully organized, and objectively controlled. Staff involvement and commitment is needed: Who is going to do what and when? Along with this, some sort of visible structure is necessary to insure consistency, understanding, and completion of the fundamental principles relating to the security factor.

The modern middle school professional knows that the only realistic solution for providing for security lies in utilizing teachers as well as counselors. When all teaching members of the staff are included in a guidance capacity, both the efficiency and effectiveness of the entire school's affective efforts are increased, thereby enhancing the security factor. Whether these teachers assume their additional role under titles such as "teacher-advisor" or "student advisor" is not critical. Their function is what is important: to provide for student security through attention to affective education. As such the "advisor-advisee" program in the middle school is one of great value. It is an integral part of any effective mode of organization.

THE ADVISOR—ADVISEE PROGRAM

Rationale

One need only refer to the recent publication about effective middle schools to understand the critical importance of implementing a meaningful advisor-advisee program as part of the school's organization. In the publication, *"An Agenda For Excellence,"* the National Association of Secondary School Principals states that schools must: "Institute student advisement programs that assure each student regular, compassionate, and supportive counsel from a concerned adult about his or her academic progress, adjustment to school, and personal adjustment. While this does not replace professional counseling, it provides a consultation system to give students immediate assistance with their problems."[14] Recently the Carnegie Council, in its study, *"Turning Points,"* emphatically recommended that middle level schools need to have "small group advisories that ensure that every student is known well by at least one adult."[15]

Parents are also strong advocates for advisor-advisee programs. In a new publication from the National Middle School Association, the authors state that when interviewing parents, they asked, "What would you like for the middle level school to provide for your child?" The second most frequently cited type of response was "I want to know that when my child is in school that he/she knows at least one adult well enough to go to if support is needed."[16]

Further support for the advisor-advisee program can be found in the many middle schools that have already made it part of their overall program. Many schools still have not implemented advisor-advisee programs, however. They have provided for many other components of effective middle schools, but for reasons that vary, the students in those schools do not have the opportunity to have their total affective needs met. Michael James concludes that, "Until the establishment of the middle school movement with its advisor/advisee, homebased, or teacher/advisee programs, relatively little has been done to implement fully programs that were directed at developing the socio-emotional side of youth."[17]

Definition

In order to fully understand the functions, goals, and activities of an advisor-advisee program, one should initially consider a definition of the concept. Alfred Arth, in an unpublished paper, defines the program as "a preplanned period during the school day which affords the students an opportunity to discuss with peers or an adult both academic and humane school life space concern in order to assure optimum efficiency in relation to the disposition of the challenges of the learning environment."[18] The important consideration in this definition is that the program is preplanned and organized. It is built into the regular school schedule and occurs each day.

Purpose and Goals

A successful program in any school must possess a clear statement of purpose and a list of goals. The National Middle School Association provides the following statement as an example of a purpose statement:

> The advisory component is a planned program in which school staff members develop special relationships with their students as they help them understand self and others and learn to cope with and be happy in the world in which they live.[19]

Another example of an advisor-advisee program statement of philosophy and objectives is found at Jefferson Middle School in Jefferson, Wisconsin. Their statement is as follows:

> PHILOSOPHY: The advisor-advisee system in the Jefferson Middle School is a function of the school guidance program whereby an advisor (teacher) and his advisees meet daily for the purpose of developing, in a family atmosphere, personal and interpersonal skills and building warm, human relationships.[20]

Page Middle School (Lamphere Schools) in Madison Heights, Michigan, provides the following rationale and benefits for students.

> RATIONALE: The Student Advisor Guidance Experience (SAGE) serves as an extension of the guidance function of the middle school. As such, it can provide an "early warning" system to detect those students who may be experiencing social or emotional adjustment problems. This program makes an effort to enhance students' self-concept and improve interpersonal relationships. More simply stated, SAGE serves as a home base for many children who may need an atmosphere of security and reassurance during the crucial years when physical, social, intellectual, and emotional changes occur at a dramatic rate.

> BENEFITS FOR STUDENTS: Students who develop a positive relationship with an adult learn more in school and feel better about themselves. Students who feel better about themselves feel better about school, society, and people in general. Students who feel good about other people are capable of caring and tend to be more successful. These simple cause-and-effect statements describe what happens to students who identify with their SAGE group and find that at least one person cares about them and is willing to care over a span of years. This caring encourages students to work harder in school.[21]

Each school must work carefully to develop its own vision of a teacher/advisor program. This vision must be stated in writing and become the guiding beacon for all subsequent advisor-advisee activities.

Implementation

There are some important points of caution which need to be noted in relation to the advisor-advisee program. It is relatively easy to attain staff agreement that such a program is a relevant and meaningful part of any effective middle school. It is another matter entirely to achieve consensus among staff members that the program should be part of their middle school.

Prior to developing a program, an assessment must be completed to determine the school's readiness for an advisor-advisee program. Researchers Henderson and LaForge provide four steps to consider. They include the following.

1. The morale of administrators, teachers, and students. Teacher-advisor (T-A) programs are most successful when they are implemented in healthy school environments.
2. The school's position on affective education. A T-A program can become an integral part of the instructional process when policy-makers, administrators, and faculty members acknowledge the relationship between the cognitive and affective domains of students.
3. The support of the school administration. A T-A program cannot become a reality without administrative support. School administrators demonstrate support by a willingness to provide time for the program in the master schedule, provide paid in-service training, and allocate a reasonable budget for materials and resources.
4. The presence of a guidance and counseling program. T-A programs are not a replacement for a school counselor or a guidance and counseling program.[22]

Every effort must be exerted to insure that the staff is *buying* into the advisement program. This is not a simple task to achieve. In an article about the teacher-advisor program, the authors state, "Despite the importance of advisory groups in middle schools, there has been considerable resistance. Usually some 20 percent of the teachers quickly embrace the concept while another 20 percent are skeptical or clearly negative and are reluctant to be involved."[23] Clearly, then, there is work that must be done with the staff of any school.

A sure way to hasten the program's demise is to implement by administrative decree. The top-down method of program implementation will surely lead to a genuine lack of enthusiasm for most administrative recommendations. Administrative support is critical for the advisor-advisee process, but a carefully developed structure with which to disseminate knowledge to the staff about the philosophy, goals, and structure of advisement programs will most likely result in obtaining necessary support for its implementation.

A school can initiate its efforts by providing for in-service sessions devoted to the study and discussion of the advisor-advisee program. These should be conducted by knowledgeable consultants. Such an introduction calls for a standard frame of reference to be developed, around which the staff can evaluate and increase understanding about the program. Any myths, fallacies, misconceptions, or misunderstandings about teacher advisement can be resolved during this process.

It is extremely important to be aware of all sources of teacher resistance that may result when the advisor-advisee program is presented to the staff of any school. Dr. James Costar of Michigan State University lists eight points of resistance that may be encountered. It is not inappropriate to review these points of resistance with the staff at an in-service meeting. Complete honesty and openness is essential. Give the staff ample opportunities to discuss each point of resistance. This will go a long way toward developing ownership and confidence in the program. These include the following.

1. Lack of understanding.
2. Lack of time for guidance.
3. Lack of sufficient skills for guidance.
4. Lack of suitable materials.
5. Lack of interest in students.
6. Resentment of counselors.
7. General resistance to change itself.
8. Fear that students are unprepared.[24]

Each of the points of resistance must be acknowledged, and efforts must be expanded to overcome them during the provided in-service.

Subsequent in-service sessions can be devoted to discussing advisement content and examining already existing programs. This should definitely include on-site visitations of such programs. The study of available literature and research will contribute to increasing the likelihood of a staff *buying* into implementing an advisor-advisee program for its school. After a year of study of the advisor-advisee concept, most middle school staffs will be ready to make a decision regarding its adoption. Total staff consensus must be arrived at for the program to truly succeed.

We must never forget that the program will succeed, fail, or continue to exist primarily as a result of teacher attitude. Consistent support for the staff must be provided. Gordon Vars states, "Asking a teacher to be both instructor and advisor to a group of students requires a shift in roles that may be difficult for some."[25] When we acknowledge this, it will be easier to understand concerns and make any reasonable effort to resolve them.

A timetable for implementation can be broken down into several steps. Too much unfamiliar activity in too short a period of time will result in a difficult and unsuccessful implementation. A staff is much more agreeable and cooperative when it is part of the planning. It pays to observe a cautious, deliberate period of implementation. During an in-service presentation to a middle school staff, Costar recommends using the following seven steps for achieving a successful program.

1. Principal must actively support the program.
2. Thoroughly orient and train the staff.
3. Organize a Steering Committee that must include the principal.
4. Begin implementation with a core of volunteers.
5. Provide continued in-service for the volunteers.
6. Acquire and/or develop group guidance materials.
7. Begin with one grade at a time.[26]

The benefit of such a timetable is that it will allow for the program to utilize volunteer staff members who are the most enthusiastic about the advisement concept. They will be the most likely to achieve success. Such efforts will undoubtedly be recognized by others among the staff. For the most part, this initial success will be contagious. Continued in-service opportunities must be conducted with the rest of the staff at this time as well. It will take three years for total implementation, but the results will truly be worth the wait.

It is difficult to locate specific objective studies that provide quantitative data about the effectiveness of advisor-advisee programs. The outcomes most likely will deal with the overall climate and various other components of the middle school. In a recent article, the authors state, "In middle grade schools that have highly supportive advisory group programs, principals are more likely to report that their guidance programs meet the needs of the schools."[27] Some schools have utilized surveys, analysis of attendance rates, and studies of behavioral referrals. The most conclusive evidence comes from those involved, however. They state simply, "It makes a difference!"

The boxes that follow will provide further insight into and details of successful advisor-advisee programs.

**BOX 13.1
Sample Activity**

OBJECTIVE

Students will continue to develop openness, trust, self-confidence, and mutual respect. Being aware of one's talents can increase self-confidence. Sharing those talents can promote respect and trust.

PROCEDURES

1. Ask each student to think about and then list their talents on a sheet of paper. Talents must be positive and in good taste.
2. Ask each student to pick one of those listed talents and write a slogan that tells about the talent.
3. If applicable, ask each student to draw a symbol that identifies the talent.
4. Explain what a calling card is and how it is used to introduce someone; to promote that person's talents. Explain that today we will each design our own calling card. When completed, the cards will be attached to each AA folder.
5. On scratch paper, sketch your personal calling card using the talent, slogan, and symbol already developed. Add name, address, and phone number.
6. As you approve each card, ask each student to make a final copy on a 3" by 5" index card.

Example. John J. Jones is good at math so he gives himself the title "Math Master". He also picks a slogan and he includes his address and phone number. To attract interest he illustrates his card with math symbols.

$3x - 2y$	$26/4 - 15/7$
John J. Jones	
"Math Master"	
Have a Problem ? I Have the Solution	
123 N. Fourth St.	Phone: 765–4321

Source: Adapted from the John Page Middle School SAGE Program.[21]

BOX 13.2
Teacher–Advisor Responsibilities

Teacher-Advisors

Provide a warm, caring environment in order to facilitate achieving T-A goals.

Plan and implement advisory goals.

Assist advisees in monitoring their academic progress.

Be a good listener and respond to advisees' needs.

Refer advisees to appropriate resources, such as the school counselor, when necessary.

Communicate with parents of advisees.

Help advisees set goals for academic work and social concerns.

Counselors

Help develop T-A activities.

Coordinate T-A activities.

Motivate and encourage implementation of T-A activities.

Coordinate in-service T-A training for advisor.

Respond to referrals about advisees from advisors.

Communicate with teacher-advisors about their advisees.

Serve as a resource person for teacher-advisors.

Administration

Generate a total school philosophy that supports the advisor-advisee program.

Promote the program within the school and community.

Obtain and maintain support from the Board of Education and central administration.

Provide appropriate in-service training for teacher advisors.

Develop a management system for the program.

Allocate time and space within the school for planning and implementation.

Source: Adapted from the John Page Middle School SAGE Program.[21]

BOX 13.3
Scope and Sequence

ADVISOR-ADVISEE TOPICS FOR GRADES 6–8
Sample Topics

Topic	Grade 6	Grade 7	Grade 8
Self-Concept	Me—a unique individual	Who am I within the community?	Building self-confidence, self-esteem
Family Life	Who am I within the family?	Adjusting to my changing role within the family	Breaking away
Substance Abuse	Identification Physiological effects	Peer pressure Community agencies	Decision making Value judgment Peer pressure
Prejudice	Handicapped Awareness	Race and Culture Stereotyping	Sex equity Sex biases Stereotyping
School Survival	Change to middle school	Living in a middle school	Change to high school
Coping Strategies	Dealing with emotions	Divorce and death	Coping with situations that cannot be changed
Responsibility	Self-control Organization	Self-discipline Responsibility	Becoming a young adult

---

Source: Adapted from the John Page Middle School SAGE Program.[21]

BOX 13.4
Advisor–Advisee Sessions

TIPS FOR ADVISORS

1. Be yourself. Build your own kind of relationship with your students.
2. Be flexible. Veer away from plans if necessary. Tune in to your students.
3. Review purpose and ground rules when necessary.
4. Include processing as part of the activity.
5. Provide follow-up lessons where applicable.
6. Student referrals to counselors are available and should be used when appropriate.
7. Keep all items from year to year pertaining to your advisees, such as report cards, progress reports, etc.

Introduction for Advisors

1. At the beginning of each session, put desks in a circle. (Optional).
2. Take attendance sometime during the session.
3. Read all activities in order to know what to prepare for each session.
4. Complete "Advisory Activity Evaluation Form" for each activity.
5. If any issues occur which you feel are worthy for discussion, please feel free to use them as topics for your group.
6. No letter grades are to be given on report cards.

Student Rules

1. Everyone should have an opportunity to talk and participate in some meaningful way.
2. Listen to the person who is speaking.
3. Do not interrupt someone when they are talking. No one should put down ideas in this sharing activity.
4. Stay in your own space.
5. Some answers may be better than others, but there are no right or wrong answers. Your ideas are as important as those of anyone.
6. It's OK to pass—sometimes.

Source: Adapted from the John Page Middle School SAGE Program.[21]

SUMMARY

Guidance and its relationship to middle school students is an aspect of education that is most complex. The issues and concerns that have been examined require commitment and involvement that transcend the narrowly focused interests of any one component of the school program. All components must truly begin to establish primary focus on the central core of middle school education—the student. Teacher, principal, counselor, support staff, and parents must be the mutually supportive team components that develop and maintain effective school practices for this very fragile group of youngsters. The transescent student is truly at an age when affective educational practices such as guidance can make school a most rewarding and beneficial experience. We know what we need. We know what to do; now let us begin.

ENDNOTES

1. Cole, Claire G. *Guidance in Middle Level Schools: Everyone's Responsibility*. Columbus: National Middle School Association (1988): 4–5.
2. Ibid, p. 14.
3. Meyers, John W. *Involving Parents in Middle Level Education*. Columbus: National Middle School Association (1985): 2.
4. Cole, op. cit., p. 12.
5. Eichhorn, Donald H. *The Middle School*. New York: The Center for Applied Research in Education, Inc. (1966): Special Printing by the National Association of Secondary School Principals and the National Middle Schools Association (1987): 86.
6. Merenbloom, Elliott Y. *Developing Effective Middle Schools Through Faculty Participation*. Columbus: National Middle School Association (1982): 6.
7. *This We Believe*. Columbus: National Middle School Association (1982): 12–13.
8. Purkey, William Watson. *Inviting School Success*. Belmont, Calif.: Wadsworth Publishing Co. (1984): 6.
9. Myrick, Robert D. and Linda S. Myrick. *The Teacher Advisor Program*. Ann Arbor: ERIC Counseling and Personal Services Clearinghouse (1990): 5.
10. Beane, James A. and Richard P. Lipka. *When the Kids Come First: Enhancing Self-Esteem*. Columbus: National Middle School Association (1987): 53.
11. Cole, op. cit., p. 8.

12. Cole, op. cit., pp. 10–17.

13. Capelluti, Jody and Donald Stokes, eds. *Middle Level Education: Programs, Policies, and Practices*. Reston: National Association of Secondary School Principals (1991): 31.

14. *An Agenda for Excellence*. Reston, Va.: National Association of Secondary School Principals (1985): 4.

15. *Turning Points: Preparing American Youth for the 21st Century*. Washington, D.C. Carnegie Council (1989): 40.

16. Hoversten, Cheryl, Nancy Doda, and John Lounsbury. *Treasure Chest—A Teacher Advisory Source Book*. Columbus: National Middle School Association (1991): 3.

17. James, Michael. *Advisor-Advisee Programs: Why, What, and How*. Columbus: National Middle School Association (1986): 3.

18. Arth, Alfred A. *Advising/Guiding At the Middle Level*. Williamsburg: National Association of Secondary School Principals ML III Conference (1986): 1.

19. Van Hoose, John. *The Ultimate Goal: A/A Across the Day*. Columbus: National Middle School Association (1991): 4.

20. Jefferson Middle School (Lamphere Schools). "Advisor/Advisee Program." Jefferson, WI (1986): 1.

21. John Page Middle School. "Student Advisor Guidance Experience. Madison Heights, MI (1986): 2.

22. Henderson, Phyllis and Jan La Forge. "The Role of the Middle School Counselor in Teaching-Advisor Programs." *The School Counselor*, Vol. 36 (May, 1989): 348–349.

23. Myrick, Robert D., Marilyn Highland, and Bill Highland. "Preparing Teachers to be Advisors." *Journal of Educational Public Relations*, Vol. 10, No. 4 (1986): 7.

24. Costar, James W. *Focus on Improving Your Middle School Guidance Program*. East Lansing: Michigan Association of Middle School Educators (1988): 24–25.

25. Vars, Gordon F. "Getting Closer to Middle Level Students: Options for Teacher-Adviser Guidance Programs." Schools in the Middle; a Report on Trends and Practices, National Association of Secondary School Principals (January, 1989): 2.

26. Costar, James. "Presentation to the Page Middle School Staff." Madison Heights, MI, 1981.

27. Epstein, Joyce L. and Douglas J. MacIver, "National Practices and Trends in the Middle Grades." *Middle School Journal*. 22: 2 (November, 1990): 37.

Social Development of Transescents

A TIME OF CHANGE, CONFUSION, AND FRUSTRATION

Junior high and middle school students are perhaps the most interesting of all children to teach. It is during these years that dramatic changes can be seen in these young people. Physically, they have entered puberty; their bodies are developing the reproductive capabilities of adulthood. Psychologically, they are dealing with more abstract concepts and applying principles of inductive reasoning to complex problems. Emotionally, they are struggling with the frustrations of escaping from adult domination and experiencing the anxieties of accepting the responsibilities that go with independence. Socially, they are beginning to break away from same-sex groups as they explore opposite sex relationships. The middle grades teacher has the opportunity to help students as they experience the transition from childhood to adulthood.

The one consistent characteristic of middle grade students is that their individual growth and development patterns are irregular and unique. Middle school children, or transescents, are caught between two worlds. They are neither children nor adults. At times, they are expected to behave in a grown-up manner, making responsible decisions, and at other times, they are expected to be submissive and willing to accept the directions of elders. Confusion and frustration result when the transescent's perceptions of appropriate responses conflict with the behavioral expectations of parents and teachers. The 13-year-old who is expected to clean her room without adult prodding—but is told to be off the telephone at 9:00 P.M. without argument—has experienced this frustration.

Helping students develop social skills has long been recognized as an important aspect of the school program. Social development refers to the ways an individual learns how to become integrated into groups. While this integration is a lifelong process, certain crucial developments occur during the transescent years which can influence how successful social relationships will be in later stages of development. Maslow's hierarchy of needs at level three has particular application on middle grade youngsters (*i.e.,* "the need for belonging and being loved, for close and affectionate relationships with others"). *Belongingness* Maslow later defined as a basic need that could be satisfied by "family, a community, a clan, a gang, friendship, affection, love" (Maslow 1968, 199–200).[1]

Unfortunately, the literature that deals with the implementation of middle grade concepts does not provide much guidance for specific practices schools can include to prepare students for new and different social development. However, schools can build activities into the curriculum that promote positive social growth experiences.

It is important to realize that issues related to social development are not the sole domain of a social development program. They are integrated throughout other aspects of the middle grades curriculum. Much of the help students receive in developing positive social skills comes through teacher knowledge and practices that encourage positive social development. Some important aspects of social development at this time include (1) group membership; (2) self-concept; (3) ethnic identification process; (4) sex role identification; (5) peer approval; (6) independence from adults; and (7) a search for sophistication (Merenbloom 1988, 35).[2]

Social development of students can be placed into the context of understanding the cultural forces of the school (Eichhorn 1968, 40–57).[3] In this sense, the relationships students develop with others is much of what creates the cultural milieu of the school. Some middle grade experts include aspects of social development as part of the guidance program (Wiles and Bondi 1986, 83–91).[4] It is also possible to include social development activities in the classroom curriculum (Messick and Reynolds 1992).[5] Presented in this chapter are some ways that social development can be woven into enrichment and exploratory programs.

Developing new social relationships is a difficult but meaningful task for middle school students. Social development begins to take two directions in middle school: first in the same-sex group and then with opposite sex relationships. Same-sex groups begin to take new shapes. Students shift around as same-sex groups change because of maturity or particular interests (*i.e.,* academically gifted classes, athletics, or socio-economic factors). Thus, the typical middle school has easily identifiable group categories: the preppies, the hoods, the goody-goodies, the athletes, the nerds, the school leaders, the druggies, and so on. While there is generally little movement from category to category, there are subgroups within each category, and for most students, there is much searching to find a place where one is accepted. Unfortunately, some transescents never find acceptance.

Power struggles occur frequently within the groups. With popularity among peers comes the perception that one holds a power position. Those who hold power positions do much to define the importance of others in the group. Among other things the leaders determine who one should and should not be seen with, which couples should be matched together, whether academics are or are not important, what places are accepted hangouts, and what activities are worthy of pursuit.

Exploration of one's role with the opposite sex is also an important part of social development at this time. It is important for students to learn who thinks they are worthy and to learn how to get the attention of those they want to see them as worthy. The same-sex group will often define who is worthy of attention and may even play an influential role in how couples get together. Generally, there are many opportunities for boys and girls to interact socially. Lunch periods, dances, athletic events, parties, and free time at school are when these opposite sex explorations take place.

The vast majority of opposite sex relationships do not last very long. For many students, getting "dumped" becomes a monthly process, and getting matched with another occurs very quickly. By about ninth or tenth grade, relationships become more enduring, and more intimate (McEwin and Thomason 1989, 5;[6] Thornburg 1980, 218).[7] As most parents quickly discover, the telephone is a major source of transescent social life. Transescents talk on the phone for long periods of time or simply put the telephone to the ear for long periods of silence.

Fitting into a satisfying group and developing opposite sex relationships take considerable social skills, skills that some students never develop. For these students, transescence is a time of loneliness and alienation; they come to see themselves as unattractive and different. Lack of adequate social integration has been identified across all adolescent age groups as a major factor in adolescent suicide rates (Lester, 1991, 57;[8] Connell and Meyer 1991; 117).[9] Coder et al.[10] found in a survey of school counselors in Kansas that significant numbers of middle grade and junior high school students physically tried suicide and "verbally expressed suicidal intentions" during the previous school year (1991, 358–361). Teachers, administrators, counselors, and parents must provide opportunities for all students to have meaningful, successful, and positive social experiences.

THEMES OF CHANGE

The program of social experiences which the middle school provides must recognize that many changes occur within transescence. Four themes of change emerge as students enter transescence. Emerging from the problems and stresses of transescence are: (1) the theme of self-acceptance; (2) the theme of sex role relationships; (3) the theme of independence; and (4) the theme of broader horizons. These themes can be used to create a rationale for the development of social activities designed for middle school children. By providing activities based on these four themes of change, the school can help the transescent engage in social experiences which are appropriate for these unique social needs and which will also lay the foundation for successful social development in subsequent stages of growth.

The Theme of Self-Acceptance

As students enter transescence, a number of physiological changes begin to take place. The onset of puberty brings dramatic physical changes that signal the end of childhood. Bones and muscles that used to work perfectly have begun to grow, and the once coordinated child becomes a clumsy, awkward transescent. What was considered to be a cute kid turns into a creature who is half-child, half-adult, subject to acne, covered with baby fat in the wrong places, and subject to hormonal imbalances that cause a rash of emotional outbursts. The menstrual flow of girls and the appearance of facial and body hair of boys are other signs that a new and different body is emerging (Kagan 1972).[11]

Appearance becomes an obsession. Boys work to develop arm and chest muscles, girls accent their breasts, boys grow moustaches, girls experiment with makeup, clothing must be a name brand, and considerable time is spent grooming. All of this is in the belief that desired social positions and success at school revolve around how one's appearance is accepted by others. Social life for those who are fat, unattractive, immature, or poor can be a disaster.

These physical changes bring about a need within the transescent to redefine attitudes about self. As the transescent struggles to gain mastery over a changing body, there may be a loss in confidence and in physical abilities. Unfortunately, these changes occur with such irregularity among peers that comparisons give little concept of what is normal. In addition, this lack of knowing what is considered to be normal development can cause the transescent to experience a great deal of concern and anxiety in regard to one's own individual growth.

Physical growth changes have a considerable influence on self attitudes. Self-acceptance is at the center of changes created by physical development. Girls, in particular, struggle with body image. A review of the literature on body image revealed that between the ages of 10 1/2 and 18 years there is a continuing dissatisfaction with body image. The percentage of young women who are unhappy with their bodies ranges from 44 to 85 percent (Paxton *et al.* 1991, 362–363).[12] This problem becomes so severe that approximately five percent of girls and one percent of boys in middle grades and high school suffer with bulimia (Stein, 1991, 207).[13] With a new and changing physical image comes the regaining of physical agility and the recognition that adulthood with all of its impending responsibilities must be integrated and accepted by the transescent.

The theme of self-acceptance represents one of the problem areas confronted by the transescent. Success is the key goal for social activities that help students come to terms with their new changing bodies and help them accept a new concept of self. Teachers must encourage social experiences that provide opportunities for personal success and promote self-confidence. For example, if social recognition in school is based primarily on athletic prowess, the slow developer who already has feelings of self-doubt and inadequacy may never gain a feeling of confidence and self-acceptance. But if teachers believe there should be many ways to gain social recognition, they can provide a variety of activities that call for differing kinds of human strength.

The Theme of Sex Role Relationships

The physical changes occurring within the transescent's body have implications for changes in social relationships. The impending capacities for reproduction call for certain expected social behaviors. Society expects boys to learn how to fulfill masculine roles and girls to fulfill feminine roles. In addition, there are expected courting behaviors that exist between the sexes. During the transescent years, boys and girls learn the social behaviors which are associated with each sex.

In order to learn these social behaviors, close peer group relationships form. One of the functions of the peer group is to help the transescent define the appropriate sex role. Learning to conceptualize, react, and behave as a member of one's own sex is very important to the development of the individual's self-concept (Alexander and George 1981).[14] As the transescent learns the appropriate behaviors for his or her own sex, each also learns how to react and respond to the opposite sex.

Two very important concerns need to be considered as teachers develop social experiences which help students define their respective sex roles. The first of these concerns has been voiced by those who feel that many of the traditional behaviors society has expected should not be within the exclusive domain of a particular sex group (Garskof 1971;[15] Epstein and Goode 1971).[16] For example, there is increasing pressure for boys to learn to cook, to care for babies, and to assume other homemaking responsibilities. Girls are repairing automobiles, joining sports teams, and learning how to participate more in the business and scientific world. The second concern deals with the tensions which are created when the middle school promotes social activities that encourage courting behaviors.

The school can provide a social context which allows boys and girls to understand that the concepts of masculinity and femininity refer more to

biological than cultural differences. Certain cultural sex role distinctions between men and women change with time and circumstance. Thus, women
are driving trucks, men are doing the family shopping, and raising children
is becoming more of a cooperative effort. Rather than teaching students to
assume assigned sex roles, the school can help students understand the wide
range of potential individual roles they can perform in society.

The transescent should be given opportunities to establish relationships
with the opposite sex without the pressures of having to fulfill what should
be a future sex role. That is, at the age of 11 or 12 there should not be
worries about dating, who is going steady with whom, or how to display
sexual prowess. Transescence is the time for boys and girls to learn to regard one another as persons rather than as sexual stereotypes. In the middle
school, there needs to be an emphasis on social activities that orient the
goals of boys and girls toward the accomplishment of common purposes.
Activities that expect students to participate in pre-courtship behaviors
should be discouraged.

The theme of sex role relationships presents several implications for
the development of social experiences in the school. Projects and activities
that allow for the cooperative contributions of all students can illustrate that
both boys and girls have much to offer. Competitive events can be healthy
as long as the competitors are evenly matched. Body size and physical development should be given more consideration than age and sex when
matching competitors. ''Mixer'' type activities can introduce boys and girls
to more adult-like social roles without the pressures of one-on-one relationships. A social program that provides cooperative type activities, competitive
events based on fair contestant matching, and social events that promote informal pairings can help students develop positive sex role relationships.

The Theme of Independence

The transescent's need for independence should be considered in planning
the social activities of the middle school. Many parents and teachers have
had anxious firsthand experience with the transescent's often truculent demands for more freedom. They want to stay out later at night, they want
greater financial resources, and they want to make more decisions regarding
the development of their own lifestyles. A challenge to any of these demands brings that oft-used refrain, ''But everyone does it.''

The transescent's striving for independence is a source of frustration
for both youngsters and adults. In one sense, transescents want to be dependent but they also need to be independent. Emotionally there is the need to
be loved, to be accepted, and to feel a sense of belonging. But the transescent
also wants the adults who fulfill these emotional needs to grant social independence. Conflicting signals occur when adults expect responsible social

behavior from maturing transescents but treat them as children in other respects. In school, these conflicting signals are seen when teachers expect students to work at their studies independently and with inner direction, yet demand that students raise their hands to ask for permission to use the restroom.

Van Hoose and Strahan (1988, 30)[17] describe this dependence-independence conflict in the following way: "It is also common for middle level students to ask teachers or parents for ideas about how to proceed with an experiment, what to say in a social situation, or what to wear. Then they often promptly reject whatever is suggested. They want adult input but also want to be able to accept it or reject it on their own terms. This move from dependence to independence often causes an adult to become frustrated, irritated and, at times, have indigestion or heartburn."

In addition to the dependence-independence dilemma, there is the problem of helping transescents understand that as they gain social independence, they must assume responsibility for their own behavior. No longer can they claim the immaturity of childhood as the reason for irresponsible acts. Transescents need to be given opportunities to make decisions about what acceptable and unacceptable social behavior is. The manner in which they fulfill their desires and achieve their goals must be in accordance with society's expectations for responsible behavior.

A planned program of social experiences can help students overcome many of the problems associated with independence. As transescents gain independence, they must make more choices regarding their own behavior. Given opportunities to select from among alternatives and to realize the consequences of choices, the transescent can begin to achieve independence. Some of the ways to help students with the problems of independence are to involve them in the planning of activities, provide a wide range of activities from which they can choose, have students collect and manage money related to their clubs or projects, and allow students to accept the responsibility for the success or failure of their projects.

The Theme of Broader Horizons

In addition to the physical and emotional changes occurring in middle school students, the school's program of social activities must acknowledge some very important intellectual developments among transescents. For example, many transescents are capable of understanding more abstract concepts—abstract concepts which enable them to make generalizations concerning their place in the universe. Middle school students exhibit an interest in the problems of ecology, they question the workings of government, and they begin to show a consciousness of world problems. Transescents begin to understand that the world is larger than their immediate surroundings.

As transescents' intellectual curiosity broadens, so do their social relationships. In expanding their explorations of the world, transescents seek out others with similar interests. They join groups that reflect their intellectual interests. Involvement in community service projects, student government, and clubs that promote specialized skills such as writing or photography can play an important role in the student's social activities.

The transescent's widening intellectual interests present two opportunities for social experiences offered by the school. First, the activities must have graduated structures which allow the student to explore specific areas of interest with a sense of direction. With a gradation structure to follow, the student can progress from simple to complex concepts. Second, the program of social experiences must be broad and it must offer much variety. To nurture growing interests in the world, the transescent must be given opportunities to sample from many areas which help to stimulate intellectual curiosities.

CHARACTERISTICS OF THE SOCIAL EXPERIENCES FOR MIDDLE SCHOOL STUDENTS

The themes of change emerge from the unique growth patterns of transescents. The characteristics of the social activities appropriate for transescents are an outgrowth of the themes of change. By providing social experiences with the following characteristics, the school can develop a social program which is unique for middle school students rather than adopting modified versions of activities that are appropriate for students in other developmental stages of growth.

1. *Success-oriented.* With the pressures of adjusting to physical changes, transescents do not need a social system that is based on athletic prowess. They should be given opportunities to receive social recognition for skill development in many areas. Activities which allow students to gain social status and help to enhance their self-concepts are very necessary. Recognition and success can be achieved when students can exhibit collections or show expertise in a particular hobby area, contribute to the school newspaper, have art work displayed in prominent places in the school, participate in dramatic presentations, organize a musical group, or join the debate society.

2. *Group-structured.* Activities in which students can socialize without the pressures of pairing can help students achieve some social poise with the opposite sex. Mixer activities where students participate together can help them to establish many types of relationships. A gradual introduction to dating can be achieved by providing opportunities for boys and girls to socialize together in

group activities. Group activities such as bowling, ice or roller skating, hiking, gymnastics, folk dancing, chorus, and band can provide a wholesome social context for students.

3. *Fair competition.* Competitive events among middle school students can sharpen skills, build self-confidence, develop school morale, and provide entertainment for spectators. However, care must be taken to insure that contestants are evenly matched. Pitting strong against weak, skilled against clumsy, or intellectual against ignorant for the sake of ''separating the sheep from the goats,'' is detrimental to developing youngsters. Intramural sports, homeroom against homeroom service projects, talent shows, arts and crafts fairs, and noncontact sports can provide healthy and positive competitive activities where boys and girls can socialize.

4. *Goal-directed.* Social activities which are directed toward accomplishment of a goal will help boys and girls learn how to work together to achieve a common purpose. Students should be given the opportunity to work at a common interest without the pressures of developing boy-girl relationships. Students who are socially ready to begin dating activities can do so, however, the primary emphasis should be placed on the achievement of the common goal. Sexual pairings should be incidental to the attainment of the common purpose. Goal-directed social activities could include developing ecology projects; preparing testimonial programs; tutoring; presenting a consumer, job, clothing, arts and crafts, or science fair; working with school beautification projects; participating in fund-raising projects; preparing for an interschool band, dramatic, or art contest; and organizing a talent show.

5. *Provides for decision making and responsibility.* Transescents need to learn how to make sound decisions and assume the responsibility for their behavior if they are to achieve independence. Social responsibility comes when students establish relationships with others, based on fairness and lack of prejudice. Examples of activities which help students make decisions and assume responsibility are student council; fund-raising projects that hold students responsible for handling money; junior achievement; and the business aspects of clubs and organizations; library, office, and audiovisual helpers; associations for future teachers, farmers, and homemakers; and career exploration clubs.

6. *Organized structure.* The transescent's social activities should have an organized structure to accommodate developing intellectual abilities. Structure provides a variety of entry points for students at different levels of intellectual development. Opportunities to experiment, to develop problem-solving skills, and to learn new

things in interest areas can be accomplished by joining specialized clubs and organizations. The transescent can progress from simple to complex or from beginner to expert with others who have common interests and who also have similar levels of understanding. Social activities in the school which provide structured intellectual experiences are clubs for woodworking, debate, photography, creative writing, science, ham radio, journalism, electronics, geology, automotives, and art and music appreciation.

7. *Wide variety.* Social experiences ought to reflect the transescent's growing intellectual curiosities. By providing a wide variety of activities, the transescent can explore and enlarge horizons. As attentions are turned outward, the transescent develops interest in the world at large. Social activities which can capitalize on this intellectual curiosity include clubs for pen pals, service, school newspaper, stamp and coin collecting, environmental conservation, debate, travel, current events, world affairs and scouts.

SOCIAL ACTIVITIES FOR THE MIDDLE SCHOOL

The list of suggested activities at the end of this section can be used to develop social experiences for middle school students. However, care must be taken to insure that the activities of the school are appropriate for transescents. The four themes of change we have discussed reflect the special problems of children between the ages of ten and fifteen. Therefore, the characteristics of social experiences for middle school children are different from those of other developmental groups.

All too often, the unique needs of transescents are ignored in the rush to accelerate developmental growth. Concerns have been expressed for many years that we have a tendency to value social precociousness as a sign of advanced human development (Gordon 1962;[18] Mead 1973).[19] Unfortunately, transescence is often regarded simply as an early stage of adolescence and not as an important and meaningful time in itself. Thus, the social program of the middle school often consists of watered-down versions of high school activities. The middle school student deserves to have social experiences which have been designed for transescents and not for other age groups.

What is perhaps most frustrating in the construction of a social program for middle school students is how to provide for the wide variations in transescent interests, capabilities, and development. In the middle school there will be boys with childlike features in body and voice, and other boys, not much older, who are tall, well developed, and ready to shave. Among the girls there will be variances that are just as wide. Even wider variations can be found when transescent boys are compared with girls. Girls will tend to be more advanced than boys, particularly in terms of social development.

The social activities of the school must recognize the many differences in the developmental rates of transescents. For example, some girls may be ready to date when they are in middle school while other girls are not certain they are interested in boys. There will always be some boys who are constantly engaged in horseplay while others want to organize an electronics club. The school needs to have a broad program of social experiences with many levels to accommodate the many developmental differences among transescents.

Therefore, while the following list gives many examples of appropriate middle school activities, it is still necessary for the faculty to mold them into experiences for middle school students. Understanding the themes of transescent changes, building in the seven characteristics derived from them, and allowing for variations in developmental growth are all a part of adjusting these activities to transescent needs. Also, these activities are for all students. There is no need to make them gender specific.

In most cases, it is arbitrary to categorize these activities as curricular or cocurricular. It is hoped that the activities themselves will suggest many ways the school faculty can develop social experiences regardless of how they are classified.

Curricular Activities

Career planning	Math puzzles
Consumer education	Mechanics
Contemporary problems	Modern music lyrics
Cooking	Money management
Creative writing	Nutrition
Current events	Panel discussion
Debate	Personal grooming
Electronics	Personal conditioning
Environment problems	Public speaking
Gymnastics	Remedial or speed reading
Home management	Weight watching
Home repair	Woodworking
Interior decoration	World affairs
Journalism	

Group and individual research or exhibition projects in:

Art	Science
Language arts	Social studies
Music	

Cocurricular Activities and Mini-Course Topics

Art appreciation
Arts and crafts
Astronomy club
Automobiles
Balsa models
Band
Bible club
Bicycle club
Biology club
Book club
Camping
Candle making
Carving (wood, soap,
  cornhusks, apples)
Ceramics
Chess club
Chorus
Cinema
Coin and stamp collecting
Conditioning
Conservation club
Copper enameling
Creative writing
Crewel design
Crocheting
Dancing, folk, modern
Decoupage
Dramatics club
Drawing
  Cartoon
  Commercial
  Graphic arts
  Mechanical
  Poster
Ecology
Electricity
Electronic games, computers
Embroidery
Family history
Fashion design
Flying

Foreign language clubs
  African
  Asian
  French
  German
  Latin
  Russian
  Spanish
Games
Gardening
Geology
Guitar
Handicrafts
Hiking
Indian lore and arrowheads
Jewelry making
Junior achievement
Knitting
Literacy magazine
Macrame
Magic club
Math club
Model building
Motors
Music appreciation
Musical groups
Mystery club
Newspaper
Officiating sports events
Outdoor education
Pen pal club
Pet care
Photography
Poetry club
Pottery making
Predicting weather
Puppet theatre
Puzzles
Radio broadcasting
Radio club (ham)

Reading club
Rock collecting
Rocketry club
Rock polishing
Rug hooking
Science club
Science fiction
Scouts
Sculpturing
Service Clubs
  Audiovisual
  Library
  Messengers
  Office
  Ushers
Shop
Soapbox derby
Spectator sports
Sports
  Archery
  Baseball
  Basketball
  Bowling
  Fishing (fly casting)
  Golf

Gymnastics
Ice Skating
Kickball
Roller skating
Self-defense
Skiing
Table tennis
Tennis
Touch football
Track
Tumbling
Volleyball
String art
Student council
Study skills
Talent show
Terrariums
Travel club
Tropical fish
Tutoring
Weight lifting
Winter camping
Woodcrafts
Woodworking

SUMMARY

Among the many and often difficult changes which middle school age students must adjust to are new and different social relationships both at school and at home. A diminished acceptance of parental guidance is accompanied by a greater importance given to peer group opinions and standards.

Four themes of change emerge as students cope with the problems and stresses of transescence. These are (1) self-acceptance where the problem of accepting and adjusting to a series of rapid physical changes can seriously affect a person's self-image and self esteem; (2) sex role relationships change with the advent of an interest in the opposite sex and a struggle to find the appropriate behavior towards others; (3) the growing need for independence, which must be balanced with a gradual development of readiness to exercise decision making and responsibility; and (4) broader horizons develop as the awareness of transescents widens to include more abstract concepts and a larger world than they were previously aware of.

The social activities of the middle school must recognize not only these general themes but also the many differences in rates of development among individual students. Selection of both curricular and cocurricular activities can be key provisions in meeting these social development needs.

ENDNOTES

1. Maslow, Abraham H. *Toward a Psychology of Being.* New York: D. Van Nostrand Co., 1968.

2. Merenbloom, Elliot Y. *Developing Effective Middle Schools.* Columbus, Ohio: National Middle School Association, 1988.

3. Eichhorn, Donald. *The Middle School.* New York: Center for Applied Research in Education, 1968.

4. Wiles, Jon, and Joseph Bondi. *The Essential Middle School.* Tampa: Wiles, Bondi and Associates, Inc., 1986.

5. Messick, Rosemary, and Karen Reynolds. *Middle School Curriculum in Action.* New York: Longman Publishing Group, 1992.

6. McEwin, C. Kenneth, and Julia Thomason. *Who They Are How We Teach: Early Adolescents and Their Teachers.* Columbus, Ohio: National Middle School Association, 1989.

7. Thornburg, Hershel. "Early Adolescents: Their Developmental Characteristics." *The High School Journal* 63 (March 1980): 215–221.

8. Lester, David. "Social Correlates of Youth Suicide Rates in the United States." *Adolescence* 26 (Spring 1991): 55–58.

9. Connell, David K., and Robert G. Meyer. "Adolescent Suicidal Behavior and Popular Self-Report Instruments of Depression, Social Desirability, and Anxiety." *Adolescent* 26 (Spring, 1991): 113–117.

10. Coder, Tamara L., Richard E. Nelson, and Laura K. Aylward. "Suicide Among Secondary Students." *School Counselor* 38 (May, 1991): 358–361.

11. Kagan, Jerome. "A Conception of Early Adolescence," in *Twelve to Sixteen: Early Adolescence,* edited by Jerome Kagan and Robert Coles. New York: W. W. Norton and Company, 1972.

12. Paxton, Susan J., Eleanor H. Wertheim, Kay Gibbons, George I. Szmukler, Lynne Hillier, and Janice L. Petrovich. "Body Image Satisfaction, Dieting Beliefs, and Weight Loss Behaviors in Boys and Girls." *Journal of Youth and Adolescence* 20 (June 1991): 361–379.

13. Stein, David M. "The Prevalence of Bulimia: A Review of the Empirical Research." *Journal of Nutrition Education* 23 (September/October 1991): 205–312.

14. Alexander, William, and Paul George. *The Exemplary Middle School.* New York: Holt, Rinehart, Winston, 1981.

15. Garskof, Michele Hoffnung (ed.). *Roles Women Play: Readings Toward Women's Liberation.* Belmont, California: Brooks/Cole Publishing Co., 1971.

16. Epstein, Cynthia Fuchs, and William J. Goode (eds.). *The Other Half: Roads to Women's Equality.* Englewood Cliffs, New Jersey: Prentice-Hall, Inc., 1971.

17. Van Hoose, John, and David Strahan. *Young Adolescent Development and School Practices: Promoting Harmony.* Columbus, Ohio, National Middle School Association, 1988.

18. Gordon, Ira. *Human Development: From Birth through Adolescence.* New York: Harper and Row, Publishers, 1962.

19. Mead, Margaret. ''Are We Squeezing Out Adolescence?'' In *The Middle School: Selected Readings on an Emerging School Program,* edited by Louis Romano, Nicholas Georgiady, and James Heald. Chicago: Nelson-Hall Company, 1973.

PART

Student Services and the Community

Auxiliary Staffing

Student Services

17

Community Relations

PART V

The work of the classroom teacher can be enhanced when auxiliary staff members are available to assist them in a variety of ways, as discussed in Chapter Fifteen. In addition, Chapter Sixteen points out that student services are important in the middle school as they offer the expertise of trained professional personnel, which teachers can make use of in meeting the particular needs of students.

In Chapter Seventeen, discussion is centered on the concept that school and community must work together to make the education of students as effective as possible. Using community resources, both human and material, in the school program, encouraging members of the community to visit and feel a part of the school, and having teachers and students participate in constructive community projects and activities can all do much to forge a desirable school-community relationship.

Auxiliary Staffing

DEFINITION

Overall staffing of the middle school has been termed an operation of the highest priority. Because it is so important, let us clearly delineate between the terms "staffing" and "auxiliary staffing." Within the context of middle school structure, staffing refers to the overall process of recruiting, selecting, and placing appropriately qualified and professionally trained personnel. Auxiliary staffing refers to the process of recruiting, selecting, and placing highly diversified personnel that complement and assist the professional staff. These include volunteer parents, teacher aides, clerical aides, student volunteers, and other important categories of support staff.

THE NEED FOR AUXILIARY STAFFING

Auxiliary staffing is needed to provide the individual help students require. Recent research has reinforced the realization of educators that large numbers of transescents begin the middle school years with significant instructional needs in several areas. Several causes contribute to the effect of such a problem. One is the reality that school financial structures, such as foundation programs, provide limited opportunities for first priorities within school programs. To combat this problem, many schools use federal assistance to fund programs. In such causes, the programs are for the most part funded by external-to-district dollars and therefore are usually restricted in operation to perhaps only the primary grade years of school. Students who have participated in such programs are then frequently returned to the classroom for the remaining elementary school years, thereby losing the individually focused attention that was so vitally needed. Typically, a pattern of linear regression then follows and the students begin the middle school years with a significant educational disadvantage. Such a disadvantage is particularly severe in its future implications for learning unless there is some remedial intervention.

Another rationale for auxiliary staff is efficiency. Program variety tends to increase in the years after the elementary school years. In such period years, and particularly beginning with the middle school years, a differentiation of staffing becomes possible and feasible. A resultant benefit of staff differentiation to students and taxpayers is that effective use of available staff resources is optimized. Teacher aides, clerical aides, student volunteers, and others provide the auxiliary services that are most effectively met when considering auxiliary staff training, background, and peer association.

DETERMINING AUXILIARY STAFFING NEEDS

Let us assume that we are starting from "square one" in analyzing auxiliary staffing needs for a school.

1. A first consideration would be to determine the size of the student population to be served. Included in such preliminary thinking would be how many and what type of professionals are available to serve the students directly. An appropriate ratio of students to teachers can be figured. Second in priority would be the task of listing students for consideration of auxiliary staffing services. Appropriate professional staff should be given the responsibility for evaluating priorities of student needs. Such a needs assessment could, for example, be done by the guidance staff, teaching area team, central office professional staff, or individual teacher, to name a few possibilities.

2. When analyzing the needs assessment data and when considering priorities for educational services, particular attention should be given to several areas of student historical information. Such information is frequently maintained in official student records. It is important to avoid giving too much consideration to a singular indicator, such as one test score, when determining needs priorities. Look for the total picture! Historical information includes records of achievement, absence data, examples of former homework, information concerning unusual physical or emotional problems, interest inventories, nonstandardized test results, and teacher comments or evaluations. The overall objective in determining needs priorities for students is to analyze records for trends in student development so that a maximum utilization of program design is possible.

3. After specific needs have been determined, the next step is weighing each identified student need. Weighing refers to the importance attached to each need as determined by professional staff. The weighing may either be determined by consensus of the evaluation group(s) or decided by the obvious nature of the analysis data.

4. The fourth step is making a needs profile. Such a profile would list in descending order the identified needs of a particular student.

5. The fifth step involves assembling into groups those students whose needs profiles have similar characteristics. Group size can be determined by matching available resources with appropriate student numbers. It is important to match the descending order of needs as closely as possible. Such matching—for example, beginning sounds or inferred meaning in reading comprehension—facilitates the future assignment of auxiliary staff.

6. The recruitment, selection, and placement of auxiliary staff is greatly enhanced if steps one through five can be accomplished prior to the end of a school year at the time when auxiliary staffing program(s) are planned for a succeeding year. Why accomplish steps one through five before the end of a school year? The answer becomes quite clear when one rethinks the confusion of school year closing activities and further recognizes that such tasks, as formerly outlined, may easily encompass a four or five month period. Assemble as many components of the auxiliary staffing program as far in advance as possible. Be prepared to find the solutions to unknown problems which will likely arise. Advance preparation limits the number of new problems and helps enhance the initial operation of the program.

Following development of the needs assessment profile, a study group should determine what student needs should be set as priorities. The study group may be composed of teachers, administrators, and guidance development staff. It is also advisable to include, if possible, a school psychologist. Such an individual will assist in the interpretation of psychological tests and may additionally be able to provide invaluable insight into a student's apparent needs.

Also important for inclusion in such an important group are parent participants, who may be involved in analysis of student's personally identifiable data. Take care to avoid violation of the intents of Public Law 93-380 unless access to information is released by parent/guardian. Participants could be involved in providing input when priorities for service to students are determined. Parent involvement in determining priorities for student service helps to insure the overall effectiveness of the auxiliary staffing program. Such involvement by parents also serves to create open lines of communication between and among school, parents, and community at large.

One middle school community capitalized on the strong interest that parents have in their children's schools in a positive, constructive way. With parent leadership and teacher/principal cooperation, they organized a WASP group (Women's Auxiliary for School Programs) of volunteers who were willing to donate one or more hours per week of time to serving as unpaid volunteers. They even designed an inexpensive emblem that each person proudly wore while on duty. The end of the school year saw their efforts acknowledged in a modest but well-attended luncheon provided by the board of education. The benefits to the school included better communication between school and home and a stronger commitment of support from parents for ''their'' school's programs. It also led to a realization by middle school students that education was a total community effort and therefore must be important. And it gave many hundreds of hours of free and needed assistance for teachers.

After priorities for student service are set, the task of determining type and number of auxiliary staff can be initiated. Several questions may be considered. Are teacher aides available? Is an extension of teacher services necessary? Is more individual attention to needs of the student indicated? Are student peers likely to be beneficial in such an instance, as opposed to adult volunteers or other auxiliary staff? Many other questions, of course, are possible and likely. All questions represent a point of view and should be considered before final decisions are made.

When considering aides, it is important to remember that teacher aides differ from so-called clerical aides. Teacher aides usually are assigned tasks that become an extension of instruction planned and assigned under the direct supervision of the teacher. Clerical aides are frequently assigned tasks involving the recording of data; that is, the scoring of tests made and administered under teacher supervision and the scheduling of student library/media time, recess/playground, lunch supervision, etc. The deciding factor between aide description lies in the educational preparation and experience area of the aide. Individuals with some college preparation in education or education-related areas are frequently recruited as educational teacher aides. Individuals with business related backgrounds are frequently recruited as clerical aides. In any event, place your available aides into the area(s) where they will complement the goals of the program and additionally into the areas where good working relationships with staff are likely to occur.

Tasks for Teacher Aides

1. Work with small groups of students on work assigned by teacher.
2. Help in administering tests.
3. Set up and operate A.V. equipment as needed.
4. Tutor individual students under the teacher's supervision.
5. Assist students in library searches and the use of tapes, etc.
6. Prepare basic materials for follow-up instruction.
7. Arrange displays of interesting materials related to topics of study.
8. Prepare charts, overhead transparencies, etc.
9. Grade papers as assigned by teacher and share evaluations with teacher.
10. Search out and secure supplementary material from library or Instructional Media Center for use in classroom studies.
11. Supervise playground activities.

Tasks for Clerical Aides

1. Prepare and duplicate instructional materials: Typing, dittoing, etc.
2. Help with record keeping, lunch money, attendance, test scores, etc.
3. General housekeeping chores, such as straightening bookshelves, etc.
4. Assist with classroom discipline.
5. Playground or lunchroom supervision.
6. Prepare charts and overhead transparencies.
7. Set up and operate A.V. equipment as needed.
8. Supervise playground activities and lunchroom periods.
9. Assist teacher with field trip arrangements and supervision.
10. Record and organize learning materials in the classroom and in the IMC.
11. Help students learn proper use of tools and equipment.

It should be noted that some duties are double listed and may be handled by either teacher or clerical aides.

Student volunteers are another valuable resource. Advantages lie in potentially strong relationships that are often developed among students, helping to increase student motivation. Student volunteers should be assigned tasks under the direction of teachers or other auxiliary staff. This might release a teacher from additional direct responsibility and increase flexibility of the program as well. In any case of assignment, an adult should be in charge of student volunteers. It is wise to clearly establish in the student volunteer's eyes who is in charge. Avoid any confusion or potential grief by communicating this clearly.

Student volunteers are sometimes chosen from the same school where auxiliary services are being offered to students. In other situations, student volunteers may be chosen from a school of the same type or of a different type. A middle school student volunteer, for example, could be used in an elementary school. Student volunteers are less frequently chosen to serve in higher schools. For example, elementary school students are not usually selected to assist students in the middle school. High school volunteers would assist students in the junior high/middle school and junior high/middle school students would serve students in the elementary school. It is also frequent practice to permit students to assist others at their own grade level. For example, students at the sixth-grade level could assist other students at the sixth-grade level. In cases where levels are the same, student volunteers should be clearly superior students who are self-directed in their ability to conceptualize an assignment and follow directions from a supervisor.

The scheduling of student volunteers is improved if secondary or middle school student volunteers are selected to assist other students. Such advantage is the result of study sessions/halls which are frequently scheduled for the afternoon. Scheduling for such times is conflict-free and places priority on the expectations of classroom or area teachers. If elementary school student volunteers from middle schools are recruited, all attempts should be made to avoid conflicts in those students' schedules of required classes. Elective classes or activity classes may offer less conflict but still should be respected in terms of scheduling. A possibility may be the scheduling of these student volunteers for the elementary school either immediately before the school day or immediately after the school day. This creates supervision problems, but the hurdle may be cleared if afterschool professional staff are available to include in their supervisory responsibilities the observation of student volunteers. In case of student volunteer scheduling before or after school, the maximum time per session should not exceed 30 minutes. Parent resistance will likely become a problem if parents feel that their offspring are being used to that particular student's disadvantage. This point should be cleared up when communicating with the parents. Careful planning insures benefits to the school and student resulting in an image to parents and school that enhances the entire operation.

One particularly interested group of student volunteers may be found among those aspiring to become teachers. While the middle school may be too early an arena for the formation of a chapter of Future Teachers of America (F.T.A.), valuable preformal training and preservice experiences become an advantage for such students. The opportunity for service as a student volunteer could also be planned as a valuable component of the guidance department's career education program.

PROGRAM DESIGN

The following example of an auxiliary staffed program is suggested for inclusion into varied types of educational or physical plant school structures. Variations on the following suggestions are certainly possible, limited only by the creativity of the designer(s).

The components of this include utilization of categories of auxiliary staff as follows:

1. Parent volunteers
2. Teacher aides
3. Clerical aides
4. Student volunteers

Program design at this point also assumes that:

1. Student population to be served has been determined.
2. Student needs in service group have been analyzed.
3. Student needs have been ranked in priority.
4. A needs weighing has been completed.
5. A needs assessment profile has been constructed.

During the first days of the new school year, a meeting should be scheduled for all staff who have the responsibility for primary instruction in the needs assessment area selected for service. If reading is chosen as the area, then all teachers of reading would assemble as a group. The specific purpose of the meeting is to collectively decide upon a scheduling plan, and work out details and anticipated problems concerning communication. It may be helpful to have such a meeting chaired by the building principal or appropriate designee. Overall instructional plans for the school year should be reviewed. Such review would include an analysis of each quarter or period as well as short-term and long-term goals. Goals of each type should be specifically stated so that later evaluation can be more realistically accomplished.

Following the discussion of short- and long-term goals, the structure for educational services by auxiliary staff can be discussed.

One type of structure is a concept called "Action Lab." The action lab is a designated area within the middle school where students are scheduled for small group instruction and/or individual support, and/or remedial assistance. The lab is staffed at all times during the school day with available auxiliary staff. A rotation of such staff occurs during the day. The early morning action lab session should always begin with teacher direction and each late afternoon session should ideally end with teacher closure. This is to say that a service area teacher (perhaps reading) should be present to welcome students along with the auxiliary staff serving the first session. Such an arrangement gives extra stability to the day's activities and also tends to remind students of the importance of the program. An example of auxiliary staff rotation could be:

- First morning session number one, parent volunteers.
- Session number two, teacher aides.
- Early afternoon session, student volunteers.
- Last session, clerical aides.

1. During the first morning session, the teacher(s) in charge outlines the activities of the session. Such activities, in this or other sessions, could include but not be limited to seat work, audiovisual presentations, monitoring or oral reading, tachistoscope reinforcement, rote-recall vocabulary building, etc. Parents are scheduled during the early morning sessions because that is when many of them are available to volunteer. Typically, the parent has either ushered the offspring out the door for school or driven them there. In the latter case, parents are already at the school site so a duplicate trip is avoided.

2. The second session, involving teacher aides, is complementary to the parent volunteers. It is also an important extension of teacher-directed activities that have probably occurred in the classroom session. Teacher aides are usually directly assigned to teachers during the first part of the school day. This occurs for many reasons. However, one of the most important reasons is the fact that language arts activities usually occur in the early morning, and here the teacher utilizes the teacher aide to facilitate small group instruction. By scheduling the teacher aides into the second session, an extension of teacher direction is gained in the action lab. Another advantage of scheduling teacher aides into the second session occurs as a result of two adult groups of auxiliary staff closely following each other in succession.

3. The third session (early afternoon) is probably the most appropriate time to schedule student volunteers, when it is most convenient for both students and professional staff in cognate areas. Concentrated cognitive activities are usually scheduled during the morning hours. Elective subjects, art, music, study sessions, and physical education are most likely to be scheduled in the afternoon. Experience has shown that staff conflict is more easily resolved if student volunteers are scheduled during the more flexible times. Student achievement does not suffer in the cognate areas and make up work possibilities are more easily planned if student

volunteers are scheduled for auxiliary staffing services in the afternoon. Avoid staff conflicts to insure the significance and impact of the program.

Student volunteers may need to be supervised, depending on their ages and maturity levels. Each situation is different, so appropriate solutions are necessary.

4. The fourth (closing) session is scheduled with clerical aides. Such aides may serve at least a twofold purpose during the final session. First, they are involved with recording necessary data from all sessions as supplied by volunteer staff. Additionally, they are responsible for assisting the professional teacher with whatever tasks become necessary for closure of educational activities for the day. Data collection may involve the recording of seat-work results such as taking attendance for each session, keeping library records, etc. Clerical aides can also change bulletin boards, with teachers supplying suggestions. Don't be afraid to give the clerical aides some leeway in supplying ideas for bulletin board illustrations. If inconsistency develops between program design and bulletin board illustration, the remedy between teacher and clerical aide is simple. Tactfully redirect the aide, perhaps giving a few extra samples or illustrations, and new ideas will likely be generated as a result of teacher direction, tact, and interest.

EVALUATION

With an educational program, it is important to provide a planned evaluation design. The following design is suggested as one measure for evaluating program effectiveness. Careful analysis of program effectiveness will help provide direction for changes necessary in improving the total auxiliary staffing program. Evaluation data should be used to strengthen program elements which may appear to be only marginally meeting student needs. It is important to consider the sharing of evaluative information with other professional staff. Such sharing will facilitate total educational planning within the school. It will also tend to reinforce or refute other data, thereby creating another dimension to the information gathering process concerning student achievement.

When possible, it is an advantage to include objective testing within the auxiliary staffing program. Such testing should of course fall within the stated purposes of evaluation in the school district. Restrictions may exist in the district concerning the number or kinds of tests administered, so it is important to be in tune with the district philosophy. If appropriate and consistent with school district testing practices, objective testing within the auxiliary staffing program will appeal to other staff members. They may see such testing in the action lab, for example, as supportive of the need to monitor student performance. Such testing will also assist guidance staff members as they plan educational programs for action lab students. In any case, be careful to clearly state or communicate the purposes of the action lab testing to avoid the perception that schools test for limited or unsound educational reasons.

The evaluation design should include at least three elements.

1. Written and oral feedback to teachers from auxiliary staff concerning their observations of students. Such observations from auxiliary staff need to be directed and will likely be included on printed forms. Directed information varies with the situation, but is determined early in the school year when analyzing priorities to be considered for service. Examples of observation could include study habits, behaviors, eye problems, emotional indicators of potential problems, etc.
2. Teacher evaluation of assigned student seat-work as supplied to teacher auxiliary staff members.
3. Teacher-made tests and the administration of standardized tests.

The written and oral feedback from auxiliary staff should be structured as indicated above. Structure assures the uniform collection of data and applies the evaluative model more fairly to all students.

Indication of feedback structure might include for each group.

1. Parent behavior records.
2. Teacher aides' seat-work corrections and primary data on such to the teacher(s).
3. Student volunteers' correct response records for teacher-made test and resultant administration of such.
4. Clerical aides' general housekeeping records as may be assigned.

Included here would be the record of bulletin board charges inclusive of the topical area of instruction.

Professional teachers should be totally responsible for the evaluation and control of student seat-work quality. The work habits of students, determined by teachers and aides, may be helpful in analyzing student needs and how improvements in achievement may likely be attained. Finally, all tests, whether teacher-made or standardized, should be considered as another indicator or element of the evaluation design. In no case should a single test alone be interpreted to be the absolute indicator of student performance. Testing practices dictate that when inconsistent test data are obtained, other measures of student achievement (including different tests) should be administered. Such opportunities for insight should be provided at periodic intervals for the purpose of assuring an adequate sample.

When standardized tests are a part of the total school testing program, every attempt should be made to correlate testing of students in the action lab program with the total school testing sequence. Such a decision to uniformly test is cost effective and additionally serves to limit disruptions during the school year.

Consideration should be given to testing for aptitude as well as achievement. If both measures are obtained, and particularly at the same time, a comparison is possible in that student performance may be compared with individual student aptitude. Advantages in such a testing design may be especially realized when, for example, school administration personnel or school board members compare student performance in one school with the performance of students in another school while taking into full consideration the variables in each school.

Let us remember that the bottom line for any middle school testing program is to maximize student actualization of innate abilities into skill development.

SUMMARY

The use of auxiliary staffing can maximize the efforts of the regular classroom teacher, and it is hoped, increase the learning opportunities for middle school boys and girls who need further attention. Teacher aides, clerical aides, and student aides can succeed with an assessment of the needs of each middle school child who is given this special assistance. With this assessment data, the classroom teacher can design appropriate activities with the aid of the auxiliary staff.

Using such staffing, parents, senior citizens, and other community members not only serve boys and girls, but also obtain positive insights as to the fine efforts by classroom teachers.

REFERENCES

Cahan, E. D. *Past caring: A history of U.S. preschool care and education for the poor, 1920–1965.* New York: Columbia University, 1989.

Cheek, D. W., and Leonard J. Waks, eds. Technological literacy IV: proceedings of the national technological literacy conference. Virginia: 4th National Technological Literacy Conference, February 3–5, 1989.

Hamburg, D. A. *Early adolescence: A critical time for interventions in education and health.* New York: Carnegie Corporation, 1989.

Harrington, D. and Schine. *Connections: service learning in the middle grades. A survey conducted by the early adolescent helper program.* New York: Center for Advanced Study in Education, 1989.

Marchant, G. J. *How many and why not more?; A survey of issues in education.* Paper presented at Annual Meeting of the Mid-western Educational Research Association (Chicago, IL), 1989.

Reform Plans: Implications for principals discussed by chairman of task force on education of middle grade students. NASSP-Bulletin, 1989.

Schine, J. *Young Adolescents and Community Service.* Washington, D.C.: Carnegie Council on Adolescent Development, 1989.

CHAPTER

Student Services

SPECIAL NEEDS OF STUDENTS TODAY

Embedded in middle school philosophy are a variety of major needs geared to the special and unique traits of the young adolescent. These needs are social, physical, emotional, and academic. As middle school students make the transition from elementary school to high school, auxiliary student services can give young adolescents the support they need.

The attention of middle school educators to the needs and directions of young adolescents who are, indeed, at the "turning point" of their lives has been dramatized by the Carnegie Council on Adolescent Development.[1] The council points out that middle school students are caught in a changing technological society enveloped in social change while they are in the process of rapid change themselves from childhood to young adulthood. This transitional period of exploration of the preadult world is the perfect time to individualize the complete growth and fullest development of the middle level students.

Although preparing students for the future has always been a mission of teaching, the future for which educators today are preparing students is more complicated than in the past. Today educators are faced with contemporary demands that historically have not been part of the daily routine of a teacher's responsibility. In addition to the demands of a complex society, middle school teachers are faced daily with the dynamic needs of the young adolescent. The ups and downs of a middle school learner are addressed by the NASSP's Council on Middle Level Education.

Student learning capacities change more rapidly and more often during their middle level school years than in either elementary or high school. To improve early adolescent intellectual development and achievement, middle level schools must identify the kinds, degrees, and ranges of diversity in ability, achievement, interests, and social development which will create the most effective learning environments. No single pattern will fit all situations.[2]

With the uniqueness of the middle school learner and the changing society, middle school educators recognize the need to have and to utilize support resources to help their classroom educational programs. Diagnoses and evaluation of needs and interests of students, in coordination with support services, can enrich and expand the learning and growing processes of the young adolescent. Student services available from within the school organization and community sources can provide needed additional support for the classroom teacher.

Defining Student Services

By definition, student services provide educational opportunities which normally cannot be provided in the classroom. With the middle school philosophy advocating a student-centered curriculum, it is difficult for a classroom teacher to successfully address the unique needs of individual students. Therefore utilization of student services is paramount in middle schools. Student services available for middle schools should be reflected through the unique needs of the young adolescent as suggested by the New York State School Boards Association.

> . . . pupil support services address student needs, almost panoramically, as a series of often overlapping factors which inhibit academic and social development of the individual. As the school program, curriculum, and instruction become more oriented to a student-centered philosophy too, so, must systems of pupil support services.[3]

For the purpose of this chapter, the definition of student services for the effective middle school is programs that support and/or enhance the learning process of students within the regular core classroom curriculum. Student Services might include such programs as: Exceptional Education Needs Services; Instructional Services; Counseling and Guidance Services; Extracurricular Activities; and Community Support Services.

To better organize support services for middle school students, a unification effort through middle school organizations and centers for the young adolescent should concentrate on joint efforts to develop a mission statement, a common vocabulary of goals and objectives, and definitions of student support services. Presently, a disparity of terminology in the literature of student services, especially in middle school, creates a clouded picture or misinterpretation of what student services are appropriate for middle school students.

School organizations, state departments of education, universities, colleges, and educational professional organizations need to join together in their attempts and programs to prepare our students for the future. These collaborative efforts contribute to the restructuring of contemporary educational experiences for our young adolescents. However, with a variety of layers of support to develop the youth, services often become overlapped or neglected in the process. When this duplication or neglect occurs, the process becomes confused. As different terminology is developed, replication of services is hidden in the guise of difference in language and terminology.

STUDENT SERVICES ARE IMPORTANT

For The Student

Within the past few years schools have seen additions to student support services in: At Risk Student Programs; Drugs and Other Alcohol Programs (DOA); Gifted and Talented Programs; Student Equity Programs for gender, ethnic, and other multicultural/nonsexist education needs populations; and Teen Parent Programs. The new expanding and comprehensive responsibilities of student services still provides the underlying function—to make the total learning environment as efficient and effective as possible. Current research on educational trends in middle schools by the New York State School Boards Association demonstrated that 57 percent of the reporting districts have special intensive counseling programs and 55 percent have substance abuse programs.[4]

Student services provide a variety of functions in a school organization. As more demands are placed on school districts through state departments of public education, the dynamic American society, and the unique needs of the young adolescent, the role of student services has become more diversified and intensified. It is important that changes in student services address positive images and success of students as well as students with special needs.

> Pupil support services must be broadened in purpose and function. Rather than focus on weakness of youth and schools, educational policy makers and communities should see the child as part of a school community and larger community.[5]

For The Teacher

Student Services are important to the teacher, because they can provide valuable insight into the emotional, intellectual, psychosocial, cognitive, physical, and experiential background and development of an individual. With a diagnostic-prescriptive approach, teachers can provide the support services needed by the students, therefore allowing various auxiliary services to provide personnel specialized in complementing the teacher's expertise.

With a variety of individuals and organizations working towards the same result—the successful welfare of the students—the groups of individuals must be organized as teams. Decisions should be based on the needs of the students, communicated to all team members, and agreed on as a team in order to provide effective successful delivery. Schools and communities need to communicate, explore options together and acquire mutual trust to create the clearinghouse of excellence desired in a support system. Toy Watson encourages the use of cooperative efforts of team members to enhance maximum results for the students in the learning climate.

> . . . the concept of the Pupil Services Team in education as an effort to provide for the needs of the total child and to make the educational experiences for each pupil relevant to his or her own individual needs. With the advent of new legislation mandating that this be done for pupils suspected of being handicapped and the growing recognition that this should be the goal for all children, Pupil Services become increasingly vital to the educational purposes.[6]

STRATEGIES FOR MIDDLE SCHOOLS TO PROVIDE STUDENT SERVICES

Some of the basic services in auxiliary Student Services include special education, guidance, psychological, social work, medical/school nurse, and speech and language. These services can be clustered in four major categories:

- 1. *Instructional Services*
     teacher assistants
     parent helpers
     paraprofessionals
     remedial reading program
     reading specialists
     reading consultants
     learning disability programs
     special tutors

educable mentally retarded programs
emotionally disturbed classes
gifted and talented programs
enrichment programs
instructional learning centers
media specialists
instructional consultants
speech and language therapists
supervisory staff
physically handicapped
visually handicapped programs
hearing handicapped programs
multiply handicapped programs
mentors
community service
business and industry specialists
transportation
occupational therapy
summer programs
bilingual education
resource room
orthopedically handicapped programs
education for employment
multicultural programs
gender inclusive programs
Literacy Enrichment Academic Programme (LEAP)
PLUS
I.D.U. (Interdisciplinary Unity)
Venture
environmental code
technology education

2. *Counseling and Guidance*
Advisor-Advisee (AA)
counselors
psychologists
social workers
principals
assistant principals
nurses
community agencies
parent counseling and training
peer counseling
DARE programs

AOD programs
Choice Initiatives
Power of Positive Students (POPS)
Teaching Our Pupils Success (TOPS)

3. *Extracurricular Activities*
interschool social activities
interschool physical education programs
intramural activities
special interest and club activities
exploratory programs
band

4. *Community Resources*
county human services
religious sponsored organizations
mental health clinics
4H
Boy and Girl Scouts
Girls Inc.
business and industry
Choice Initiatives
Boys and Girls Clubs of America
Police Sponsored Youth Programs

As teachers perform in a student-centered teaching style rather than a subject-centered teaching style, the learning environment becomes based on known strengths and weaknesses of individual students in conjunction with the common needs, interests, and skill development of classmates. The types and numbers of student services available to teachers are dependent on a variety of variables such as the size of the district, philosophy of education, mission statement of the board for student services, state mandates, teacher receptiveness and readiness, community support, state support, and the district's financial status.

Regardless of the school organization, student services cannot be supplied quickly in response to urgent need. For effective student service to exist, there has to be an effective organizational format. Auxiliary student support can vary from volunteer service to paid services in instructional and non-instructional areas. Such support can include playground duty, lunchroom duty, secretarial assistance, bus duty, grading papers, field trip supervisors, school bus attendants, and small group instruction. Other support services might be inclusive of a variety of specialized personnel; reading specialist, psychologist, school nurse, and social worker.

PLANNING, PROVIDING, AND
EVALUATING STUDENT SERVICES

Whatever types of services are utilized, parents, teachers, support personnel, and the community must work together as a team with a specific plan. Some suggested steps in a successful student support program include:

1. Individuals who have ultimate planning responsibility should be involved in the evaluation of the program.
2. Strong instructional leadership should be confirmed.
3. The role of each team member should be carefully defined.
4. High expectations for student achievement should be held by all team members.
5. It is essential that all team members remember that the purpose of support services is to enhance student learning, not merely reassign responsibilities.
6. An orderly and positive school climate that supports learning needs to exist.
7. Use of support services should result in the most effective use of time and talents of the student and all personnel.
8. Strong emphasis on basic skill development should be practiced and encouraged.
9. There should be planning and inservice preparation for teams after initiation of a new program in student services into part of the existing programs.
10. Teachers should be familiar with the district's support system.
11. Regular monitoring of student progress and monitoring of services in the program should be part of ongoing program evaluation.
12. Research and examination of services available in other districts or communities that are not available presently in your school organization should be undertaken.
13. All team members, especially the classroom teacher, should be committed to the concept of support services and to the actual services rendered.

The middle school team concept is an important aspect of Student Support Services. A successful team has to be committed to the team and to the concept of student services. Other important qualities of teamwork include:

1. Having a regular meeting time and place. The team should meet at least monthly.
2. At the meetings, discussion of events and evaluation of program should be addressed.
3. Team members should come to the meetings prepared and organized.

4. Frequent communication should occur between team members. The team leader/director can be responsible for this.
5. An agenda and minutes from each meeting should be utilized and recorded.
6. The team needs to stay current with other districts and with the research on effective and successful student services.
7. Competition, mistrust, and ownership cannot occur. Clearly agreed-upon goals need to be stated.
8. Specific expectations of each team member need to be defined to prevent any misunderstandings.
9. Each school organization may have its own organizational structure of the team function, therefore, the school district should have a clearly articulated action plan.
10. Depending on the size of the district, each team could have a team leader or director. However, if this is not possible, the Director of Student Services might then act as the leader. If a district doesn't have a Director of Student Services then the principal or counselor may need to organize the team, after which team members may determine the leader.

After a mission statement is articulated, a commitment from the board of education can provide a sense of direction and success that may not presently prevail in some school organizations. Then as new demands are made from the state department of education, society and the young adolescent, the school will be in a proactive position and can provide appropriate services.

Student services available to the teacher can provide valuable insights into the emotional, intellectual, psychosocial, cognitive, physical, and experiential background and development of a child. With a diagnostic-prescriptive approach, teachers can provide the support services needed by the students, thereby allowing various auxiliary services provided by specialized personnel to compliment the teacher's expertise.

Minimal auxiliary services expected of a school district are usually suggested by the state department of education. For example, the Wisconsin Department of Public Instruction (DPI) includes these services:

Alcohol and Other Drugs (AOD)
Children at Risk
Learnfare
Compulsory School Attendance & Truancy Prevention
Counseling and Guidance

School-Age Parent Programs
Student Immunization Law
Suicide
Pupil Nondiscrimination
Exceptional Educational Needs

Within each of these areas, the Wisconsin DPI provides guidelines for the development of the integrated student services. Availability of student services can be school-based, school-community based, or inclusive of all organizations designed to provide pupil support services.

The number of possible auxiliary services may be more than many school districts can oblige. In the case where schools may not be able to provide students with all the appropriate or available services directly, they may still be able to share services cooperatively with other school districts. Or the state might have group services available. For example, in 1964, the Wisconsin Legislature developed Cooperative Educational Service Agencies (CESAs), replacing the then existing County Superintendent of Schools structure to help insure that support services would be established and available to the students who need them.

The state of Wisconsin is divided into 12 CESAs. The purpose statement of CESA reads:

> The organization of school districts in Wisconsin is such that the legislature recognizes the need for a service unit between the school district and the State Superintendent. The Cooperative Educational Service Agencies are designated to serve educational needs in all areas of Wisconsin by serving as a link between the school districts and between the school districts and the state. Cooperative Educational Service Agencies may provide leadership and coordination of services for school districts, including such programs as curriculum development assistance, school district management development, coordination of vocational education and exceptional education, research, special student class, human growth and development, data collection, processing and dissemination and inservice programs.[7]

Each CESA serving those schools in their district which pay for the services is autonomous in determining its programs. For example, CESA 3 serves 32 school districts in southwest Wisconsin. CESA 3 has focused its divisions as: Curriculum Development; School District Management and Development; Vocational Education; Exceptional Education; Research Collection, Processing and Dissemination of Data; Human Growth and

Development; Inservice and Staff Development; and Media Services. Many of their programs overlap from division to division. Some of the CESA 3 programs include:

Action Centered Consortium in Equity for Students and Staff (ACCESS)
Chapter 1
Curriculum/instruction
Education for Employment
Human Growth and Development
Job Training Partnership Act (JTPA)
Local Vocational Education Coordination (LVEC)
Media Production
Regional Media Center
Family and Consumer Education
Gifted and Talented
Alcohol and other Drugs (AOD)
Team Parent Program
Academic Decathlon
Safety Education Program
Pupil Nondiscrimination
Spanish Pilot Program

Iowa has a similar state program, Area Education Agency (AEA), providing comparable types of services to all public and nonpublic schools. The primary difference between the CESA and AEA programs is that in Iowa, school districts have a required membership to AEA while the CESA membership in Wisconsin is voluntary. Approximately 75 percent of the AEA services are support services for special education. Most of Iowa's AEA services fall under two divisions:

1. *Special Education*
    special education nurses
    intinerant teachers
    special education consultants
    speech-language pathologists
    hearing clinicians
    school social workers
    school psychologists
    physical and occupational therapists
    work experience coordinators

transition coordinators
juvenile shelter teachers
special education curriculum lab.
2. *Instructional Services*
cooperative purchasing
curriculum consultants
delivery services
Iowa Network for Obtaining Resource Materials for Schools
(INFORMS)
inservices
media consultants
lending library
production services
professional library
staff developmental programs
multicult-nonsexist (MCNS)
talented and gifted consultants
computer consultants
contest and special projects

Organizations like CESA and AEA are especially important for smaller school districts that cannot individually afford many of the student services essential for the development of the young adolescent.

EXAMPLES OF SOME STUDENT SERVICES PROGRAMS

A variety of exceptional student services programs has been created throughout the country to address the needs of middle level students.

Cities in Schools (CIS) has become a national program which embraces county agencies like Boys and Girls Club of America, 4H, Boy and Girl Scouts and other agencies that work directly with families. What is important about the CIS program is that it encourages and functions by expanding the school organizations' services, development of community wide partnership, and networking. CIS involves three phases of involvement:

1. An organizing body is created and becomes the governing body. This board becomes a nonprofit organization and is comprised of public and private sector members;

2. A city wide team is created with a director and two agency coordinators. Agreements from human services are established for positioning staff members; and

3. There is an on-site education center with a site director and team members who work with small groups of students and parent volunteers.

Futureprint is an intensive reading program designed for 7th and 8th graders in Ontario, California. Multilevel high-interest reading materials are used in a non-threatening environment which encourages high motivation, student responsibility, success, and student contract for study.

Maximizing Achievement Potential Toward Excellence (MAPS) is a program designed to increase the achievement of students at risk in Frederick County Public Schools in Maryland. It provides for parent involvement as well as support from the guidance components for faculty and students. The MAPS program links the school to the community and the student's home since they each contribute to the child's growth and development.

A more specific plan of auxiliary student services is offered in a middle school in a local rural school district in southwestern Wisconsin. It includes preschool through grade 12, involving 1,200 students, 400 of whom are middle schoolers. Here is an outline of this plan:

LANCASTER PUPIL SERVICES PROGRAM (WISCONSIN)

    I. Developing Guidance
        A. Learning
        B. Personal/Social
        C. Career/Vocational
    II. Health
        A. Regular Curriculum
        B. Here's Looking at You 2000
        C. Human Sexuality
           1. Sex Respect
           2. Values and Choices
        D. Child Protective Behaviors
           1. Officer Friendly
           2. Helping Hand
           3. Advisor/Advisee
        E. Great American Smokeout
    III. Student Assistance Programs
        A. Alcohol and Other Drug Abuse
           1. Staff Training
           2. Groups and Classroom
           3. Drug Abuse Resistance Education (DARE)
           4. Curriculum and Concerns Persons Group
               a. Grief and Loss
               b. Changing Family
               c. Depression and Suicide

    B. Self-Esteem
      1. Staff Training
        a. Assertive Discipline
        b. Self-Esteem, the Transferable Skill
        c. Power of Positive Students
      2. Group Work and Classroom
    C. District and General Building Programs
      1. Power of Positive Students Program (POPS)
        a. POPS Saying of the Day
        b. POPS Person of the Week
        c. POPS Lunch Treat
        d. POPS Breakfast for All (teachers, students, family members)
        e. POPS Weekly Drawing
      2. Faculty and Staff Public Relations Photographs

  IV. Gifted and Talented
   V. School-age Parents
  VI. Delinquency and Truancy
 VII. At Risk
    A. Grey Area Students
    B. Teen Parents
    C. Delinquency/Truancy
    D. Career Resource Lab
VIII. Advisor-Advisee
  IX. Education for Employment
    A. Career exploration
    B. Wisconsin Career Information Services (WCIS)
    C. Classes
   X. Special Education
    A. Laws and Parent and Child Rights
    B. Programs
      1. Trainable Developmentally Disadvantaged
      2. Physical Therapy
      3. Occupational Therapy
      4. Handicapped Conditions
        a. Gross Motor Skills
        b. Fine Motor Skills
        c. Self-Care Skills
        d. Perceptual Motor Skills
        e. Sensory-Motor Skills
        f. Social/Behavior Skills
        g. Prevocational Skills
        h. Oral-Motor Skills

SUMMARY

This chapter addressed the various issues of student services in middle school education and gave examples of existing middle school programs. The chapter also suggested that in addition to the knowledge base of the core needs of a middle school student services program, the development of a clearinghouse of current programs would be an asset for districts attempting to create or expand their student services. As districts are attempting to meet the needs of their students and the demands of state departments of education, duplication often occurs. Presently, a variety of creative student support programs exist throughout the country. They could be shared.

Encouraging the development of auxiliary student services permits a cornucopia of services to be available in many places to support the academic and developmental success of the young adolescent. Until a collection of national programs exists, there are two recommended resources. A recent outstanding publication inclusive of a variety of student services for middle students is *Promising Practices and Programs for the Middle-Level Grades.*

A second resource that provides a strong program for at-risk middle school students is *In the Middle: A Technical Team Report Addressing the Needs of At Risk Students During the Middle Learning Years.* (Both are listed in the references.)

For more information regarding pupil services for middle schools contact:

Your State Department of
Education

National Middle School
Association
4807 Evanswood Drive
Columbus, Ohio 43229-6292
(614) 848–8211

Center for the Young Adolescent
128 Doudna
University of Wisconsin–
Platteville
Platteville, Wisconsin 53818
(608) 342–1276

The Center for Early
Adolescence
University of North Carolina at
Chapel Hill
Suite 223, Carr Mill Mall
Carrboro, North Carolina, 27510
(919) 966–1148

Center for Research and
Development on Elementary
and Middle Schools
The Johns Hopkins University
3505 N. Charles Street
Baltimore, Maryland 21218
(301) 338–8000

International Association of
Pupil Personnel Workers
2025 Juneway Dr.
Long Beach, Indiana 46360
(219) 872–4975

National Alliance of Pupil
Service Organizations
(NAPSO)
1250 N. Pitt
Alexandria, Virginia 22314
(617) 730–2444

Wisconsin Department of Public
Instruction
125 South Webster Street
Post Office Box 7841
Madison, Wisconsin 53707–7841
(608) 266–1879

ENDNOTES

1. Carnegie Council on Adolescent Development, *Turning Points: Preparing American Youth for the 21st Century.* (New York: 1989): 809.

2. NASSP, *Middle Level Education's Responsibility for Intellectual Development.* (Reston, VA: 1989): 18.

3. New York State School Boards Association, *A Kaleidoscope of Student Needs, New Challenges for Pupil Support Services.* (Albany, NY: 1987): p. 4.

4. Ibid., p. 8.

5. Ibid., p. iv.

6. Toy F. Watson. *Pupil Services—The Team Approach Part 1: The Team* Paper presented at the Annual Meeting of the National Association of Social Workers. (New Orleans, LA: 1985): 2a.

7. Cooperative Education Service Agency #3, *Resource Directory.* (Fennimore, WI: Fall, 1989): 1, and Wisconsin State Statutes Section 116.01 (CESA Purpose Statement).

REFERENCES

Carnegie Council on Adolescent Developments, Task Force on Education of Young Adolescents. From an abridged version of *Turning Points: Preparing American Youth for the 21st Century.* New York, 1989. The Carnegie Council is a program of Carnegie Corporation of New York.

Cooperative Educational Services Agency #3, *Resource Directory.* Fennimore, WI, Fall, 1989.

Keystone Area Education Agency, *Take a Look at Keystone Area Education, You'll Like What You See.* Publication of Information Services for Iowa special education field offices.

National Association of Secondary School Principals. *Middle Level Education's Responsibility for Intellectual Development.* Reston, VA:, 1989.

New York State School Boards Association, *A Kaleidoscope of Student Needs: New Challenges for Pupil Support Services.* A New York State School Boards Association position paper, Albany: NY: 1987.

Palmer, Joan; Cynthia Caldwell; Lorraine Costella; and Russell Eschbacher; and Willie Foster; Thomas Groce; and Judy Mauriello. *In The Middle: A Technical Team Report Addressing the Needs of At-Risk Students During the Middle Years.* A paper submitted to The Commission for Students At Risk of School Failure, Maryland State Department of Education, 1990.

Watson, Toy. *Pupil Services—The Team Approach. Part I: The Team. Part II: Record Keeping.* April 1985, New Orleans, LA: Paper presented at the Annual Meeting of the National Association of Social Workers. January 31–February 3, 1985.

Wisconsin Department of Public Instruction. *Promising Practices and Programs for the Middle-Level Grades.* Madison, WI: 1991 Judy Peppard, Middle Level Educational Consultant, (608–267–3833).

Community Relations

THE MIDDLE SCHOOL AND ITS ENVIRONMENT

Schools do not exist in a vacuum, and middle schools are no exception. Interactions between the school and its community are frequent and can be far reaching in terms of their impact. Every day when students leave school and return home, they take with them their impressions, their reality, of what happened in school that day. Yet when they are asked what they did at school, they often respond by saying "nothing." However, in many other ways, some of them quite subtle, they convey to their parents and others the meaning that middle school has for them.

Parental concerns about the education of their children change as youngsters leave the elementary school and enter middle school. In earlier years, parental attention was focused mainly on whether their child had learned to read and whether they had friends among their classmates. Now, in the middle school, parental concerns shift to some of the more specific domains of academic achievement. Enlightened parents are also concerned with whether their child is developing a healthy self-esteem. Often, however, direct parent involvement in organizations such as the PTA begins to wane. Middle school educators are challenged with finding creative ways to cause parents to want to maintain their contact with the school.

Unlike elementary schools, middle schools typically serve a larger segment of the community. And they are the focus of parental attention for a brief three years. By design or not, everyone associated with the middle school has an impact on the rapport that is developed and nurtured between the school and community. In fact, support personnel, secretaries, janitors, cooks, and bus drivers, etc., often have more frequent and intimate contacts with community members than do teachers, counselors, and administrators.

Community members trust these people to know what is going on. In the eyes of community members, they are very credible. For this reason, it is imperative that your support personnel is up to date on the latest information about the middle school.

THE MIDDLE SCHOOL MUST "SELL" ITS PROGRAM

A community's impression of what is going on in the middle school is its reality. That impression is formed more by what middle school people do than by what they say. For example, when all staff members act in a highly professional manner, their behaviors convey clearly that they care about the students. However, most communities are comprised of a diversity of people. Parents and other community members have had wide-ranging experiences that often predicate how they view the middle school and the expectations they hold for it. For some parents, school was an experience of success and high achievement. For others, school was a disaster and led to low achievement or possibly dropping out. Some parents will insist that you are not assigning enough homework. Others do not understand why the school should expect their child to turn in work on time.

With all the diverse hopes and aspirations that people have for their middle school, it is imperative that the school maintain a low-key, but regular, contact with its clientele. Too often, middle schools mount a community relations program that might be depicted as a "peaks and valleys" approach. In this kind of program, the school sponsors a hard sell, short-term program on an "as needed" basis. However, the valleys in between are protracted periods of time when the school maintains no outreach program to the community. This approach is an especially poor strategy to use in building and nurturing an understanding and strong support for the middle school.

Every member of the middle school staff is a potential contact and spokesperson for the school and its program. Following are some suggestions for how staff members can project a positive image for the school. A low-key approach to community relations evidences much give and take (two-way communication) between the middle school and community members. All parties to this communication are sensitized to each other's changing goals and aspirations. Do not expect that anything done will please everyone. However, with good, open communication, people will probably know why some things are changing while other things remain as they are. This means that good reasons must be given for making changes. Today, most people are unpersuaded when told, "Take my word for it."

Community relations for today's middle schools very much involves the use of marketing strategies. Just "telling it like it is" will not get the job done. Marketing efforts must target more than just the parents in the community. It is estimated that only about 27 percent of the adults in the typical community today have children in school. But every registered adult is eligible to vote! Using marketing strategies gives your citizen population reasons for having confidence in the middle school and its programs.

Banach (1988) suggests that schools might use some of the marketing strategies popularized by business and industry where they target a particular audience. Specific tactics, such as creating bumper stickers stating that "my son/daughter is on the middle school honor roll" or ". . . is in the middle school orchestra," could be used. The aim is to keep the middle school in the public's eye with positive messages. Creating a school logo and motto that can be put on the school menu is another example.

Middle school educators need to create and avail themselves of a complex network of both internal and external communication. The network is not just "there" waiting for you to use it. It has to be created and recreated as position holders change. For example, the education editor for your local newspaper may change often since the position typically is entry level and does not enjoy great status within the hierarchy of the newspaper. You make a solid investment in good community relations when you make a personal effort to reach out to meet these people. Initially, it is important just to get to know them and for them to get to know you. Later, when you are sponsoring an event that you want them to cover, they may be more receptive to your request.

Local civic groups and clubs provide an excellent avenue for direct communication with community members, including those who do not have children in the middle school. Often, the administrative team in a school district will divide the responsibility among its members to join local organizations. Especially if you happen to be new in the community, it is to your advantage to join, be a good listener, and gain a sense for the metabolism of the community.

Your expression of a sincere interest in what is important to *them* will greatly accommodate your developing a good rapport with community members. Once you enlarge your visibility in the community, you may be called upon periodically to present to a club or group some aspect of what your middle school is doing. Occasionally, middle school administrators assume the arrogant position that only they can tell the middle school story. What they may miss is the opportunity to invite a current middle school teacher to make an informal presentation to the group on what he or she is doing *today* in the classroom. This can be a much more powerful message than just having the middle school administrator talk about the general aims and goals of the middle school and what others (teachers) are doing.

Internal and external communication are not serial activities. Both are going on at the same time. Because a lot of information is being exchanged, it is important that the middle school's official communications speak with one voice. There needs to be one consonant message. And even with that, you can be sure that there will be a wide range of interpretations in the community for what that message means. For example, you need to be attentive to some communications that are more credible than others to parents. A descriptive piece sent home explaining what the middle school is doing will tend to be less credible than the *actual* pieces of work produced by your students and taken home. The difference lies in one piece being only an artifact describing the intent of the middle school. The other represents what the student has done.

One of the most commonly overlooked and underpracticed skills in developing good community relations is *listening*. As educators, we get all caught up in and sometimes carried away with telling, explaining, explicating, justifying, etc. As a simple matter of fact, you just cannot listen while you are talking. This is a bit like an unsophisticated discussion group where no one is listening to what others are saying. Rather, each person is waiting to speak. In fact, when no one is listening, what has been said is of no consequence and contributes nothing to your knowledge of what is going on and how others feel about it.

As you think through the several interactions that are to occur between your middle school and people in the community, it is important to differentiate between what you want to convey and what they may want to know. What you think community members need to know may, initially, be of little or no interest to them. Your initial task is to ferret out what there is in what you want to convey that will pique their interest. If you are able to provide a persuasive reason for people to become involved, people's receptivity to your communications will be heightened appreciably. One strategy that you can use is to try to anticipate questions that people might have and address them in the context of your message.

Educators at all levels, middle school folk notwithstanding, are word people. We use a lot of words orally and in print. And in doing this, we often fail to capitalize upon other communication formats that are at a lower level of abstraction and often communicate much more concretely. Charts, graphs, pictures, and representations often can serve our ends much more powerfully than just words. A lot of what we communicate is conveyed metaphorically. But do we really think through whether the metaphor has an understandable meaning to the people who are the intended recipients of the communication? The challenge here is to simplify something that is complex without making it simplistic.

Even if you possess good listening skills, you are not going to get much, if any, feedback from individuals and groups in your community unless you creatively devise ways and means by which people can reach you to express their thinking about the middle school. When a middle school educator is one-on-one with a parent, the parent will tend to focus on how his or her son or daughter is doing in school. This is a time for you to focus on the individual student's accomplishments, not to orate on the goals, visions, or aims of your middle school. Conversely, when you are talking with a group of parents or citizens, this is a time when you can be more generally informative of what you are attempting to do and how you are going about doing it.

Many middle schools traditionally reach out to parents through parent-teacher conferences and open houses. And these activities are valuable. But there are other things you can do to enlarge upon citizen knowledge of your middle school. One effective practice has been opening the school to adult visitation during a regular school day. This gives parents and others a "real world" view of the middle school in action. When you do have open houses or parent-teacher conferences, are you attentive to the different hours your patron community members are at work? To assure that parents and others have equal access to your activities and events, you may have to schedule them at unusual times. This may necessitate some added negotiations with your support and professional staff regarding extending hours of work.

Sometimes, inadvertently, we shoot ourselves in the foot in our interactions with community members. One example of this has been the growing number of fund-raisers different middle school groups have sponsored throughout the school year. When this approaches a saturation point, you can expect to hear a hue and cry from the community that "your middle school students are at my door nearly every week raising money for this or that. . . . " Many middle schools have found a solution in having one big fund-raiser each year. They then apportion the proceeds among the school's many activities, much as the United Way allocates the monies collected during its once a year drive.

THE MIDDLE SCHOOL MUST KNOW WHAT THE COMMUNITY VALUES

Since the middle school is about at the halfway point of the K–12 experience, it has the opportunity to articulate with the public the developmental flow of activities from the elementary school through to the high school. While middle schools provide a range of exploratory activities for students, they also are party to the continuing development and nurturing of knowl-edge and skills in common subjects such as English, science, mathematics, and social studies. Parents are interested in the logical flow of these learn-ings as they move from the simple and concrete to more abstract under-standings. Middle school educators are ideally placed to tell this story and dispel the myth that the school's curriculum is little more than a hodge-podge of inarticulated activities that teachers have dreamed up for student consumption.

MIDDLE SCHOOL NEWS SHOULD BE PLANNED AND REGULAR

The people responsible for your local media will, from time to time, come to you with a request for news. If you have been content to just let your middle school "continue to happen, day by day," you have missed some fine op-portunities to take note of and record events and activities that come under the aegis of *timeless news*. This is news that can be maintained on file for future use. It is news that does not have to be publicized immediately to be timely. It may take the form of a series of pictures or slides that can be used for a photojournalism piece, a videotape that might be used in a public ser-vice time exposure, or the historic emergence and development of new com-ponents in your school's program, such as studies in field ecology. It is really sad when the media people reach out to you and you have *nothing* to offer them about all of the diverse activities occurring daily in your middle school.

As incredible as it may seem, community members often *assume* that you, as a middle school educator, will have seen and/or heard anything ap-pearing in the public domain and, too, that you will have an informed opin-ion about what has been said or written. People really know better. But they see you as an *informed*, professional educator. For this reason, at the least, it is important for you to access thoughts and ideas as they appear in the popu-lar media. And if you want to maintain an informed opinion, you will want to establish and maintain a regular contact with your professional literature. Some of the ideas that surface in the public's eye are half-baked and need to be exposed for what they are. For example, periodically an element of zeal-ous parents may demand that the middle school form teams in contact sports and engage in interscholastic competition. Middle school educators need to have the hard facts at hand to explain what some of the psychological and physical dangers for students are in activities such as these. However, do not let yourself get caught up in *always* being a naysayer to new ideas. Sometimes people *will* have a better idea. You will always benefit from being a thoughtful listener.

Being honest and forthright with your community is usually appreciated. If you start to tell stories that just are not so, at the least you better have a very good memory for what you have said. Sometimes you may find yourself having to do something that is not educationally sound. For example, unexpected changes in your student demographics may suddenly create a severe overcrowding in your middle school. To alleviate the situation in the immediate moment, your board of education may decide, wisely or unwisely, to redistribute sixth-graders from the middle school to less crowded elementary schools. The decision may have been predicated on sheer numbers of students and classroom space available. In a case such as this, the better part of valor lies with telling your community *why* this decision was reached. If, on the other hand, you want to erode your credibility, a good way to start is by rationalizing the decision with the community with excuses for why moving sixth-graders back to the elementary schools is educationally sound. Faced with scarce resources, middle school educators and citizens should understand that they cannot do all they want to do. Sometimes compromises have to be found in which the least damage is done, as the decision affects the entire school system.

PROVIDE FOR PARENTS' QUESTIONS AND REACTIONS TO MIDDLE SCHOOL PROGRAMS

Elementary school parent groups tend, in general, to be highly supportive of the school's program. However, parent groups at the middle school level begin to act more like high school booster groups. They begin to develop their own agenda and lobby hard for it. While it is important to recognize that these parent groups are supportive of the middle school and provide a vital link with the community, the members must come to realize that they are advisory in nature and not a part of the formal organization. Parent groups that are very active and successful at fund-raising sometimes will use tactics that hold middle school educators and even the board of education hostage. In essence, they will tell you what is to be done with funds raised or they will withhold them. What has happened is that a "we-they" situation has been permitted to emerge. And it is tough to deal with it after the fact. Thoughtful middle school educators address this matter with the leadership and membership of parent groups so that there is a clear under-standing of what the school's priorities are. It also needs to be clear that the goals of the school will not be subverted by special interest groups.

With many school districts moving to some form of site-based man-agement, there has been an unfortunate blurring of the role of parent groups, which range all the way from advising to making decisions. If good rapport with the community is to be valued, parent groups need to have a clear understanding of their role and what they can and cannot do. Because this is new ground, boards of education need to revisit their policies so that all parties to the school's activities become fully informed. Some recently formed groups include a mix of parents, other community members, teach-ers, and administrators. Often each member will have equal voting rights. When this is the case, the group becomes the decisive body, not individual members.

If, on the other hand, you have one or more groups of parents in your middle school that have volunteered or been designated to sit in an advisory capacity, you have an obligation to inform them of the differences between advising and deciding. Simply put, if you are not receptive to parent and community input and advice, it is probably wise not to form such groups. However, if you are this disengaged, your tenure for leadership in the mid-dle school may be quite short.

USE PARENT ADVISORY GROUPS WISELY

When you do seek advisement, you obligate yourself to take seriously the advice given. If not, it will cease to be given or you will be bypassed in the process. In the interest of maintaining rapport with an advisory group, when you decide to take action that contravenes the advice given, you owe the advisory group a persuasive rationale for your action. They may not accept the rationale, but if none is given you leave the impression that you have ignored their input.

Middle school educators are well versed in teaching and learning strategies that are effective with children and youth. However, they may be less aware of tactics and strategies that are appropriate for working with adults. Good community relations hinges on how effectively you are able to work with adults. Rather than pedagogy, human relations provides guiding principles for working successfully with adults. These principles are useful to observe when you are working with your professional colleagues, your support staff, and with parents and other community members. As you map out what you are going to do and how you plan to do it, keep in mind that adults, unlike young people, tend to be quite self-directed; they generate their own need to become involved and learn. Adults are experientially rich and use this as a resource in their endeavors. Adults tend to have rather specific purposes for what they want to do and what they feel they need to learn. When adults acquire new knowledge and skills, they seek opportunities to apply this right away. Adults are problem-centered in their learning while youngsters tend to be subject-centered. And maybe most importantly, adults expect to be involved in planning, diagnosing needs, formulating objectives and evaluating their accomplishments. In general, the successful climate for working with adults is one characterized by informality, respect, and collaboration.

Some educators construe community relations as developing and maintaining placid relations between the school and community. Especially for middle school educators, this is a rather unrealistic expectation. More often than had been the case at the elementary school level, you are going to be seeing parents about the unacceptable behaviors of their children. Some of these meetings will start as being confrontational. Parents will become increasingly aware of state mandated programs you must offer and maintain but with which some of them may disagree. In short, you are going to have to deal with conflict and controversy.

You can take the stance of seeking to quell conflict when it arises. However, if you do, you will find yourself spending an inordinate amount of time putting out brush fires. A more productive stance might be to treat conflict and controversy as an opportunity. Often disagreements arise simply as a result of ignorance or a lack of information. But even well-informed parents and community members may disagree with some things you are doing in the middle school. Sometimes differences emerge from a variance between the ethos of the community and what the school sees as being necessary and good for students. Typical among controversial issues are sex and health education, observation of religious holidays, school boundaries, school closings, and school discipline codes.

The appropriate place in which to address district-wide policy is at the school board meeting, not the middle school. Information sharing at the building level can often defuse some of the rancor imbedded in these issues. Your choice of pronoun to use in talking with community members can heighten understanding and improve their receptivity to listening to what you have to say. For example, consider using *we* rather than *you* or *they*. Consider using *our* rather than *my* or *your*. This careful choice of pronoun use helps generate collective community concern for schools. And it tends to diminish the emergence of adversarial rhetoric.

SOME WAYS TO IMPROVE
SCHOOL-COMMUNITY RELATIONS

In addition to general admonitions noted above, there are other regular opportunities available for enhancing school-community relations in the middle school. The following are some examples.

When a Student Is Absent—Usually someone from the middle school will call home to confirm if the student is ill. This is an opportunity to express the hope that the student will be able to return to school soon. If the illness is protracted, it is an opportunity for the school to see that assigned work is sent to the student's home.

Events—Musicals, Plays, Sports—While middle school youth are beginning to spread their wings away from their parents, they still appreciate it when their parents show up to see them perform. These events afford middle school staff members an opportunity to visit informally with parents and community members. These are also opportunities to arrange for senior citizens to attend and enjoy community youth performing, and help them develop a fuller appreciation of the school's educational program for which their taxes are paid.

Media—However exciting you may find the day-to-day events in your middle school, they are not typically seen as being newsworthy. Be creative. For example, take the school choir to an extended care facility to sing for the shut-ins. Use the human resources available in your community. Invite some senior citizens to the school to demonstrate the art of quilting and have them stay for lunch with the students. Activities such as these *are* newsworthy!

School Orientation—Invite soon-to-be sixth-graders *and their parents* to a middle school orientation. Talk about the middle school philosophy and have some summarized pass-out materials. Introduce teachers, counselors and other support personnel. Schedule small group follow-up meetings to respond to individual questions.

Parent-Student Handbook—Some of the ground rules change from the elementary to the middle school. Both parents and students need to know the rules. They need to know whom to contact with particular problems. Parents and students can work with teachers in preparing this document. Students also need to know their rights *and* responsibilities. If there are graduated punishments for unacceptable behavior, students need to know what they are.

Hotline Information—There should be a number that anyone can call with a question 24 hours a day. An informed source can use this to quell rumors or just provide accurate information. Community members should know that calls will be responded to as soon as possible but no later than the next day unless there are extenuating circumstances.

School Census—During the annual school census is an opportune time for middle school educators to visit briefly with both new and long-standing members of the community. Keep your census takers fully informed on middle school matters so that they can accurately respond to questions they might be asked.

Teacher Orientation—While new teachers have a lot to learn about the middle school, they usually also have a lot to learn about the community. Community organizations and groups can be programmed into a segment of the orientation or invited to have their own receptions for new middle school personnel. And do not forget to include your substitute teachers in the orientation.

Other Outlets—The Jaycees, local realtors, and physicians for children should be regularly provided with up-to-date descriptive material on the middle school. Always note the person that anyone can call for further information.

There is no "canned" program of public relations that can be adopted as a template for middle school. Every program has to be tailored and periodically updated. What you do and how you do it will depend upon a myriad of variables, including the diversity of people in your community, what issues are hot at the moment, the personalities of all the participants, and the level of your commitment to creating and nurturing a sense of communion between the community and its middle school.

REFERENCES

Achilles, C. M., M. Nan Lintz, and W. W. Wayson. "Observations on Building Public Confidence in Education." *Educational Evaluation and Policy Analysis*, 11:3 (Fall, 1989): 275–284.

Banach, W. and B. Bradway. *Mastering Marketing*. Pitman, NJ: Communication Briefings, 1988.

Joyce, A. B. *Written communication and the school administrator*. Boston, MA: Allyn Bacon, 1992.

Kindred, L. W., E. Bagin, and D. R. Gallaher. *The School & Community Relations*. 4th Ed. Englewood Cliffs, NJ: Prentice Hall, 1990.

Kunesch, L. G. and J. B. Bakker. ''Parent involvement in school restructuring.'' *Policy Briefs*, 9 (1990): 1–4.

Lutz, F. W. and C. Merz. *The Politics of School/Community Relations*. New York: Teachers College Press, 1992.

Saxe, R. W. *School-Community Relations in Transition*. Berkeley, CA: McCutchan Publishing Corporation, 1984.

Wayson, W. W. and F. Lutz. ''The dissat-factor: Recent discoveries in the dissatisfaction theory.'' *Educational Administration Quarterly*, 25:4 (1989): 358–376.

Wayson, W. W., et al. *Handbook for Developing Public Confidence in Schools*. Bloomington, IN: Phi Delta Kappa Educational Foundation, 1988.

West, P. T. *Educational Public Relations*. Beverly Hills, CA: Sage Publications, 1985.

Wilcox, D. L., P. H. Ault, and W. K. Agee. *Public Relations Strategies and Tactics*. New York: Harper and Row Publishers, 1989.

INDEX